Swedish
Mentality

Åke Daun

Swedish Mentality

Translated by Jan Teeland
Foreword by David Cooperman

The Pennsylvania State University Press
University Park, Pennsylvania

Grants for the English translation of the original Swedish version of this book have been given by the Marianne and Marcus Wallenberg Foundation and by the Swedish Institute.

Library of Congress Cataloging-in-Publication Data

Daun, Åke, 1936–
    [Svensk mentalitet. English]
    Swedish mentality / Åke Daun ; translated by Jan Teeland.

        p   cm.
    Includes bibliographical references and index.
    ISBN 0-271-01501-2 (cloth)
    ISBN 0-271-01502-0 (paper)
    1. National characteristics, Swedish.   I. Title.
    DL639.D3813   1996
    155.8'9485—dc20   95-14585
                                                                                  CIP

Second printing, 1999

First published in Sweden as *Svensk Mentalitet*
Copyright©1989 Åke Daun
English translation copyright©1996 The Pennsylvania State University
All rights reserved
Printed in the United States of America
Published by The Pennsylvania State University Press,
University Park, PA 16802-1003

It is the policy of The Pennsylvania State University Press to use acid-free paper for the first printing of all clothbound books. Publications on uncoated stock satisfy the minimum requirements of American National Standard for Information Sciences—Permanence of Paper for Printed Library Materials, ANSI Z39.48-1992.

Contents

Foreword

by David Cooperman

A few years ago a Swedish TV crew was in Minnesota filming a program for Swedish television about third- and fourth-generation Swedish-Americans in small towns. "They're more Swedish than real Swedes!" said a director when asked about his impressions of the Minnesotans, astonished at what seemed a clearer reflection of his own image. Many Swedish visitors to Swedish-American centers in Chicago or Minneapolis also consider attitudes and values among third- and fourth-generation urban Swedish-Americans as variations on Swedish character themes rather than as "real" American traits.

What, then, is a *real* Swede? (Is there a *real* Swede?) Do native Swedes share a unique set of character traits that make reference to "Swedish national character" reasonable? And what are the elements of that set—behaviors? attitudes? values? beliefs? norms? All of the foregoing? How can one distinguish real from not-so-real Swedish character? These are some of the major questions Åke Daun considers in *Swedish Mentality*. The Swedish edition, published in 1989, was widely read and discussed and Daun was referred to as the "guru" of Swedish character—a trait he denied, as a typical Swede would.

In many European societies, concern about national identities and values has been increasing as a result of the advent of the European Union and because of increasing crossnational interaction and acculturation. No doubt the reception of American fastfood, of Hollywood film and television entertainment, of Euro-Disney productions, not to mention the appearance of Americanisms in non-English languages, provoked apprehension about preserving native identities while implying more basic questions about national character. In day-to-day business and government transactions, the recognition that cross-cultural misunderstandings prevent rational decisions has given rise to a growth industry for cultural and national character translators and trouble-shooters.

Such questions are also the focus of research by scholarly special-
ists in European humanities and literature. For example, a multi-
volume work on the history of Danish identity has recently been
published, including an article entitled, "What Is Danish Identity?"
Certainly one source of Norwegian resistance to entering the European Union stems from concern with preserving a Norwegian way
of life. After narrowly approving of entry into the European Union,
Swedish public opinion reflected increasing suspicion about its impact on Swedish institutions, on national distinctiveness. Following
publication in Sweden of *Swedish Mentality,* Daun wrote several essays with the general title, *Den europeiska identiteten* (1992) (The
European identity), in which he explored the relation between separate national identities and a developing contemporary transnational European culture. More recently, he has collaborated with
other Swedish scholars to consider changing patterns of Swedish
values, attitudes, and relationships as immigration patterns become
more diverse and create a multicultural character in the land. These
themes were initially the subject of articles Daun published in the
early 1980s. Over the years they have been analyzed in varied contexts, both cultural and situational, with increasing sensitivity to
their subtle multiple dimensions. Daun's approach and method have
always been comparative, but in contrasting combinations. The
Swedish-language edition of this book was subtitled *A Comparative
Perspective.* But a comparative perspective of what? Its own scholarly identity requires commentary.

The term "mentality" itself is intended to be problematic. Some
scholars might identify this book as part of the genre of "national
character studies." Other terms that come to mind are "national
identity" or "national personality structure." Each term recalls a
different orientation and can be traced to different canonical writings. And each embodies different problems of analysis and apparent weaknesses. This volume necessarily includes observations on
Swedish character, identity, and personality traits without, however,
attempting to follow in the traditions or current lines of character
or identity research. "Mentality" avoids the pitfalls of the more
traditional studies, although English-language readers might find it
slightly amorphous. Possible synonymous constructions might be
"Swedish mind-sets," or "Images of Swedishness," but these are just
as open in meaning. The conceptual and historical differences de-

noted by these variant labels help to locate the contribution and hence to understand the significance of this volume.

References to custom and character differences among peoples are found extensively in classical writings, including the Bible. Aristotle and Tacitus, among others, conjectured systematically on collective character traits of societal groups, but the referents were, variously, city-states, tribes, regional populations, or religiously differentiated societies and language groups. Singular character traits were attributed to all alleged "others," despite the fact that the peoples referred to were constituted by one, a few, or many types of social organization. Montesquieu's *On the Spirit of the Laws* (1748) includes a systematic account of finite sets of collective character traits per group that he claimed to have observed in his travels in Europe and the Near East. His speculation on the reasons for any unique set included a large number of geographical, climatic, and situational factors, often alleging one "root" cause. Thus, the peoples of northern Europe were able to secure themselves against Roman power with "an admirable wisdom," despite the absence of art and education, and almost without laws, because of the rough texture of the northern climate (vol. 1, book XIV, chap. III). The idea of the nation, etymologically a homogeneous common ancestral group, had even in early usage been extended to mean populations that shared a common ruling dynasty. The rise of democracies, constitutional monarchies, modern nation-state societies, and multinational constitutional monarchies, along with ever-changing national boundaries and increased transnational population movements, made any attempt to attribute unique character qualities to most European societies highly questionable. Yet, of course by the late eighteenth century, along with the universalist values of the Enlightenment, the presence of myths of origin, ideologies, and norms centering on the particularistic idea of "race" served to justify a spirited conception of distinct birth-related, politically organized collectives with allegedly objectively discernible traits. The Nordic societies located on the geographic periphery of northern Europe, with fewer instances of boundary-regime-migration-language ambiguities than most other European societies, appeared to exemplify the concept of racial, and hence character, distinctiveness, so long as a few exceptions were overlooked, such as the *Same,* the intricate Norwegian dialect and regional schisms, the residues of Danish influence in

Skåne, the Swedish-Finns in Ostro-Bothnia, and the small Jewish migrant populations. Nonetheless, "national character" analysis was used generally, if uncritically, by scholars, diplomats, and journalists. Ernest Barker, the English political philosopher, published a systematic, historical account of the idea of national character (1927) that appeared to justify its usage as a nontechnical, political-historical term. For others, such as Hamilton Fyfe (*The Illusion of National Character,* 1940), its usage in international affairs or in ordinary discourse was inherently deceptive and always mischievous.

The experience of the Second World War, especially the authoritarian, dominance-submissive, and rigid traits observed in German and Japanese behavior, revived interest in the possibility that "national character" had scientific merit. Under the rubric "basic personality type," and with the help of psychoanalytic anthropology, unqualified constructions of distinct, developmental "cultural" character trends became fashionable. Too often the line between national stereotypes and alleged national character or basic personality type was blurred. The old, persistent problems of fitting societies with multiple groupings and variations by ethnicity, religion, and social class into a standard characterological model were obvious. Methodological critiques were followed by the construction of more refined conceptions of national character by some scholars and by the gradual decline of the currency of the term. Some anthropologists, such as Anthony F. C. Wallace, developed concepts and models of personality-culture interactions that in principle accounted for universal, cognitive, and personality development processes while explaining how cultural-personality differences among societies may be understood. These constructions were not intended to yield valid accounts of unique sets of cultural character attributes, but they represent more sensitive abstractions that offered promise of resolving the ambiguities and avoiding the pitfalls of the older national-character formulations.

In *National Character and National Stereotypes: A Trend Report Prepared of the International Union of Scientific Psychology* (Amsterdam, 1960), the Dutch psychologists H. C. J. Duijker and N. H. Frijda assessed the advances in national-character research and the progress made in resolving the problems implicit in the concept. They precisely laid out programs for crossnational research to be undertaken at several levels and emphasized the need for crossnational comparative research. Since then, although quantitative techniques and concepts such as modal personality type have been employed to tease out patterns of attitudinal and behavioral themes and variations within cultures, no "breakthrough" of the kind hoped for in 1960 has occurred. The subject appears to have been reduced to a large number of more confined questions, at least as far as ethnographers and cultural psychologists are concerned.

Among humanities and literature scholars, especially those concerned with postmodernist themes, the analysis of collective values has tended to be rephrased and reprocessed along questions of identity. This concept lends itself to highly qualitative or interpretive approaches, emphasizing subjective accounts whereby individuals identify with categorical others, such as gender, class, racial/ethnic group, and immigrant population. Classical sociology and ethnographic reports abounded with case studies aimed at depth understanding of personal-identity development in the context of group identification. Character "traits," a discrete set of distinct behaviors, are critically avoided on grounds that individuals as well as groups are depicted as static, out-of-scale mosaics rather than as complex, self-constructed persons or groupings that require not objectified explanations but meaningful understanding.

Scandinavian identity studies have certainly kept pace with the large numbers of similar publications in the English language, but typical of such research, total societies are not the units of analysis chosen. For example, recent works have appeared on the impact on *Same* identity in the past two centuries of Lutheran church education. *Judisk identitet* (Jewish identity), a collection of essays by Swedish-Jewish scholars, reflects on specific qualities and identification questions in Jewish life. Lars Gustafsson's short but insightful essay moves from the task of undertaking a Jewish identity to the critical intellectual process of finding one's self through identification.

Daun's ethnographic publications, beginning with his published dissertation on Swedish suburban life, have included, in Clifford Geertz's terms, thick descriptions of the specific cultural contexts of personal lives. His academic concerns with social character and related identities have for some time focused on the problems involved in describing and explaining Swedishness when Sweden itself becomes less homogeneous and more multicultural. When Gustav Sundbärg wrote *Det Svenska Folklynnet* (The Swedish national character) in 1911, he could assume with few exceptions that he was referring to a coherent, ancestrally bonded population. The explicit aphoristic stereotypes, of Swedes and, mostly pejoratively, of Danes recalled an ethnically unidimensional condition in which the tide of out-migration was viewed as a danger to the continuity of "real" Swedishness. By the end of the twentieth century, immigration waves have made Sweden a far different society. What, then, is a "real Swede"? The question itself may be questioned in the light of this book. If so, Åke Daun may well have succeeded in bringing to both academics and readers interested in more than aphoristic generalizaions an awareness of the skills and understanding needed to advance our knowledge.

Department of Sociology
University of Minnesota

Introduction

The Swedes—what are they like? Not Swedish society, not Sweden as a state or political system, not its material conditions. No, the question concerns the mental imprints of the Swedish environment: what one becomes growing up in this part of northern Europe. What are typical ways of thinking and behaving, forms of socializing and patterns of communication, sets of values and perspectives? Is there such a thing as Swedish mentality?

I began to ponder these matters in the beginning of the 1980s after an exceedingly uncomfortable experience. I was approached by Donald Fields, Scandinavian correspondent for the British paper *The Guardian*, who asked me these and other similar questions. To my chagrin I found I had very little to say. At about the same time, the book *Swedes, As Others See Them* (1981) was published. The author, Jean Phillips-Martinsson, an English consultant in intercultural communication and resident in Sweden, had pioneered consultant activity in cross-cultural communication in Sweden, an activity that was then also internationally new but was proving itself to be a rapidly growing area of expertise. She wrote the book, based on interviews with bankers and businesspeople who had experience dealing with Swedes, primarily for foreign businesspeople.

At the time, I had no inkling that this was one of several consequences of a new interest in "national cultures" throughout the Western world. Today, knowledge of cross-cultural management and the implications of cultural differences for business contacts are self-evident elements in educational programs dealing with international commerce.

Those encountering immigrants and refugees—social workers, health workers, school teachers, housing managers, and the police—increasingly need to know how to deal with cultural differences. In recent years Sweden has taken in, by European standards, a relatively large proportion of refugees. Of the total Swedish population of about eight million, people originally from other countries and their children comprise about one million. Indications of rising xenophobia have fueled a public debate on the distinctiveness of Swedish culture, on the willingness and unwillingness of native Swedes to accept other cultures, foreign traditions and habits, differing values and religious beliefs. Sweden's negotiations for membership in the European Union (EU) have highlighted the Swedes' acceptance of and resistance to the idea of adapting themselves to non-Swedish values and points of view—that is, to other mentalities.

The publication of this book in Sweden, in 1989, marked the first time a native Swedish social researcher had attempted to describe Swedish mentality since the population statistician Gustav Sundbärg had in 1911 completed a federal commission on the Swedish emigration to America. In his book *Det Svenska folklynnet* (The Swedish national character), a by-product of the emigration study, he regrets that Swedes seemed to find it remarkably easy to adapt to the great land in the West.

After the Second World War it was more or less taboo in Sweden to discuss "national character" (the subject was generally considered scientific nonsense). As a reaction to Nazi racial theories, all talk of distinctive national traits was discredited. Two circumstances reinforced this attitude. One was the relative lack of cultural minorities and of foreigners coming from cultures very different from the Swedish; both existed, of course, but in general the population was remarkably homogeneous. There were no real grounds for thinking in terms of cultural differences.

The second circumstance related to the very core of Swedish national identity, the idea of Sweden as a modern country, and one distinguished by justice and rationality and remarkable economic success. Given this notion, it was possible to hold to the proposition that Swedes actually did not have any special culture—in contrast with people in other countries, who were thought to be entrenched in their sundry picturesque customs and irrational religious beliefs. Swedes could spontaneously accept the description of certain holidays—Midsummer, for instance—as particularly Swedish, but could hardly accept that Swedes were clearly distinguishable by any psychological profile. This helps to explain why descriptions of Swedes by foreign researchers and journalists—there are quite a lot of such studies—have received little attention in Sweden. Neither the American psychiatrist Herbert Hendin's book *Suicide and Scandinavia: A Psycho-Analytic Study of Culture and Character* (1964) nor the British journalist Paul Britten Austin's book *On Being Swedish* (1968) has been translated into Swedish.

This state of opinion changed radically during the 1980s. In Sweden the myth of Swedes as a people lacking cultural ballast has gradually been replaced by a variety of national stereotypes—even in research projects. It has become immensely popular to discuss Swedishness and Swedish identity. By writing this book I have inevitably helped to establish or reinforce these stereotypes.

It is worth noting that interest in national character stretches far back in history, and also that this interest has varied from period to period (see van Heerikhuizen 1982 and Dundes 1986). In only the last fifty years, a remarkable number of efforts in this genre have been published, especially in the United States and, even more, in Japan. Well known are Margaret Mead's *And Keep Your Powder Dry: An Anthropologist Looks at America* (1942) and David Riesman's equally classic *The Lonely Crowd* (1950). Others include the study of the German character by Adorno et al. (1950), Geoffrey Gorer's book on the English (1955), and Luigi Barzini's on Italians (1964). Fernand Braudel (1986), a leading figure in the French *Annales* school, could be mentioned here along with other explorers of the French (e.g., Peyrefitte 1976).

The Society for Intercultural Education, Training, and Research (SIETAR)—presently SIETAR International—was established in 1974 as a forum for the exchange of research and its practical applications. The closely associated Intercultural Press Inc. publishes books on, for instance, cultural encounters in various contexts. Examples of these handbooks include Alison R. Lanier's *Living in the U.S.A.*, first published in 1973, which according to the publisher's blurb is a "fast-paced, readable survey of what Americans are like and how they conduct their lives." More analytically penetrating is Edward C. Stewart's *American Cultural Patterns: A Cross-Cultural Perspective* (1972). Particularly applicable to business is Martin J. Gannon's *Understanding Global Cultures: Metaphorical Journeys Through Seventeen Countries* (1994). Highly reputed in the field of intercultural communication is Edward T. Hall. One of his widely read books is

Understanding Cultural Differences: Keys to Success in West Germany, France, and the United States, written with Mildred Reed Hall (1990).

The question is, of course, whether a nation is a meaningful unit of analysis at all. To those familiar with sundry postmodernist deconstructions of the concept of culture, any such project is by definition futile. What a multitude of shifting patterns of behavior and life styles is contained within that geographical area known as Sweden! What a false impression of coherence, uniformity, and continuity scientists are forced to create out of the real chaos of diffuse structures and random contexts that constitute the actual reality!

Such a view is both reasonable and empirically valid, but disregards the purpose of any particular inquiry. There is always the option to disregard irregularities and multiple variations in order instead, on other levels of abstraction, to seek regularity and consistency. This is particularly true when working from a comparative perspective.

What Swedes share is different from what Americans, for example, share. This book should be read in this way: not as a consummate portrait of Swedes but as pictures of Swedes compared with other nationalities—from a contrastive perspective. In some respects, Swedes resemble many other people; the value Swedes place on modesty, unpretentiousness, and moderation recalls the Japanese, for instance. In other ways the differences are striking—for example, the strictly separated sexual roles in Japan versus the gender-crossing tendencies in Sweden (Daun 1986). What one points to as Swedish from a contrastive perspective thus depends on which other cultures are used for comparison. It would be virtually impossible without such implicit or explicit references to describe a national mentality per se; hardly any other language exists.

One question readers might ask is how widespread a phenomenon must be to be defined as typically Swedish. Must it encompass a majority of the population? Or will it suffice that a certain personality type among Swedes is the most usual, the "modal" among several others? In this book the term "modal" will crop up, for example, in the phrase "the modal Swedish personality," only to remind the reader that Swedishness is a matter of prevalence. The personality tests that I include have not led to any quantitative description of a modal personality structure, only to frequencies of different personality traits. However, I have assembled a number of traits that in my view are relevant to a description of a modal Swedish personality structure.

Comparisons with cultures other than the Swedish are fundamental throughout. This means, as several others have claimed, that one characteristic—sadistic propensities, for instance—can be limited to a small minority of a nation's population, let us say 7 percent, but still be considered typical. This is because comparisons may show that sadism occurs far less in other countries. Thus an underlying assumption is that the relatively greater occurrence of sadism, say, correlates with more general features in a society, that it reveals something essential that distinguishes just that society from many other—but not necessarily all other—societies.

That the question of national identity is far more complicated than what is implied by the above will be apparent when I address the subject of shyness. Should Swedes be described as shy if shyness ("high communication anxiety"), according to one measurement method, applies to 25 percent of the population? The answer is probably yes, since figures for the Japanese, who in comparable measurements appear to be extremely shy, do not exceed 36 percent (Daly and Stafford 1984), and since certain other peoples show smaller frequencies.

The behavior among Swedes that is generally referred to as shy or reserved has, I believe, several different causes. Shyness is not only "communication anxiety" and social insecurity. Verbal passivity may depend upon avoidance of conflict, but it can also be due to indifference, which I discuss in more detail later. The portion of Swedes who behave shyly—what non-Swedes interpret as shyly— may consequently be greater than the portion of Swedes who in a questionnaire declare that they actually feel great communication anxiety in certain situations.

One of the bases for my description of Swedishness is some thirty years of living near immigrants in Sweden and approximately five years of traveling, studying, and working in other countries. Without these experiences it would have been much more difficult to observe Sweden from, at least to some extent, an outsider's perspective.

In 1981 I began systematically to interview immigrants of different nationalities to compensate for my inevitable home-blindness. I also participated in a survey study of interviews carried out with several hundred immigrants who replied to questions concerning what they found positive and negative about moving to Sweden. This and other studies of my own, to which I refer only limitedly, have provided bases for my assertions and suppositions regarding Swedes. In addition, I cite quite a few publications in English, written by journalists and researchers, most of them American, who have clearly and pithily communicated their impressions of Sweden. One of these publications is Thomas Anton's book *Governing Greater Stockholm: A Study of Policy Development and System Change* (1975).

Another basis has been provided by a number of studies carried out by Swedish scholars, representing widely different points of departure. I shall name several here, primarily to illustrate this multidisciplinary approach: ethnologist Billy Ehn's books on immigrants and his study of Swedish culture as reflected in children's public day-care environments; social anthropologist Ulf Hannerz's reflections on Swedish culture, with a point of departure in key words or folk concepts; Hans L. Zetterberg's lifestyle investigations and other sociological studies; linguist Jens Allwood's paper on Swedish patterns of communication; Astrid Stedje's contrastive studies of German and Swedish language use; psychologist Charles Westin's research on Swedes' attitudes toward immigrants; psychiatrist Nils-Erik Landell's studies of self-awareness; economists Kim Forss and colleagues' investigations of cross-cultural management.

A primary source has been the European Values System Study, a comparative survey that included Sweden, carried out in the beginning of the 1980s. Representative samples in thirteen European countries were asked the same questions. Corresponding surveys in the United States and Japan were added later.

On various occasions I have brought up pertinent questions at lectures and seminars in Japan, Italy, the United States, Hungary, and Norway. I have cooperated with the Finnish psychologist Carl-Erik Mattlar in Turku, with the linguist Sachiko Ide at the Women's University in Tokyo, with Pyun Kwang-soo, professor of the Swedish language at Hankuk University of Foreign Studies in Seoul, with the psychologist Christa Zimmermann-Tansella at the Institute for Medical Psychology at the University of Verona, with James McCroskey at the Department of Communication Studies at West Virginia University, and, in Sweden, with the psychiatrist Martin Eisemann at the University of Umeå and the Italian psychiatrist Giacomo d'Elia at Linköping University.

Several friends and colleagues have helped me to survey some three hundred American students at seven universities: Vernon W. Boggs, City University of New York; David Cooperman, University of Minnesota; Bert Hanson, Oklahoma State University; Sharlene Hesse-Biber, Boston College; David Popenoe, Rutgers University; Ester Rider, Georgetown University; and Robert N. Wilson, University of North Carolina at Chapel Hill. The questionnaires used a personality inventory, CMPS (Cesarec-Marke Personality Scheme), which has been used a great deal in Sweden. CMPS was constructed in 1964 by Zvonimir Cesarec and Sven Marke and was based mainly on the American psychologist Henry Murry's need variables. CMPS was translated into English and Finnish and later also into Italian, Japanese, and Korean.

Thus the empirical base for my investigation consists of the following: quantitative survey data, informal interviews with immigrants, written reports by foreign authors (academics, journalists, fiction writers), qualitative material dealing with Swedish culture and intercultural communication compiled at Swedish universities, news media material, and my own anthropological observations in Sweden and elsewhere (cf. Brannen 1992).

From this mixed material I have crystallized pictures of an overall Swedish mentality, *a Swedish theme*, which in reality (more than has been indicated by this book) varies, depending on social class, generation, gender, and geography. It is this Swedish theme that I have brought into focus, not the variations. The descriptions are often presented in generalized forms, implying that everything is much more complex on a more detailed level of abstraction. I have combined observations with statistics and have tried to dramatize Swedish patterns by means of foreigners' stories and narratives.

The qualitative material on Swedes contains a bias toward the urban middle class, which includes foreign writers and scholars in Sweden. The specific consequences of this bias are easy to understand. The kind of Swedishness I discuss scarcely refers to the countryside and only limitedly to the working class. My urban data mainly stem from Stockholm, not at all from Gothenburg, Sweden's second largest city, which actually represents a somewhat different Swedish mentality. The book also contains a male bias.

These imbalances may disturb those who would prefer a more all-around representation—and in that sense a more just picture—of

Swedes, and those whose insights into different Swedish milieus contradict the book's theses. It is, however, my basic theory—by no means original—that the "Swedish theme" appears in all Swedish environments, but in varying forms determined by particular circumstances and contexts.

The individual-based data derived from immigrants, foreign journalists, or researchers possess no independent "value as evidence." Separately they are indicators and are used as examples. Together, however, they can be used as building blocks, composing part of the whole collected material.

All data have weaknesses. Scholars working with statistics often give high priority to quantification. Qualitatively oriented researchers believe more in nuanced descriptions of concrete contexts. Survey studies with their standardized questions conceal—and oversimplify—much of reality. Personality tests are blunt instruments. Anthropological observations have other shortcomings, especially if the aim is to make empirical generalizations. Reliability is difficult to check, and the subjective elements that exist in all social science easily break through. For the time being, we shall have to accept this, but these weaknesses should not be forgotten.

Nor should the reader forget that, as I have already underlined, what is described are patterns and prominent features: there is no national character that encompasses all Swedes. Even when I generalize, it does not mean that Swedishness exists in any uniform guise. Nor is Swedishness clearly delimitable or permanent: Swedishness *in reality* fluctuates in time and space and between different social contexts, but here I have been guided by the educational aim of nailing it down as clearly as possible.

The book also contains analyses of contexts and processes. How are Swedish traits connected? What are their historical roots? Many answers to these questions are necessarily speculative. It is difficult to investigate mentalities historically; there is a risk, as one of my Swedish colleagues has pointed out, "that one picks out from the past those facts that suit one's observations without really being able to show any causal connection" (Frykman 1993, 129). This is undoubtedly true, but there is no other way to explain a mentality. What we can do is simply construct psychologically plausible models of the generative processes, to find hypothetical links between given facts that make sense. Every theory invites a challenge.

The negative streak in the overall picture of Swedish mentality that emerges in this book is due to two circumstances. One is that the immigrants and other foreigners who have commented on Swedes are often, albeit by no means always, negative. In the above-mentioned quantitative field survey of immigrants in Stockholm county, their negative attitudes toward Swedes were a striking finding, and contrasted with positive attitudes toward Swedish society (Daun 1985). Swedes were considered cold, distant, and discriminating, and many immigrants straightforwardly admitted to difficulties comprehending the Swedish psyche. Since my book focuses on Swedes and not Swedish society, these demerits based on foreigners' experiences are particularly prominent.

The second circumstance is my own approach. My role in the construction of the presented reality is unavoidable. Discussions of *reflexivity* in anthropology have called attention to this side of the research process. Where do I stand? What do I think of Swedes? There is little space here to answer such a question, and I would find it hard to give an unequivocal answer. However, I have incorporated enough of other people's views of Swedes to be able critically to look at Swedish culture and at my own personality, formed in a Swedish environment—certainly not an environment that I share with other Swedes in all respects, but one that is common enough.

But as with many immigrants, my own cultural encounters lead to defensive positions. Inevitable bonds with my Swedish upbringing force me to insist emotionally on this given identity; I can never wholeheartedly join in with the critical chorus in which foreigners are free to participate. For I feel, after all, secure in my Swedish role, with its Swedish patterns of communication and ways of responding.

Try to overlook the negative tone. This book is not meant to feed a debate, even if it has provoked some of my compatriots. It is in the nature of the subject to be provocative. Everyone who has lived long in Sweden possesses enough competence to comment on Swedes. However, I would reiterate that throughout this book Swedes are seen from the *outside*, or obliquely, even when comparisons are not explicitly made with other cultures. Perhaps you have to have experienced living in another country or, like myself, shared your life with a non-Swede (preferably a non-Scandinavian) to avoid referring all generalizations about Swedes to your own personal experience of them—which is what almost all native Swedes do. To look at yourself and people of your own kind, your own culture, from the outside is exceedingly difficult.

Culture

Experiences

Although every day we are exposed to outside influences through reading newspapers and watching television, we are most profoundly affected by our own lives, by our living conditions, by direct experiences and impressions. Some of this we take in consciously, sometimes enthusiastically. Other impressions reach us unreflectively, but these too are filed away in the brain. Nothing goes unregistered—not even the sounds that penetrated our mother's womb in our very first moments of life.

Just this, our sensitivity to all impressions, explains why people differ so much from one another. We have been brought up in different ways by different adults, have lived in different places, and are thereby exposed to a variety of impressions—some of them similar, some of them not. As small children, we had our own set of playmates and, for that matter, our own sort of toys. Some of us grew up with only one parent, some with foster parents. It is easy to illustrate further how we have been exposed to diverse impressions and how we have therefore stored different experiences. This is one of the two points of departure for personality research; the second is that people differ biologically.

But all people do not differ to the same extent. This is partly because of biological similarities between some individuals but also because of experiences they have shared—that is, external impressions received when growing up and throughout one's life. Those who grow up in the same environs, in a particular kind of community, perhaps in a neighborhood where people from only one social class live, share similar experiences. Children are exposed to class-related experiences; to a degree they imitate their parents' language as well as food habits, leisure activities, and much more.

The images people have of their physical and social surroundings are shaped by their common points of view. When people share some basic living conditions, they are also likely to share experiences and thus become similar to each other in certain respects—especially when growing up. Children growing up with only one parent have certain experiences in common, as do children who live in the countryside, children of teachers or of parents working shifts.

However, people's similarities and differences are mixed together. All children of teachers do not live in the same kind of neighborhood, and shift workers do not all raise their children in the same way. The overall effect may seem to be a muddle of similarities and differences, but there is a certain system in these "intersecting" experiences. Most shiftworkers' family backgrounds lie in the working class, and this affects their educational level, which in turn has other systematic consequences.

Thus certain life experiences are connected, not in every individual case, but typically, as tendencies. If we regard this phenomenon from a national perspective—indeed, from an international one—we understand better the patterned qualities of work groups, neighborhoods, and social classes. We encounter patterns, but these patterns only exist approximately; more specifically, the same individuals may differ from one another and merge into other groups and population categories. This complex reality is subjected to varying cultural definitions. Anyone seeking a "Swedish culture" will find a multicultural Sweden, not necessarily a single, uniform national culture. What appears are different local cultures, professional cultures, youth cultures, class-bound cultures, and minority cultures, such as those of the blind, homosexuals, Gypsies, and members of religious sects. But upon closer scrutiny these also fall into subgroups, which in turn break down into more or less unique individuals.

It should now be evident why "culture" is an abstraction: one has to abstract what is common and simultaneously ignore what is different. One has to isolate certain similarities from a reality that in fact has a motley content. In this sense culture is only given through its chosen definition.

Values

I have been occupied with what people know or believe that they know, but there is also an evaluating side of human experience: what people want.

Along with obtaining knowledge of the surrounding world, children learn to "grade" things—beginning with their own activities. To eat, to sleep, and to do number two get plus points; to put stones and grass in their mouths earns them minus points. By praise and rewards, admonishment and punishment, children learn to distinguish what is good from what is bad (according to their parents' views). This learning process continues with direct instructions and through imitation of parents and older siblings and friends.

People seldom arrive at their values on the basis of their own deliberations and independent judgments. Children never do. Values are internalized in those social contexts where people live and work. Nor do scholars arrive at their scholarly values all by themselves and on the basis of independent judgment. To a great extent they take over general perspectives, theories, and methods encountered earlier among fellow students and inspiring teachers. They are shaped even more by the "trends" present in the scientific community they eventually become part of.

People tend to stick with the familiar, to a well-known environment and to those modes of living they are used to. Values belong to the identity of the individual. Almost independent of the particular quality of the content (according to any chosen objective criteria), we award special plus points to "our own." Someone who has early on begun to use sugar in coffee prefers things sweet; others immediately react with distaste when sugar is mistakenly put in the cup. A simple mechanism, similar to that behind such trivialities, steers most people's values.

The Swedish way of life is generally preferred by Swedes, not because Swedes have arrived at that conclusion by close thought or meditation, but because they know it so well. They have got used to habits like "going to the country," eating crispbread, speaking in a low voice, and avoiding controversial subjects in conversation. Most of what Swedes do they do because their Swedish friends and class comrades do it, which also means that Swedish society is primarily organized for the satisfaction of native Swedes' specific interests.

Just as people's experiences differ because they live different lives in different surroundings, so are their values differentiated. No individual appreciates and dislikes the same things to the same degree as another individual; everyone is unique in this respect. However, people's values, as their experiences, form into systematic patterns. People of the same class, profession, age, or gender, and inhabitants of the same region or community, often share some general value orientations, preferences or distastes, at least in terms of frequencies compared with other population categories.

The European Values System Study (see Harding and Phillips 1986) provides examples of the links between people's experiences and their values. One question in the study was, "Do you really look forward to going back to work when the weekend is over or do you regret it is over?" Among the Swedes interviewed, fewer blue-collar workers looked forward to work (30 percent) than middle-class people (40 percent), which is probably related to the fact that much of the former's work is dirty and monotonous and generally less stimulating than the latter's. Responses to this question also differed between men (37 percent) and women (31 percent), possibly because of the conflict between housework and professional work, which conflict women especially suffer from. The difference here may also be due to the fact that more women than men have monotonous, nonindependent, and badly paid jobs. This hypothesis was supported by answers to another question, "How much pride in your work do you feel?" Fifty-five percent of the men but only 44 percent of the women answered, "A good deal."

What has thus far been said about values should not be taken to mean that they cannot change, even when, for instance, the spirit of the times, working conditions, or one's social circle remains the same. We all know this: A life crisis, for example, the premature death of a relative, may give one a new perspective on existence, and certain values may be awarded a higher priority. Discussions with a close friend who has found a new direction can also provide an impetus to alter one's own point of view. A book can awaken new interests. But more than anything else, what shapes our scale of values, idiosyncrasies, and dreams of the future is culture: in Sweden, Swedish culture, with its multifarious historical roots and connections with religion, economy, social organization, habitation, demography, climate, and nature—albeit modified by the individual's own environment, his or her particular social class, gendered upbringing, and so forth.

Violations of Values and Norms

The above may have given the impression that humanity is totally dependent on external forces: people *receive* experiences and values; there is no free choice.

However, even within a circumscribed, culturally homogeneous milieu, where people are well acquainted with the applicable rules of behavior, individuals break the rules. The reasons for this are both individual and situational. Some individuals, because of their personalities, are more obedient than others; they dress as they are expected to, observe etiquette, celebrate all the conventional holidays. Some know the rules but break them now and again because of time, ignorance, aggression, or aversion to all conformity or simply because they are contrary; others, because of forgetfulness or absentmindedness. Some deliberately contravene norms in order to convey a message—for example, provocatively refuse to invite a disliked relative to a wedding party.

The European Values System Study gives examples of age-related norm contravention, which show that deviations also follow certain patterns. In one question, the respondent was asked to react to different norm violations, one of which was "To claim social benefits you have no right to." Ten alternative answers were given, and the two most extreme stated that this action "can never be justified" and "can always be justified." Sixty-four percent of the Swedes in the youngest age group (18–29 years) replied "never," while 78 percent in the middle age group (30–49 years) and 88 percent of those over 49 gave the same answer.

A certain portion of the population—the younger in greater numbers—thus consider they have a "right" to go against a norm, a right that is denied by the very formulation of the question. The explanation for the variation in responses among the age groups may be that the younger age groups have still not internalized society's norms to the same degree as the others. This is one explanation for the as yet not wholly explained fact that criminal acts are committed to a greater extent by young people than by old. A complementary explanation is that the younger violator of norms has grown up in a time when affiliation with Christian morals is not as likely as it was before. Willingness to subordinate oneself to collective norms has diminished; more people—especially young people—make individual assessments of what they can gain or lose given one or another alternative. The norms of groups of youth can in part be considered de facto norms—not deviations from another set of internalized norms, as they may appear to older generations.

Those who most often make use of "social benefits" are persons with limited economic resources, and therefore one could expect that proportionately more of those with relatively weak resources would not categorically answer "never" to the question. From the working class, 76 percent considered that "never" was justified; 83 percent of the middle-class respondents gave the same answer.

In addition, attitudes toward this question were clearly related to the degree of anonymity or informal social control where the respondent lived. In any case, the portion answering "never" was smallest in the big cities (77 percent), somewhat larger in communities with more than three thousand inhabitants (79 percent), and greatest in very small communities (82 percent). The most "honest" population was located in the least urbanized, northern part of Sweden (86 percent).

Codes and Interpretations

A young woman from the United States who came to Sweden for the first time in 1984 told me that she was astonished that "Swedes spit in public." The spitters were men. I had never thought about the matter as something that distinguished one country from another, but her observation was confirmed by my own daily experience. I even had colleagues at the university who spat. It is unclear how general this behavior is throughout the country, but spitting is most likely class related. The young woman recalled that spitting was forbidden in America, that one risked being fined (a legacy from the ravages of tuberculosis, I was told later). Shortly after this I met an English woman who had been living in Sweden for twenty years. I asked her what most surprised her on first acquaintance with Sweden and Swedes; "That people spit," she said.

Culture is a system of codes. A certain way of dressing, a garment, a hairstyle, a way of moving or of pronouncing a certain vowel, intonation, views of child-rearing—all these and many more function as signals linking a person with a certain category in the population. But the code system varies in significance for different groups. Spitting, which among its genuine practitioners is done smartly and with a sort of nonchalance, can be taken by many Swedes to be positive and a powerful masculine expression. In other Swedish eyes, it reveals a working-class background or is deemed negative—as a lack of refinement. To some non-Swedes, spitting can be experienced as an expression of a general primitiveness, which may hark back to the Vikings.

We human beings constantly communicate "messages" about ourselves, about our personalities and sociocultural abode. Interpretations of these messages, however, vary according to receiver. Swedes are interpreted by many immigrants as "socially closed" and "spiritually empty." These interpretations are stereotypes; that is, they lump everyone together. But it is equally important to recall that the codes of foreigners are interpreted according to systems of meaning that are applied in cultures other than the Swedish. Many Swedes' relatively slow way of speaking, for instance, can be taken as "arrogant," even though there are no real grounds for such an interpretation (see Phillips-Martinsson 1981).

One reason Swedes are considered "complacent" is their relative taciturnity, their tendency to listen rather than talk. In countries with a heavily stratified social structure, those in superior positions normally do not associate informally or converse to any great extent with their subordinates. When a Swede present in a group of French businesspersons, for example, is a colleague on the same level as the others and not their superior or boss, his taciturnity is interpreted according to their scheme of things as smugness—"as if he (the Swede) thought he was something."

Punctuality is a virtue in Sweden, but it is not always so positive elsewhere. In Sweden a working day can be planned in detail, with meetings beginning at ten, one, and three o'clock. The times can be written into a planning diary months in advance. It is assumed that the meetings will end by a certain time. To Swedes, this means efficiency and organization, of which many are proud. But to a foreign colleague, "to end on time" can indicate lack of interest, since it may entail an abrupt stop. It may appear that Swedes display an unsympathetic and impractical rigidity when it comes to human relations.

Codes and the value systems of cultures are of vital importance when trying to understand encounters between people of different nationalities. The interpretation and evaluation of a single code depend on cultural context and may vary considerably, depending on that context. A foreigner's perception of a Swede as "self-satisfied" or "smug," on the basis of the latter's taciturnity, exemplifies a misinterpretation that is made when people ethnocentrically judge others' character traits from the frame of reference of their own code system.

An interesting illustration of this misjudgment is the Finns' perception of Swedish men on the basis of the specifically Finnish form of communication, which is characterized by much greater taciturnity, slowness, and communication anxiety than that of native Swedes. According to several sources, Finns consider Swedish men "womanish"—or, in other words, suffering from a lack of "manliness." To Finns the ease with which Swedish men talk with anyone about anything—a trait generally ascribed by Finns to women—is incomprehensible. The Finns even have a term of abuse for Swedish men—"homo," that is, homosexual—that refers to this allegedly feminine character trait: "A real man should not talk unnecessarily."

This is a good illustration of how descriptions and interpretations of cultural characteristics depend upon the culture within which the descriptions are made. The Finnish perception of Swedish men contrasts greatly with many Swedes' national image of themselves as relatively reserved, and contrasts even more with the perceptions of Swedes held by Europeans outside Scandinavia.

From her work in the Organization for Economic Cooperation and Development (OECD) in Paris, Jean Phillips-Martinsson has reported the impression the Swedish delegation made on the representatives of other countries: "[W]e had nicknames for all delegations and the Swedish delegation was nicknamed 'The Quiet Men'— they attended meetings, yes, but rarely participated. They arrived punctually, were always very polite and well-dressed, but stuck together and rarely opened their mouths!" (1981, 18).

Personality

In contrast to culture, which is a collective phenomenon, personality is both collective and highly individual. Personality is collective only to the degree that individual traits are systematically observed in a population; for example, more Americans than Swedes seem to be characterized by an extroverted personality (Daun, Burroughs, and McCroskey 1988).

Despite all the sophisticated personality research available, it is still not possible to predict how, for example, a person with a certain sociocultural heritage, brought up in a certain way, will place on Eysenck's extroversion scale, which shows how extroverted or introverted a person is. This unpredictability is due to the almost infinite number of factors affecting an individual's personality (Cook 1984,180). The individual personality is unique.

Psychotherapeutic and psychoanalytic treatment takes account of a patient's particular background, even if many of his or her experiences can be sorted into more generally relevant categories. Aptitude and intelligence tests register unique individual traits or capacities, but they do so with instruments constructed on the basis of general talents. Personality research is occupied with widely divergent population categories such as children, criminals, smokers, overweight people, and with personality traits such as introversion, aggression, affiliations, and the need to dominate. The research devoted to the personality structures of certain population categories—smokers, for example—is also important for the understanding, and thus also the clinical treatment, of individuals.

The study of "national character," or mentality, is mainly concerned with those personality traits and psychological predispositions that have systematic consequences for behavior among groups and populations. These psychological predispositions may be registered in terms of significant tendencies in comparison with other groups or collectives. The concept of personality traits has, for example, immediate relevance with regard to a universally occurring value such as work and work performance, but not with regard to an empirically more limited value such as the preference for highly spiced food (but a link with personality may possibly exist here too: an inclination toward sensuality or sensuous pleasure). A great many customs that are generally not described as related to personality are nevertheless presumably rooted in it; a probable example of this is the Swedish habit of frequent thanking, reflected in common phrases like *tack för senast* (roughly, "thanks for your hospitality"; literally, "thanks for the last time we were your guests") and *tack för maten* ("thanks for the food/meal").

In the Swedish as well as the German tradition, the study of national character is also called "folk psychology," which stresses the psychological nature of this research. In the United States, less burdened with racist biological heresies, the term "national character studies" (along with "psychological anthropology")—so loaded with negative connotations in Sweden and Europe—is still used in respectable circles. On the other hand, the anthropologist and folklorist Alan Dundes has reported that Columbia University Press refused to use the original subtitle, "A Study of German National Character," in one of his books published by that press in 1984. It was changed to "A Portrait of German Culture Through Folklore" (Dundes 1986). I also pondered "culture"—"Swedish culture"—as an alternative term, in order to avoid the negative charge of "national character." Because of the uncomfortably broad meaning of the concept of culture, however, I decided to use "mentality"—referring to the French school of historical research.

The American culture and personality research initiated by Ruth Benedict and Margaret Mead especially, and by the psychoanalyst Abram Kardiner, was inspired by the Gestalt psychology that emerged during the second decade of the twentieth century. Research was also influenced by Freud, and anthropologists carried out practical research in close cooperation with psychiatrists (see Bock 1980). A psychological dimension was thus established right from the start.

Culture and personality, like national character, basically lost their academic interest toward the end of the 1950s, partly because of a generation shift, but also because of methodological difficulties. One attempt to counter these difficulties was the statistically oriented "cross-cultural correlation approach," which used *inter alia* the "Human Relation Area File," established at Yale by George Peter Murdoch. This register made it possible quantitatively to compare data from hundreds of different societies.

Research on "national character" did not cease, but it became largely the dominion of psychologists and psychiatrists, particularly in specialties such as cross-cultural psychology and transnational psychiatry. The latest addition to the terminology is "cultural psychology," whose main proponent is Richard Shweder (see Stigler, Shweder, and Herdt 1990; Shweder 1991). Psychological anthropology today could be described as a comparatively small research area in terms of the number of scholars involved, but it exists nonetheless as a formal section in the American Anthropological Association.

In Sweden and other countries—at least in Europe—the 1980s brought a break in trends. First of all, in Swedish social science research, multiple disciplines now pursue themes like national identity, cross-cultural relations, mentality, cultural barriers, and so forth. Second, aspects of national cultures are generally studied (less often, national cultures "as a whole"). And third, a contrastive, culturally comparative perspective prevails, partly as a result of interest in intercultural communication.

Personality Traits

In every study of personality, one must first choose levels of detail or abstraction. In a dictionary, G. W. Allport and H. S. Odbert (1936) found around sixteen thousand adjectives with some sort of applicability when describing people, of which about four thousand represented permanent personality traits. With all the rarely used words removed, there are several hundred left, according to James Peabody (1985, 21) in his commentary on "The Allport and Odbert problem."

The large number of words for personality traits does not mean, however, that an equal number of personality traits actually exist. There are almost always words that express different attitudes toward the same trait, for instance, "thrifty" and "stingy," "generous" and "extravagant." Others express different gradations on the same positive or negative scale. This complicates the description of personality as an objective phenomenon but also implies that the number of traits should be much more manageable.

The "number" of personality traits is dependent upon those who observe or study personalities. Levels of detail or abstraction are products of our intellect: the objective reality can be anatomized and classified in precisely those categories that we subjectively choose. Regarding personality, such a classification may achieve finer and finer levels of detail until we reach the level represented by the unique individual. The same applies to the concept of culture, which likewise can be used for ever smaller entities until we reach the level of the individual household or family.

If one tries to characterize a population group or people of a certain nationality, the degree of detail will necessarily be crude. In her study based on foreign businesspeople's view of Swedes, *Swedes As Others See Them* (1981), Jean Phillips-Martinsson proceeds from a relatively abstract level—one might even say a schematic approach—and the number of personality traits she describes as typically Swedish are consequently easy to grasp. Swedes are described by the interviewees as taciturn, serious, stiff, boring, superficially friendly, unsociable, punctual, inflexible, arrogant, and overcautious.

When a group of Swedish pupils in the ninth grade (15–16 years old) were invited to assess "foreigners" (Takac n.d.), the ten most frequently mentioned characteristics were unruly (mentioned by 57 percent), loud (57 percent), lively (54 percent), dirty (49 percent), talkative (46 percent), disgusting (45 percent), irascible (45 percent), lazy (42 percent), old-fashioned (42 percent), and cool (39 percent). What we can glean from these judgments is not only Swedish teenagers' negative attitudes toward foreigners but also their attitudes toward themselves. Their national self-stereotype is a peaceful person who dislikes unruliness and disorder and prefers calm, and who may be described as clean, quiet, industrious, and modern.

The pupils' comments on foreigners mix real personality traits (e.g., liveliness) with judgments that are better described as cultural values (e.g., old-fashioned). It is interesting that one can diminish the number of traits by confining oneself to the *typical* or the quantitative (e.g., the ten most often mentioned). Any comparative study of a personality typical of a nation involves a level of abstraction that likewise limits the degree of detail.

It is also possible to collect certain personality traits under a larger, common heading that represents a continuum, for example, "tight versus loose control over impulse expression," which according to Peabody's study, *National Characteristics* (1985), encompasses a large part of the total personality variation.

Violating One's Personality

I discussed breaking norms in the preceding chapter. Culture prescribes rules and conventions for behavior; for example, in Sweden one holds a fork with the convex side up (in contrast with the custom in the former Yugoslavia), eats with the fork in the left hand (in contrast with what is done in the United States), and holds bread in either hand (in contrast with Indians of India). Naturally, it is entirely possible to break such customs or behavior, even though it sometimes, if not always, leads to negative sanctions—like raised eyebrows, meaningful looks, or critical comments.

It is more difficult to violate one's culturally linked personality. The personality is a more deeply integrated part of the individual than are cultural rules and regulations, and is more difficult to get rid of. For people who are calm and thoughtful in the typical Swedish way, it would be nearly impossible to violate these personality traits by being lively, quick, or temperamental. Only actors manage such transformations. Conceivably, very loquacious Swedes (such do exist) sometimes "bite their tongues" when they realize they have been talking too much. However, it is difficult for the socially insecure person to behave aggressively and outspokenly.

For a consultant in intercultural communication giving advice to businesspeople who wish to be successful with their foreign contacts, it is rather meaningless to propose patterns of behavior that run counter to their personalities. Even so, it may be pedagogically useful to point out to Swedes doing business with the Japanese that they can carry on with their typically Swedish, reserved, taciturn, and markedly polite style of communication; it blends in well with Japanese culture.

Compared with trying to display personality traits that one actually does not possess, it is relatively easy to learn another country's etiquette; for example, in Japan one does not talk business over lunch. Even if customs are ever so entrenched, people can, without exerting a lot of will power, learn to break their own culture's dictates, especially if it is a matter of *refraining* from doing something, for instance, not "thanking for the last time" as Swedish custom prescribes. But try to talk fast and ardently when you are a phlegmatic person who also has both feet planted firmly on the ground! There is little doubt that many Swedes would never manage that.

Basic Personality and Modal Personality

One important step in the American research on culture and personality was taken when the concept of "configuration"—launched by Ruth Benedict, referring to a more or less coherent pattern of thoughts and actions—was replaced by the concepts of *basic personality structure* (BPS) and *modal personality* (MP). This development occurred mainly under the leadership of the psychoanalyst Abram Kardiner and the anthropologists Ralph Linton and Cora Du-Bois. The fundamental methods and concepts regarding BPS were presented by Linton in the book *The Individual and His Society* (1939). To Linton, even though the configuration model was superior to the functionalist way of studying cultural integration, it actually suited only those cultures dominated by an *idée fixe*. With the concept of basic personality structure Linton instead wanted to emphasize that cultural integration occurred among the *individuals* participating in the culture. While Benedict and Mead considered personality and culture as nearly identical entities—personality was culture—Linton and Kardiner tried to understand the causal relation between the two. "Culture is integrated, they say, because all members of a society share certain early experiences that produce a specific basic personality structure, and because this BPS in turn creates and maintains other aspects of the culture. This assumption leads to a division of culture into two parts: *primary institutions*, which produce a 'common denominator' of basic personality, and *secondary institutions*, which are produced by the BPS" (Bock 1980, 87). (The remainder of the current section, as well as the next, "Personality and Culture," is largely based on Bock 1980.)

In her book *The People of Alor* ([1944] 1960) Cora DuBois gave an account of fieldwork in the Dutch East Indies. Her data reported childhood experiences to a great extent, as did earlier studies by Linton and his predecessors. But her material was richer and more systematic. Cora DuBois's ambitious project was received well, but it was also criticized by some, partly because the methods regarding data on individuals—for instance, the Rorschach tests—permitted alternative interpretations. Another objection was that the eight collected autobiographies demonstrated much too diverse character types for any "common denominator" to be distinguished among them.

In any event, DuBois's detailed fieldwork and use of psychological tests constituted methodological progress, and her idea of the "modal personality" was a theoretical contribution. But the modal personality in a population refers to the most frequent type, which is not the same as the "average person" and moreover need not be represented by a majority.

In a later paperback edition of the book, DuBois conceded that in her analysis she may have oversimplified the degree of accord and disregarded the contradictions and deviations between institutions and personality. She now maintained that the use of projective tests was expected to give "multimodal rather than unimodal" results (Bock 1980, 96) and that it was likely that only a small portion of people in a society belonged to these modal groups.

A core issue when studying national cultures is generalizability. I am not in a position to determine the overall impression given by my own presentation of Swedes. If I have given a false impression of unity and accord, this is partly because I have used a contrastive perspective, which has the immediate consequence of dispensing with large chunks of cultural multifariousness. My choice to include certain Swedish traits and not others is dependent upon on which other cultures are used for comparison. The approach also requires a certain clarity, or even schematizing. My aim is to help readers note certain tendencies and phenomena among Swedes, not all equally or according to any principle of representation.

Personality and Culture

"Well-dressed" is an adjective used to depict a person, but for that reason need not be called a personality trait. What it expresses is instead a cultural attribute of a universally valid personality trait that can signify "order." "Well-dressed," however, can also be related to the personality variables "achievement" and "defense of status"—all three concepts taken from Henry Murray's scheme (1938).

Ego weakness and the need for order and achievement orientation are present in different collective "externalizations," as well as in different individual forms. The study of culture is thus partly an exploration of "cultural apparel," that is, an exploration of surface. For example, in what forms do people insist on order—in dress and bureaucratic systems—and to what sorts of performances does the need to achieve refer in any given culture? Needs as such are universal, but the ways they are satisfied vary according to culture. The present book addresses both dimensions.

The study of culture entails investigation not only of external forms, for example, how one attains prestige, but also of internal matters, for example, how strong needs are. The proportion of individuals in one culture who may be characterized as "orderly" according to certain measurement methods may thus be significantly larger than the proportion in another culture when judged according to the same methods. This difference is based on social structures and value systems and is related to culture—but is not identical to it.

In addition, personality traits have a genetic origin, to which many parents of more than one child can attest. Very early on, children growing up in the same circumstances—albeit never with the exact same stimuli (even two-egg twins)—display personality differences that are contingent on biology.

The combination of genetic inheritance and an individual's unique upbringing and life course produces a range of personalities *within* a society much greater than that *between* different societies. Such was the conclusion of a study of the Zuni, Navaho, Mormons, and Spanish Americans by the anthropologist Bert Kaplan, published in 1954. This important discovery has since been referred to by many.

Kaplan's investigations were based on Rorschach tests; so were Anthony Wallace's equally well known studies of two Indian tribes (1952). These studies clearly show that personality is culturally bound but at the same time anchored in more-specific, individual situations—in both the conditions of upbringing and the genetic inheritance. Wallace affirmed that 37 percent of the Tuscarora Indians corresponded to what he defined as the modal personality, while 5 percent of the Ojibwa Indians corresponded to the Tuscarora's modal personality type. However, 28 percent of the Ojibwa possessed the modal personality of their own society. Such research results of course refute the generalized concept of national character, that is, the notion that (more or less) all people of a certain nationality are united by a particular "character," or personality.

Kaplan's and Wallace's and other similar studies led to methodological progress, but they also had weaknesses: small samples and hardly rigorous Rorschach interpretations. The same sort of criticism has been leveled at Erich Fromm's otherwise brilliant, if methodologically rather impressionistic, studies of "social character"—for example, the German social character and the capitalistic "market personality." The psychologists Alex Inkeles and Daniel Levinson, who have commented on the method problem in particular (1954, 1969), are often cited with regard to the demand for greater representative samples and rigorous investigative instruments.

One and the same method, however, can have both strong and weak sides. In the study of personality, psychologists have used quite different methods, such as interviews, systematic observation, questionnaires with structured questions, and projective methods (e.g., the Rorschach). The structured questionnaire is considered relatively reliable, especially when the number of questions—each measuring a self-estimated variable—is sufficiently large. In addition, they generally provide a satisfactory picture of the phenomena they are intended to measure.

In Sweden the personality inventory CMPS, which I have used for my own study, has been widely used. It consists of 165 questions, with fifteen questions for each of Murray's eleven needs variables. In contrast with previous uses of CMPS, which have generally focused on the structure indicated by the eleven variables and have not devoted much attention to individual answers, my use focuses on the information that the answers to the individual questions provide. If one wishes to get close to real-life situations, these questions are exceedingly interesting. The CMPS questions are pertinent to several sides of the Swedish character usually referred to as typical.

In 1970 a random-sample survey using CMPS was carried out in Stockholm County (excluding the city of Stockholm) (see Bygren 1974). It included just over one thousand people eighteen to sixty-five years old. The population was not nationally representative but nevertheless represented a cross-section of the population with regard to social stratification, age, gender, and type of neighborhood. The survey, moreover, comprised a region to which people had immigrated from the rest of Sweden. Since my own aim is to study what is specifically Swedish, all foreign-born people were screened out of the material before I made use of it.

With reference to Inkeles and Levinson's demand that national character studies be based on relatively large representative population samples and that stringent psychological methods be used, I considered that this CMPS survey could give an adequate point of departure for a description of specific Swedish profiles. The same demand should be more than fulfilled by the European Values System Study, containing a representative sample of about one thousand interview subjects in each of the countries studied (see Harding and Phillips 1986).

What Explains Personality?

I have already discussed cultural manifestations as products of human knowledge and values, of what people "know" and what they "want." This, however, does not mean that these factors are the only ones in this generative process. Another class of explanatory factors exists in each society's techno-economic system—that is, the exceedingly tangible framework for people's actions that both facilitates and limits them. Even climate constitutes an explanatory category like other natural preconditions. Climate affects, for example, opportunities to socialize out of doors, as well as the length of the growing season.

Personality also extends explanations of culture. Freudian anthropologists explained how first a particular child's upbringing created a particular personality and how later this personality created secondary institutions "in its own image." However, the question remains, what power does the personality structure have in its influence over society's political organization, legislation, household composition, and so forth, particularly if we presume that the modal personality only includes a small part of the population? In retrospect, these anthropologists were perhaps too enthralled by this idea—not unusual with so-called single-variable explanations, whose simplicity can confer a certain grandeur. In their book *Culture Theory* (1972, 161), the anthropologists David Kaplan and Robert Manners argue instead for "a kind of limited technoeconomic determinism tempered by ideology, tempered by social structure, and, sometimes even tempered by personality."

Thus, there is a question about the explanatory power of personality. The opposite question is, what explains personality? I have already mentioned the Freudian perspective, represented by Mead, Linton, and others, which focuses on the significance of early childhood for socialization (cf. Dundes 1984). We now know that socialization does not cease after childhood, even though early experiences generally are decisive for the development of personality.

Kaplan and Manners also point to a theoretical catch in the earlier explanatory model, which construes socialization as an independent variable: how is it that different cultures have different ways of bringing up children? The authors refer to the work of Erich Fromm, who has taken upon himself the difficult task of explaining different societies' "social character," or dominating personality types.

According to Fromm's theoretical scheme, a society's sociocultural institutions are not created by—nor do they stem from—personality factors. These institutions are generated by history and at least partly autonomous. Fromm views personality and socialization (including child-rearing) as dependent variables, which are more often the results of institutions than their creators. In short, Fromm is inclined to see institutions rather than personality traits as causal factors, even if his approach is essentially dialectic.

Fromm heavily underlines the economic character of society and thinks that a society's institutional arrangements, together with its attendant socialization patterns, tend to create a personality type that is special for that society. Applying a dialectical principle, he claims that a society's institutions, together with its dominating personality type, or "social character," play a dynamic role in maintaining the cultural structure, since it also contributes to cultural change.

Based on knowledge of Swedish society's institutional arrangements and their attendant patterns of socialization, is it then possible
to understand how these preconditions create a personality type typical for Swedes? What dynamic role does this typical Swedish personality—along with social institutions—play in the daily re-creation of
the typical Swedish pattern of culture and in the transformation of
Swedish reality?

Relations

It is primarily through looking at social relations that we are able to understand encounters between the Swedish and non-Swedish, for example, between native Swedes and immigrants. In the relations between people, culture is expressed in terms of feelings and reason—two themes that are later treated in chapters of their own. However, in the present chapter, Swedish social relations are described under five headings: shyness, modesty, independence, avoidance of conflict, honesty, and homogeneity.

Shyness

The psychological phenomenon of shyness, sometimes called communication anxiety or communication apprehension, has been little investigated in Sweden, despite the well-known stereotype of Swedes as rather shy, reserved, withdrawn, stiff, and in many cases not very interested in approaching someone they do not know.

The extent of the phenomenon, however, has been indirectly noted in Swedish psychology texts. "Fear of expressing oneself in a group of people is unfortunately very common. This applies in informal groups, such as peer groups, as well as more formal groups, such as working groups and study groups. Many people sit silent, apparently passive, not venturing their opinions or their knowledge, daring neither to answer or refute points of view they do not share nor to support proposals they agree with" (Holm 1978, 8). Bo-Arne Skiöld, an expert in speech training in Sweden, has pointed out that many adults have difficulties talking in front of large groups (Skiöld 1975). Such statements about people's speech difficulties would not be made in all countries. Shyness as a personality trait is universal, but its extent is related to a cultural context.

The most detailed Swedish study of shyness is Magnus Elfstadius and Anne Pressner's psychological study "Om blyghet" (On shyness) (1984). They suggest that a *positive view* of shyness, which parallels the perception of it as a problem for certain individuals, blocks academic studies. Shyness has been associated with positive abilities such as "empathy and intuition, which particularly in the psychological and psychiatric professions are highly valued." Consequently, understanding its causes has not been considered so vital—at least, has not been considered to be so from the Swedish point of view.

Furthermore, Elfstadius and Pressner maintain that shyness is unusual in the Swedish clinical *nomenclature*. If so, the paucity of the Swedish research contrasts with that by Americans. John A. Daly and Laura Stafford's overview (1984) presents an enormous diversity and wealth of perspectives in the research on shyness. James McCroskey (Daly and McCroskey 1984, 81) writes that this field has been given much attention for more than fifty years and that it constitutes the oldest still vital area within communication research.

Stereotypes of Shyness

To dismiss stereotypes as worthless prejudices has become the convention. In fact, stereotypes sometimes hit the nail on the head, though sometimes they do not. The most "reliable" are self-stereotypes— that is, a group's views of itself, even though such stereotypes may be prone to conceit (see Stewart, Powell, and Chetwynd 1979). Stereotypes are sometimes prejudicially false, particularly in their generalizing capacity: for example, claiming that Swedes are shy, as if *all Swedes always* were shy in *all* situations. Every population is multifarious, and shyness varies according to the situation; some people are fairly comfortable in small groups but avoid expressing themselves in front of larger gatherings.

In survey research carried out in 1985 a national sample of people between sixteen and seventy-four years old were interviewed.

One of the questions asked was, "If you would choose three things to describe Swedes, what would you choose?" Thirty-three percent gave the word "stiff," the second most common answer (Zetterberg 1985, 2). The word here refers to stiffness in social interaction, which is often seen as a sign of shyness.

The same self-stereotyping occurred in a 1986 survey of a thousand Swedish school children ("International Children's Project," IPPNW 1986). The second largest response category was "stiff, reserved, boring," with which 14 percent of all the school children agreed (and 30 percent of the high school students).

Another kind of stereotype is that held by people about groups other than their own. A study of immigrants' stereotypes of Swedes, conducted by the National Public Survey of Ethnic Discrimination, revealed that one of the most widespread of these stereotypes is that Swedes are *closed* and *reserved* (Bergman and Swedin 1982, 201). A similar picture emerges in the Stockholm County Council's investigation of immigrants, "Bra och dåligt i Sverige" (Good and bad in Sweden) (Daun 1985), and in other studies of non-Swedes' views of Swedes.

Many foreigners' conceptions of Swedes are based on hearsay and rumor—that is, on already existing stereotypes. Others more or less reflect firsthand experiences of Swedes. In courses in Swedish for immigrants there is an exchange of both stereotypes and personal experiences between the students. Very likely this leads to a certain amount of homogenization in their images of Swedes.

The question of stereotypes is complicated by the vagueness of the vocabulary of everyday speech. "Shyness" is one such vague, unspecified concept. Who is depicted as "shy" depends on the perspective: Finnish people do not think that Swedes are shy—on the contrary.

The concept of shyness stands either for a personality trait (i.e., something permanent) or for a *condition* (i.e., something temporary or dependent on circumstances). It can be defined (*a*) on the basis of a statistically arbitrary distribution of normality, (*b*) according to norms given within a culture, or (*c*) in comparison with other cultures. McCroskey's point of departure is a technical distribution of normal "shyness" among the American population (16.7 percent high communication anxiety, 66.6 percent normal, and 16.7 percent low), which is then compared with other countries. The common, everyday, vague term "shyness" does not distinguish between feelings and behavior. The technical term "communication anxiety" refers exclusively to how one feels in, or at the thought of, certain situations. This is important to keep in mind. Actual behavior in natural situations is difficult or impossible to study systematically. Therefore most research on shyness is based on attitudes or self-assessments, that is, on personal descriptions.

The most usual criterion used for defining shyness is of course each culture's general conception of it. Most Swedes probably do not conceive of themselves as shy, or "stiff, reserved, boring." It is rather in situations where many may feel their own limitations that shyness comes to the fore, when they think that others expect, or at least would greatly appreciate, a more extroverted and relaxed manner—for instance, on festive occasions requiring many speeches or at gatherings with foreign guests. But the person who behaves "like people usually do" is hardly viewed by others as shy, even though he or she may feel discomfited. The psychologist Phillip Zimbardo conducted a survey in which people were asked whether and how they thought of themselves as shy. The results showed that about 40 percent of Americans generally considered themselves to be shy (Zimbardo 1977).

This result is interesting because it contrasts with the Swedish stereotype of Americans as not shy, which is also the way Americans perceive themselves as a group. The result should be interpreted against the background of those demands for and expectations of nonshy, "bold," and "aggressive" behavior associated with mainstream American culture. It means that the very same behavior could be considered shy by an American but not by a Swede—if we allow ourselves to generalize about Americans and Swedes.

Different social groups hold different values and personality ideals. Such differences are related to the identification of shyness, that is, to what is considered shyness. This is evident in the above-mentioned study of school children (IPPNW 1986, 15). Of students majoring in the humanities, social sciences, and the like, in Swedish high schools, 43 percent thought typical Swedes were "stiff, reserved, boring"; but only 27 percent of the students studying natural science or technical subjects held the same view. In Charles Westin's book *Majoritet om minoritet* (The majority on the minority) (1984), in which different groups describe themselves, the attributes "shy and taciturn" were mainly applied by young wo-men to themselves. In the whole sample of Swedes interviewed, nearly as many mentioned being, for instance, outgoing, talkative, and temperamental. However, this is not to say that these adjectives would be recognizable to immigrants observing Swedish styles of communication.

The third basis for determining shyness involves comparisons with other cultures. All descriptions of one's own national identity, of the type "Swedes are . . . ," presume comparisons with other na-tionalities. In contrast, descriptions of one's own personality are based on comparisons with other people in one's own group.

As the above suggests, it would be a different matter if people other than Swedes, namely foreigners, were to answer the question about shyness among Swedes. Their responses would depend on their own culture, that is, their particular norms and values. For example, most southern Europeans would consider Swedes more shy than the Japanese would, simply because the Japanese score high on communication anxiety scales.

Penetrating the theme of shyness is complicated by the fact that the cultural grounding of personality manifests itself in dif-ferent strengths or degrees of "commonness" in a given nation. Some individuals, as a result of heredity and personal upbringing, are more shy than others—fairly independently of the surrounding cultural expectations. What is culturally formed is the relative distribution.

The Cultural Determinants of Shyness

Donald Klopf (1984, on which this section is primarily based) refers to a comparative study of communication anxiety, "Pacific Basin Studies," which included a sample of Australians, Japanese, Koreans, Micronesians, Chinese from the People's Republic, Filipinos, and a culturally mixed group from the University of Hawaii (Caucasians, Chinese, Filipinos, Japanese, and Korean Americans). The sub-jects were all university students, eighteen to twenty-four years old, with equal numbers of men and women. They were asked to fill in McCroskey's "Personal Report on Communication Apprehension" (PRCA). The differences between the groups are given in table 1.

Table 1 Mean (X) and Standard Deviation (SD) According to PRCA and Proportion of Individuals with High Communication Apprehension (CA) Within the Respective Culture Groups

Culture	N	X	SD	% High CA
Hawaii (U.S.)	397	63.34	12.48	33.5
Australia	219	60.37	12.94	22.4
The Philippines	312	58.09	10.59	13.8
Japan	504	65.90	10.72	35.9
South Korea	73	52.78	10.59	2.8
Micronesia	153	60.78	13.35	22.8
China	184	62.18	11.23	26.0

Source: Klopf 1984, 162.

The cultural variations are obviously great. The difference between the Japanese and South Koreans is striking. Other studies cited by Klopf support these results—for example, a survey of about 4,500 Japanese university students, businesspeople, and other well-educated individuals. When they were compared with Americans and certain other non-Japanese groups, the results showed higher communication anxiety among the Japanese. The psychiatrist Tadeo Doi claims in his book *The Anatomy of Dependence* that shyness (*hitomishiri*) is typical of so many Japanese that there are grounds for designating shyness as a Japanese cultural trait (Doi 1971, 106).

The South Koreans, so different from the Japanese in certain respects, are "outgoing, talkative people who are relatively active, pleasant, industrious, friendly and fast" (Klopf 1984, 163). With our limited knowledge of the Orient, such differences may well surprise us in the West. In another study Koreans are depicted as aggressive and assertive and more temperamental than one would expect from oriental people.

The Micronesians in the study were less shy than the Japanese. They were more shy than the South Koreans and Filipinos but not very different from the Australians and Chinese. The Micronesian students in the survey included Chamorros, Chinese, Filipinos, Palauans, Caucasians, Trukians, and Koreans, who generally in their Micronesian environment are said to have a positive communication "image." In other words, Micronesians are well known for finding it easy to talk to other people. They conceive of themselves as "friendly, dramatic, animated, and impression-leaving."

Their self-stereotype conveys the message that they are interested in other people and generally demonstrate goodwill in communication situations. Micronesians believe themselves to be verbally active, to speak "picturesquely," and to have a penchant for exaggeration.

Regarding the Chinese from the People's Republic, the studies available to Klopf offered little in the way of definite stereotypes. Nevertheless, the Chinese are described as comparatively talkative, even though one investigation of regional stereotypes in China indicated that regional differences were considerable. One stereotype mentioned at least in one province, and here and there in others, was of "people talking too much." They could be open and free with their thoughts and feelings but normally avoided expressing their innermost feelings, thoughts, and problems, especially to people they did not know and especially if the feelings were negative. Others have stressed that the Chinese participate in groups that include the family as well as the immediate or extended neighborhood, the factory, and commune—groups that seldom change membership. As a consequence of this group stability, the Chinese feel comfortable in company with other group members and talk a great deal with them, but rarely express their inner feelings.

After the South Koreans, the Filipinos were the least shy. Typically, the Filipino child grows up in a large network of relations—social and kin. Maturation is not equivalent to independence, as it is, for example, in Sweden and the United States. On the contrary, it involves forming an expanding and satisfying series of dependency relations with others. It follows that the Filipinos seek the company of one another and prefer to do things in groups or through groups rather than by themselves. They cannot stand being alone for long periods. They maintain family ties and other social relations through communication, especially oral communication. Filipino children spend their childhood in an environment where the group is very strong, and they learn the art of verbal interplay, which is necessary in order to be accepted and coexist harmoniously with others. Such an environment provides no soil for the implantation of communication anxiety.

The Filipino example clearly shows that there is a correlation between social structure and personality; that the surrounding human environment nourishes certain character traits.

Shyness in Sweden

In his book on suicide in Scandinavia, the American psychiatrist Herbert Hendin (1964) reported more shyness among his Swedish female patients than among their Danish counterparts. Hendin worked one year each in Sweden, Norway, and Denmark. Compared with his Danish female patients, he found the Swedish women to be more "reserved" in their responses to interviews on emotional problems. It could take several hours to reach the sort of cooperation with the Swedish women that was possible from the beginning with his Danish patients.

A common reaction among the Swedish women, when interviewed the second or third time, was to become *embarrassed* for revealing so much about themselves. This attitude was very different from that of the Danish women, who, when interviewed the second time, often said they had thought of many other things they would like to talk about. The Swedes *blushed often*, from their crowns to their necks. They tended to blush when expressing inner feelings during the interview. Their blushing was usually a reaction to this exposure rather than to any particular subject of conversation.

Swedish men were even more difficult to reach emotionally. They were seldom spontaneously talkative, and in facial expression and body movement they tended to be constrained. When asked questions about their feelings, they were often defensive or cooperated with an air of intellectual curiosity rather than emotional engagement.

It is difficult to judge the reliability of Hendin's observations, at least with a view to using them as independent grounds for generalizations about cultural differences between the countries studied. However, his observations are supported by other evidence of shyness among Swedes, which increases the relevance of the observations. Hendin is a student of Kardiner and exposes himself to the same criticism as his mentor in regard to the small size of the sample, which in itself does not mean that their data cannot be right on target.

To get a better grip on the question, I have used McCroskey's questionnaire and also investigated Swedish university students. The first mailing was done in the fall of 1985. A subsequent expanded psychological personality questionnaire was distributed in January 1987, in cooperation with James McCroskey (Daun, Burroughs, and McCroskey 1988). In 1985, 423 questionnaires were sent to all undergraduate students registered in ethnology at Stockholm University; 77 percent returned completed forms.

Both surveys showed that Swedish students do not differ from their American counterparts in the degree of the anxiety they tend to feel in social communication. However, the two national groups differ in other ways. Although the Swedes consider themselves somewhat more competent in social interaction, they are less likely to initiate conversations. They are less willing to talk. Very likely the documented higher level of introversion among Swedes is an important explanation for this. A significant ramification yielded by these surveys is that *unwillingness to talk* cannot be treated as a universally valid indication of communication anxiety (as has often been done in this research).

The similarities in the degree of communication anxiety between Swedes and Americans are of course astounding, since Swedes are inclined to view Americans as the opposite of shy. Similarities in feelings, however, do not, in this instance, correspond to similarities in actual behavior and behavioral norms. In the United States it is negative to be shy; shy people try to hide their insecurity or try to learn to get over it. Shy persons are considered less competent, even less intelligent than others (despite the fact that investigations show that no such correlations exist). American schools place much more emphasis on oral presentation and performance generally than do Swedish schools (although this situation is changing, and oral proficiency is now given more attention); at some American universities students are graded on their ability orally to present what they have learned.

In Sweden, it is well nigh the opposite. To be shy in Sweden is not at all so negative as it is in the United States, especially in the eyes of others, even if individuals doubtless wish they were more self-assured. Swedes ascribe to the shy person admirable characteristics— reflectiveness, modesty, or unpretentiousness (which is highly valued), willingness to listen to others. A philosopher is not assumed to be loquacious. Taciturnity is seen mainly as a problem for the individual him- or herself, provided that it does not take extreme forms and that one's profession or occupation does not demand the opposite.

Paradoxically, these differences may explain why Swedish students consider themselves more skillful at communication than American students do when judging their own abilities. In America, students feel a pressure for high communicative competence, under which a larger proportion of them must think they cannot rise to the demands. Swedish students, on the other hand, under no such pressure, need worry about their abilities in this regard to a much smaller extent.

If we compare the figures for Swedish students' communication anxiety with the figures in table 1, we find that the group that comes closest to the Swedes with regard to high anxiety is the Filipinos (13.8 percent). According to the two surveys of Swedish students, the portions with high anxiety were insignificantly higher (15.2 percent [1985] and 15.3 percent [1987]). However, as has been mentioned, the Filipinos were described as particularly communicative, more than all the others except for the Koreans.

That despite this Swedes appear less communicative is explained by their relative unwillingness to communicate, which is probably connected with the introverted strain among many Swedes (Daun, Burroughs, and McCroskey 1988, using Eysenck's extroversion scale). Possibly the Swedes' stereotype of themselves as shy is a popular image that explains a more comprehensive personality trait (or set of personality traits) that is based on something else for which there is no other common term available.

Another source of knowledge about shyness is psychological personality inventories. Several of the questions in the Cesarec and Marke's personality inventory (CMPS) that aim at illuminating traits such as dominance, impulsive aggression, defense of status, autonomy, and exhibitionism also provide information on shyness and its prevalence (see Daun, Mattlar, and Alanen 1989, which contains all of the CMPS questions and responses to them).

To the question (no. 94), "When making a new acquaintance, are you the one to take over the conversation?" 67 percent of the sample of Swedes answered no. To another question (no. 26), "Do you often think back on situations which have been embarrassing for you?" 42 percent answered yes, thus describing the discomfort that socially insecure people feel when they have "made a fool of themselves," "said the wrong thing," "behaved inappropriately."

Yet another question (no. 70), "Can you easily maintain your self-confidence also, when you are together with self-confident and supercilious people?" was answered in the negative by 41 percent, the women outnumbering the men. Women's greater lack of self-confidence recurred in several answers.

Shy people typically dislike being the center of attention. To the question (no. 29), "Are you unpleasantly affected by situations where you attract attention?" 55 percent answered yes.

As we see, the percentage of affirmative answers is different for different questions. This is because their content represents different strengths or describes different degrees of the discomfort shy people feel. An extreme example would be a situation in which one were placed in the public limelight by the mass media; confronted with such a prospect several people might be expected to feel discomfort. To the question (no. 106), "Would it be a nuisance to you if newspapers and TV paid attention to you?" 63 percent answered yes.

Consequently, it is difficult to pinpoint the precise percentage of shy people in the Swedish population. Nevertheless, personality inventories are helpful because they give measurements that facilitate comparisons between different kinds of population groups. One can study how psychologically diverse groups distinguish themselves in terms of personality. One can search for possible personality characteristics for certain somatic subject groups. One can study differences between women and men, between different age groups, and between different social strata. Finally, the method makes it possible to study how distinctive features in national cultures are reflected in personality structures.

To exemplify: the inventory in Daun, Mattlar, and Alanen 1989 gives a comparison between Sweden and Finland. The answers to some of the CMPS questions suggest that Swedes are the less shy (see table 2).

Table 2 Shyness Among Swedes (26–65 Years Old) and Finns (29–71 Years Old) (The higher the figure the greater the shyness)

Question no.	Sweden	Finland
26	42% (yes)	57% (yes)
29	55% (yes)	76% (yes)
70	41% (no)	43% (no)
94	67% (no)	72% (no)
106	63% (yes)	80% (yes)

Let us examine another study. In the early 1980s, the psychologist Charles Westin carried out a nationwide investigation of Swedes' attitudes toward immigrants and other minorities (Westin 1984).

The responses to some of the questions in this survey can also be used to illuminate the subject of shyness.

One statement the interviewees were asked to comment on was "I am often afraid to make a fool of myself." The responses were divided as follows:

Very true	4%
Quite true	22%
Not very true	33%
Not at all true	39%
Doubtful, don't know	3%

In total, 26 percent thought that the statement corresponded very or quite well to their views of themselves: they were often afraid of making fools of themselves. According to this indication, one fourth of all Swedish people would be classified as shy (Westin 1984, 345). Whether that figure is to be interpreted as large or small depends on what other culture is used for comparison.

Another of Westin's questions highlights the preconditions for self-confidence—that is, the basis for feeling secure in the company of other people. The interviewees were to respond to the following statement: "I like myself." The responses were distributed as follows:

Very true	14%
Quite true	41%
Not very true	22%
Not at all true	15%
Doubtful, don't know	7%

Judging from these answers, a total of 37 percent had a predominantly negative attitude toward themselves. Remarkably many, 15 percent, did not like themselves at all (Westin 1984, 346). Among these one would not expect to find people who talk frankly and personally with others.

In a 1984 sociomedical study of women between twenty and forty years old in Österåker rural district, Nils-Erik Landell posed a number of primarily psychological questions. The investigation was a follow-up to a research project that I myself had conducted in cooperation with Landell (Daun and Landell 1982). The purpose of both investigations was to find psychological explanations to ill health—psychosomatic as well as somatic. Six hundred and forty women, selected randomly, answered the questionnaire, several of whose questions shed light on the incidence of "shyness" (Landell 1985).

One of the questions was, "Do you possess self-esteem?" The response alternatives were "yes," "no," and "between yes and no." Twenty-five percent answered no. Another question was, "Is it easy or hard for you to find friends?" and this was accompanied by five alternative answers. A total of 6 percent answered that they found it "very difficult" or "rather difficult" to make friends—quite an extreme expression of shyness.

With regard to the comments, given earlier in this chapter, on introversion as a Swedish personality trait—at least in contrast with data on Americans (see Eysenck and Eysenck 1983, 56)—the responses to the following question are interesting: "If you were to characterize yourself, would you say you were quite reserved?" Of the 635 respondents, 19 percent considered themselves "quite reserved."

Neither Westin's nor Landell's investigations permit us to see just how shy Swedish people are, compared with people in other countries. What they do indicate are certain measurements based on Swedes' attitudes toward themselves and toward their social environments. The questions represent different degrees of social insecurity, and the responses vary between 6 and 25 percent. However, this does not preclude there being Swedes whose general pattern of interaction in the eyes of many foreigners appears "reserved," "passive," or "cautious" but in the eyes of most Swedes appears normal and expected. These people, in other words, feel neither reserved nor dissatisfied with themselves. They only "imitate" their Swedish surroundings; they behave as "typically Swedish."

However, a concept like "reserved" is dependent upon the culture in which it is used. Where there is a tendency toward introversion, the likely definition of "reserved" would be more delimited than it is in an extrovert culture such as the American; that is, in Sweden the meaning of being reserved corresponds to a greater degree of reservation than it does in the United States. Even if a single individual from one culture "feels" the same way as an individual from another culture, it is still possible that they name the feeling differently. Difficulties with explaining shyness go hand in hand with difficulties with describing it.

Shyness as Culture

In Sweden it is a well-known maxim that many Swedes behave less shyly when on vacation in southern countries. The American writer Susan Sontag mentions this phenomenon in her essay "Letter from Sweden" (1969). She writes that many Swedes feel freer abroad and behave more expressively: " 'If you only knew me as I am when I'm in Spain.' Or '. . . in New York.' Or '. . . in Italy' " (Sontag 1969, 24).

The sort of remarks that this "liberation phenomenon" elicits from Swedes may be illustrated by the following, which I overheard when a group of Swedish charter passengers were getting close to home: "Oh well, put on the mask again." Sontag had the impression that Swedes are quick to defend their "national character" and that they "are saddened if you show you really mind what so evidently bothers *them* in their intercourse among themselves"—shyness, clumsiness, inhibition. "Swedes so often treat themselves as a 'case,' operating a kind of moral blackmail through the display of their vulnerability" (Sontag 1969, 24).

Many Swedes prepare themselves for giving a speech by writing it down and then reading it aloud. People less bothered by speaking are content with an outline, but even this is written down to safeguard against "losing the idea." It may be a short welcoming speech at a formal dinner or at a conference, a tribute at a birthday party, a thank-you speech to the hostess. "I am no speaker" is the classic opening to a dinner speech with a written manuscript. It is part of Swedish folklore that people lose their appetite when, without forewarning, they have to accompany the hostess to the table and are obliged to "thank for the meal" according to Swedish etiquette. For what is in fact expected is not merely thanks for the food on behalf of the guests, but a much more personal and spiritual address into which compliments on the food should be elegantly integrated.

Communication anxiety is not uniquely Swedish, nor is reading from a manuscript, but they are sufficiently common in Sweden to attract the attention of foreigners (see Phillips-Martinsson 1981). Of course, Swedes' memories are not worse than other people's. The need for notes stems mainly from "that confusion and blocking, lapse of memory, etc., that causes shy people in social situations often to function far beneath their intellectual capacities" (Elfstadius and Pressner 1984). Members of the Swedish parliament (Riksdagen) generally read from manuscripts. If members of the British houses of Parliament did that, they would be booed (according to a Swedish foreign correspondent in a television program).

One variant of communication anxiety is the passivity that comes over Swedes when they are to contribute to a discussion with many other participants. At Swedish universities few students on few occasions ask questions or make comments. English-speaking guest lecturers are sometimes astounded at the silence in the auditorium when the discussion is left open for comments or questions from the floor (see Jenkins 1968). Not surprisingly, many foreign students in Sweden find it surprisingly easy to be active despite their limited language proficiency.

"When I was studying at the [Swedish] Film Institute for two terms, Ingmar Bergman came there," a young American woman related to me.

> We interviewed him in a panel, four Swedes and me, with three hundred people in the audience. He hadn't been there for many years, so it was a great event. But no one in the audience dared to ask any questions, and the four Swedes had thoroughly prepared all their questions, but not me. I asked questions as they came up—spontaneously. Even Bergman himself answered in the same way as the other Swedes, and seemed very anxious to "answer right." Everything he said he'd said many times before, often word for word the same as he'd said in previous interviews, but he performed like an actor who's following a script but tries to sound spontaneous and natural.

According to Elfstadius and Pressner, "Shy persons are especially exposed in situations where they are to show off to their own advantage, express their own views, or subject themselves to an objective assessment."

One manifestation of shyness is speaking in a low voice, something to which Swedes are prone. People from countries where one generally speaks louder, for example, countries in the Middle

East and Latin America, have noted that Swedes generally speak quietly. According to Zimbardo (1977) the shy person is withdrawn and taciturn, and when he or she talks, it is with a soft voice. Lilly Lorénzen ([1964] 1978), in a book on Swedish customs and behavior written for an American public, says that Swedes "mumble" their names when introducing themselves. In Sweden it is considered somewhat arrogant to say one's name loud and clear, "as if you thought you really were somebody." Mumbling signifies modesty.

Another indicator of shyness is the avoidance of eye contact. Eye contact is a frequently discussed theme in studies of body language in different countries, as is its connections with social position, gender, age, and so forth. Socially inhibited people stand out through their avoidance of eye contact.

Apparently many Swedes alternate between meeting another's gaze and focusing on something else, for instance, on a point behind or beside the other person (Phillips-Martinsson 1981, 77). When Swedes listen, however, they may appear to look the other person in the eye. An American bank director, who for a time frequently visited Sweden on business, told me how bewildered she became on a visit to the National Bank of Sweden. During a conversation with a bank employee, she sat with her back to a window, and the man talking to her persisted in looking past her, out the window. He did this for such a long time and with such concentration that after a while she became curious and turned around—but there was nothing particular to see.

Isolated experiences of this sort are supported by a survey conducted by Jens Allwood, professor of linguistics. According to his study, Swedes seem "to tolerate and expect less eye contact than Greeks if [the encounter] is to be experienced as neutral; or, as a Greek respondent expressed it: 'Why do Swedes so seldom look at me—is there something wrong with me?' " (Allwood 1981).

Swedes tend to attach great weight to the impression they make on others—the import of what they say and how they say it. Views and arguments are presented and interpreted as representations of one's identity, as "calling cards," not as anything external, detached from oneself, which one can play around with or simply say without thinking. Such seriousness and concentration increase the level of psychic tension. Occasionally "staring into space" instead of into the eyes of the other person facilitates concentration on one's own words (Richmond, McCroskey, and Payne 1987). "Staring" can be interpreted as inverted attention, as introspection, regardless of culture; but this behavior is striking in the Swedish pattern of communication, especially when someone expounds at length or relates something in detail. It is possible that the social charge lessens when the eyes do not meet. This most likely explains the "downcast eyes," the token of shyness.

In certain cultures, it is thought bold to look a superior right in the eye; the downcast gaze is the expression for subordination. Shy people through their social passivity "downgrade" themselves by always letting others speak first, always holding the door for others, whenever possible meeting others halfway, being accommodating.

The American sociologist David Popenoe, who has written extensively on Sweden (1977, 1985, 1988), told me after a series of interviews in Stockholm that he had especially noted that nearly every person answered *yaa* (yes) to his questions. Almost irrespective of the question, they had opened their response with a *yaa*, which did not always indicate an affirmative answer. What Swedes do with their introductory *yaa* is express their understanding of the other person's question or statement. They are signaling that they have understood what the other has said as reasonable, relevant, pertinent to the subject—that they "have caught on." Linguists call such responses "feedbacks." In Swedish the most common feedbacks are nodding and small words like *yeh*, *mm*, *umhm*, and *yaha* (Allwood 1981). But at the same time, these seem to function as a positive indicator, a desire for "consensus": the *yaa* contributes to a pleasant atmosphere. This adaptation, which can also be seen as a sort of subordination, seems to distinguish many Swedes. Japanese culture is similar insofar as many Japanese have difficulty saying no (Kawasaki 1984).

The phenomenon has been remarked by the British writer Kathleen Nott in her book *A Clean, Well-Lighted Place* (1960, 3–4):

> [A] Swede can do quite an exceptional amount with *"ja."* On the Swedish Lloyd boat there was a conversation of which I understood nothing except *"ja"* and its variants. It was at the next table and too far away for comfortable hearing and in any case I hadn't listened to a general Swedish conversation for eight years. Over an indecipherable buzz,

"*ja*" boomed up and down, sometimes fishing up one of those particles or intensives which continentals often hook on to their affirmatives: *ja*-ha, *ja-saw, ja-visst, ja-yoosta*. And this conveyed a mixture of proper sympathy, polite attentiveness, polite and expected credulity, polite and warmhearted hypocrisy, and dedicated intention to do the right thing at all times.

Swedes' assiduous thanking can be interpreted in a similar way. "One thanks everywhere and in all conceivable circumstances, in shops, but also even on the phone phrases saying thank you replace saying goodbye," remarks Allwood, who goes on to comment that "[o]ne remarkable characteristic is that both partners in such a transaction say thank you and sequences like the following seem very common: *ja tack då, tack tack, tack, tack tack* (yes thanks then, thanks thanks, thank you, thanks thanks)" (Allwood 1981, 27). Thanking functions here as "redundant" communication, that is, as superfluously conveying the message that one is positively inclined. Over and over again both parties repeat their desire for consensus.

In some Swedish situations thanks responses are even more institutionalized, more obligatory. "It is, for example, almost obligatory to thank [the hostess] for the food, something that does not at all apply in Anglo-Saxon cultures. . . . One also thanks for the company, for example, after conversing with an unknown person in the restaurant car of a train, also something that seems unknown in other cultures" Allwood also reminds us of the special Swedish custom of "thanking for hospitality." "This obligation applies with varying degrees of force for different people in Sweden. Some people call up the hosts the day after the event to which they have been invited to thank them. Others wait until they meet the people in question and then express a 'thanks for hospitality,' even though a year might have passed since they last met" (Allwood 1981, 28).

The rituals around thanks recall a past, more hierarchical Swedish society, which even today—in comparison with the United States, for instance—curtails individual freedom in social interactions. L. Wylie (Wylie and Bégué 1970, cited by Peabody 1985) relates that as an American student in France he had said "hello" to his landlady when passing her on the street and was later taken to task for not (*a*) stopping, (*b*) taking off his hat, (*c*) shaking hands, and (*d*)

telling her where he was going. Even if that particular system of
rules does not apply in Sweden (few people today take off their
hats), Swedes have other similar rules that symbolically express
subordination.

The person expressing thanks ritually subordinates him- or herself
to the person being thanked, demonstrating a *debt of gratitude*. This
ritual has certain similarities to bowing, which also signals a subordinated status. If we assume that the insecurity underlying shyness is a
fundamental theme in Swedish culture, we would expect just such an
expression of subordination that profuse thanking suggests. An alternative or complementary explanation, to which I return later, is that
such redundant thanks are a way to reestablish a symmetrical relation—an expression of sameness in a homogeneous society.

Bowing between Swedish men (which Swedes themselves scarcely
think about and which anyway, in comparison with the Japanese, is a
rare and insignificant event) is also behavior characteristic of Sweden,
albeit apparently on the wane among younger generations. Subordination is not real but ritual. It is positively charged, like the Latin
servus, a word of greeting in Hungary and Austria meaning "I am
your servant," corresponding to the old Swedish slang word of
greeting *tjänare* (meaning servant). The phenomenon as such is not
unique for Sweden; what is interesting is its commonness.

According to information given to me by the Norwegian anthropologist Jan-Petter Blom, a stereotype among Norwegians is that
Swedes "move stiffly." Susan Sontag described the Swedish "unlibe-
rated body" and noted the limited movements of the head and
shoulders in nonverbal communication (Sontag 1969). "Delibera-
tion in movements" was mentioned also as a characteristic by the
psychologist Georg Brandell (1944). In her study of Swedes, a study
based on interviews with foreigners, Jean Phillips-Martinsson reported that a Swede's facial muscles are often stiff and that he typically sits "with his arms crossed, ties his body into a corkscrew and
his legs and feet into knots" (1981, 73).

This could be seen as part of a shyness syndrome. How people
respond with their body movements to that internal condition called
communication anxiety is discussed by Elfstadius and Pressner
(1984), though their examples are different from those given above.
In socially pressurized situations some people experience increased
activity in "the oral region," a response that goes back to the early

oral contact with the mother. "When the narcissistic basis (in the social) situation threatens to vanish, it is supplanted by equipping the oral region with something 'to hold on to.' When, for example, an individual increasingly experiences being 'suspended' or 'being outside,' he or she compensates by seeking an oral anchorage corresponding to that present in the original situation" (Elfstadius and Pressner 1984, 85).

David Kaplan (1972) mentions the habits of leaning on one's chin or stroking it, rubbing one's cheeks or poking at the corners of one's mouth with a finger, chewing on a toothpick or pen or whatever, smoking a cigarette, sucking on a pipe, even eating and drinking— in other words, activating the mouth. Since it is in the area around the mouth that the nervousness of shy people is first noticed, they often try to conceal this part of the face—for instance, by keeping a hand in front of the mouth, or having a beard or mustache. Another reaction is to keep one's muscles busy by chewing gum or continually smiling. Unfortunately, it is not only methodologically difficult to make quantitative measurements of these phenomena, it would be even more difficult to make quantitative comparisons of the frequency of these phenomena as they appear in different cultures, fascinating though it would be to know what picture of Swedish mentality would emerge from such a comparison.

Earlier in this chapter I mentioned the freedom from inhibitions that some Swedes say they feel abroad. In other contexts, too, in which the prerequisites for shyness are lacking, shy behavior can be transformed into its opposite. Swedes behave differently in the closed environment shared by family members and others close to them. They draw a remarkably strict line between private life and nonprivate, a phenomenon I return to. When Swedes are together with close friends or family, there are fewer grounds for feeling insecure, since everyone knows one another so well. Tacit questions such as "What do you think of me?" or "How can I be sure they like me?" are not prompted. Intimate friends and family see through one; and since in such circumstances the others already know one's faults and shortcomings, there is no need to be afraid of making a fool of oneself. The taciturnity and stiffness that characterize many Swedes when they are with people they do not know change among friends into louder and, above all, more open and much less cautious behavior.

Swedes' drinking habits and their behavior in connection with the consumption of alcohol help us to understand their shyness. Drinking is a particular illustration of the theme "private life versus the rest of life." One of the social and psychological functions of drinking in Swedish culture is to lessen the individual's fear of making a fool of him- or herself—for example, the anxiety people feel about saying the wrong thing. Instead, under the influence, it is permitted to be "too" aggressive, "too" sentimental, "too" loud or gay. The individual then never—or seldom—is accountable for breaking the norms. There is here a striking similarity to, for example, Japanese culture (Daun 1986). What matters to the drinker is less the physiological effects of alcohol than the "cultural ticket" to a freer and more irresponsible pattern of social interaction.

In their work on shyness Elfstadius and Pressner (1984, 31) touch upon the question of alcohol abuse. "It is tempting to view shy people as a group at risk in this regard," they write, referring to Schilder 1938 and Zimbardo 1977. "When our social habits [in Sweden] are such that alcohol is used to loosen our social inhibitions, there may be grounds for thinking that the type of patient that suffers more than others from social inhibitions also runs greater risks of developing alcohol problems."

How Can Shy Behavior Be Explained?

In research on communication anxiety, the basic theory is that shyness arises when the individual is exposed to *new* social situations. He or she is then forced to communicate with people whose basic judgment and norms are not known. This gives rise to insecurity and anxiety, and it explains why some young people behave shyly in adult contexts, why country people do the same when in a city, why people who change social class through education do so. They all become passive in the presence of relatively unknown people to whom they feel a pressure to adapt.

New situations may also follow from a transformation of the society as a whole. Old norms no longer apply. What the individual has learned during his or her upbringing is not applicable. If conventions tangibly and continually change, an adult person may acquire a permanent feeling of uncertainty. And if, in addition, society tends to be divided into more and more separate subgroups and

"subcultures," the difficulties involved in learning the "correct behavior" may increase.

That not everyone suffers from communication anxiety in a markedly changing society is due to biological inheritance as well as to
upbringing and individual environments. Certain individuals are
genetically more disposed to develop a personality very much in
line with their environments, while other personalities run directly
counter to the norms presiding over their external conditions. Moreover, individuals—through their work or habitation—are more or
less exposed to the social pressures mentioned above. The aphorism "Opportunity makes the thief" could be parodied as "Opportunity makes the shy person."

The theory may have a certain pertinence to the Swedish personality, but it does not explain very well why many Swedes are so
afraid of holding a dinner speech—among friends, among "their
own kind of people," with whose judgment one would assume they
are familiar. However, in this case, the task itself is unfamiliar, or at
least not routine, and in that sense it is more or less "novel." Nevertheless, I think a better explanation requires introduction of a cultural evaluation into the explanatory model.

Hannerz (1983) discusses the great value placed on the concept
of *duktighet*—roughly translated as ability, industry, sedulity—in
Swedish culture. The word is difficult to translate into certain languages because it contains two meanings: in part skill or capacity,
in part a moral expectation and a personal quality; one *should
be* duktig. From this it follows that at a dinner speech one cannot
say "anything unless it comes from the heart." A Swede wants to
be capable and industrious—and not only in the context of work,
since the *duktighet* ideal encompasses the whole person. The situation is complicated by another notion, namely, that you are nothing
by virtue of being an individual; on the contrary, you should not
think you "are anything special." This cultural trait, called the "Law
of Jante" (*Jantelagen*), is also a significant component in Norwegian
and Danish culture. Personal worth is gained not least as a reward
for being *duktig*, industrious, hard-working, but one is admonished
not to forget that "pride goes before a fall." Such is the Scandinavian
attitude.

A third hypothesis to explain shy behavior also has a Norwegian
connection. The social anthropologist Tord Larsen has pointed to

some of the consequences of Norway's being a small, well-integrated society, more homogeneous than many other countries (Larsen 1984). In a country like Norway, the inhabitants have reason to assume that "everything hangs together." People inside are what they seem to be on the outside; paradoxes and surprises are rare in comparison with culturally heterogeneous societies.

However, had Sweden and Norway a history of many different kinds of people—that is, ethnic, religious, and linguistic groups, living relatively separately but nonetheless interacting—then this complex situation would have given rise to another basic attitude among the nations' inhabitants. One would then not have been able so immediately or unreflectively to deduce people's inner identity from how they spoke. What a person said would primarily be understood as something "external," not necessarily or automatically reflecting anything "inner." In a heterogeneous culture people use to the maximum the information conveyed by the context and situation: who says what, when it is said, and so forth—in other words, the message behind the words. In a multicultural Sweden people would speculate much more and would make psychological interpretations; indeed, such frequent encounters with foreigners and other cultures would contribute to just such a psychological interest that Swedes are said to lack.

Even if native Swedes are no great psychologists, they do know one thing—and in an utterly self-evident way—what they say is interpreted by others as a sign of who they are, and consequently everyone should think carefully before he or she says anything. This takes time and leads to pauses, and it is assumed that those listening do not interrupt and use the pauses to take over the conversation. In Sweden—as opposed to, for example Germany and France—it is "bad to interrupt." In contrast to the French and many other nationalities, typical Swedes never express opinions that they do not hold, in order, for example, to incite discussion or to shed light on another side of a subject. The caution with words and the pauses in conversation characteristic of Swedes may be easily interpreted by a foreigner as shyness—but also as denseness, as a lack of anything to say.

A fourth, complementary explanation is avoidance of conflict: the particularly marked inclination toward consensus and "amiability" in direct contacts. I comment on this in more detail later, but for the time being, suffice it to say that in conversations one consequence of this tendency is a certain passivity that often arises when people encounter a stance very different from their own. In contrast to many other cultures, the typical Swede feels no joy or elation at opportunities "to use all his or her crushing arguments." Instead, the Swede feels some discomfort and prefers to wait and see rather than start an argument.

Since conversations between people sometimes highlight vital questions on which the parties have different views (for instance, politics, child-rearing, school, sexuality, private morality, life styles), we can assume that Swedes' avoidance of conflict, and their attendant wait-and-see attitude, contribute to the impression that they are shy, stiff, and reserved—even when the individual is actually not at all bothered by communication anxiety.

The fifth explanation focuses on the relative *indifference* of many Swedes to people outside the narrow circle of friends and relations. (Under the heading "Independence" that follows, I examine this in more detail.) This explanation, then, has nothing to do with *feelings* of shyness or communication anxiety; on the contrary, many Swedes may be socially assured but still behave passively toward people they do not know. Such behavior can be quite mistakenly interpreted as shy.

Foreigners, of course, do not always interpret Swedish taciturnity as shyness. In certain cultures taciturnity can be taken to be arrogant and dictatorial: for instance, in countries with hierarchical relations, when a superior does not deign to participate with equal enthusiasm in a discussion with his or her subordinates. Norwegians are sometimes exposed to the same sort of misinterpretation as Swedes. They are often criticized for being arrogant. "In other cultures people interpret low-key, controlled behavior, matter-of-factness, taciturnity—qualities *we* consider excellent—as arrogance," writes the Norwegian cross-cultural consultant Agnes Fife (1986, 16).

One side of the inclination to remain "independent" is a low degree of curiosity. A noncurious person divides up the world into a relevant part, containing his or her own concerns, and an irrelevant part, including everything and everyone outside these private spheres. The phenomenon as such is universal; the question is where on the scale from indifference to commitment—or from introversion to extroversion—people typically find themselves in various cultures. Or in other words, as an American colleague of mine suggested: where is the cultural point of gravitation?

It is only human to prefer to listen to gossip about friends and acquaintances than about totally unknown people. But in Sweden this boundary around "one's own world" seems to be tightly drawn, and curiosity about those outside seems slight. Kati Laine-Sveiby, an ethnologist of Finnish extraction, has commented on this seemingly slight interest in other countries' cultures and social conditions. Many Swedes live in the conviction that all people are basically the same. They regard culture as a "question of development." This means that not all people have "developed as far as the Swedes," and then, "it is neither meaningful nor interesting to inquire about something that is anyway hopelessly old-fashioned." Those who have "come equally far" are already known, and for this reason they do not attract Swedes' curiosity (Laine-Sveiby 1987, 29).

Swedish "indifference" has been compared with analogous propensities in German culture by the linguist Astrid Stedje of Umeå University. She has examined differences in attitudes toward "poking one's nose into other people's business." According to the norms revealed by linguistic material, one should not do this in Sweden, while in Germany it is tantamount to a moral decree. To Germans it is positive and desirable to "get involved," since it demonstrates responsibility and engagement. This difference is reflected both in the two languages and their uses.

Another explanation for Swedish indifference is suggested by the British psychologist Richard Lynn (1971), who has classified a number of countries with regard to their inhabitants' degree of "anxiety" or "emotionality." What Lynn shows is that people in different countries tend to react emotionally with different degrees of strength to different experiences, or stimuli. In fact, what he presents is empirical evidence that people in different cultures have different temperaments. People in "low-anxiety countries," like Sweden, England, and The Netherlands, react less strongly than do people in "high-anxiety countries," like Germany, France, and Italy.

We may conclude that in conversations Swedes are less motivated to participate actively ("less anxious to participate"—which is the meaning of "anxiety" that Lynn invokes). In Sweden the emotional reactions to what is being said are weaker than in certain other countries.

A seventh explanation for "shy" Swedish behavior is the special value awarded to politeness in Swedish culture. To be polite involves ritually subordinating oneself, showing respect through, for instance, allowing others to talk, and listening attentively. In this way, one places others before oneself.

Perhaps politeness has largely contributed to the positive attitude that Swedes in general have toward shyness as a character trait. Shy people are not pushy and unruly; they do not think they "*are* somebody*." Subordination is expressed ritually in the "bowing" that few Swedes perceive as a cultural peculiarity but that seems exotic to Americans, for example.

Even the continual thanking constitutes a ritual subordination (to which I return in the chapter "Proverbs and Mentality"). Interestingly enough, "thanks" is nowadays used instead of its opposite, "you're welcome." Both parties in a transaction may say "thanks," which may indeed have its logic but not one that has universal application. A person who hands something over to someone else or who does someone a favor often replies to the thanks received with "thanks" or "thank you." This use of language has made considerable inroads over recent decades, which could be interpreted to mean that the need for ritual subordination has increased. A more likely explanation is that greater stress on *sameness* as a superior value favors behavior communicating symmetry, balance, and reciprocity or mutuality.

Independence

Many Swedes seem to have a strong need for independence. It can express itself in a desire to be alone, to "avoid people," but also to avoid "being indebted." The precept is not to wait too long before returning an invitation, and to prefer separate bills at restaurants. The opposite of the need for independence in the first-mentioned sense is the need for contact—company—a personality trait that varies in strength from culture to culture.

One of the CMPS questions was, "Can you endure being separated from your friends for quite a long time?" In the study conducted in Stockholm county, referred to previously, 70 percent of the Swedes answered yes, whereas only 41 percent of the Finns in the Abo study answered similarly (Daun, Mattlar, and Alanen 1989). Close and deep friendships are more important to Finns than to Swedes. However, Swedes quickly establish superficial friendships more easily than do Finns (a trait among Swedes that can hardly be described in such terms when compared with Americans). This difference between Swedes and Finns was demonstrated systematically in answers to various questions.

To another question, "Do you become depressed or unhappy during periods of separation from your best friend?" 39 percent of the Swedes, 62 percent of the Finns, answered yes. Nor were as many Swedes as Finns "very anxious to keep in contact with [their] friends, even if they [had], for example, moved to another town": 26 percent of the Finns but only 14 percent of the Swedes answered yes.

One question directly concerned independence: "Is it essential to you to be free and independent?" Sixty-two percent of the Swedes answered yes (75 percent of the men, 51 percent of the women). For Finns, the need for *autonomy* is obviously not positively related to the need for company, since their need for autonomy is even greater: 83 percent answered yes. When the same CMPS questions were put to our sample of university students, there was, as expected, a much greater stress on independence—85 percent of the Swedes answered yes. A similar degree of emphasis was found among American students (86 percent), but it was appreciably higher among Italians (98 percent).

One of the questions in the European Values System Study sheds light on the more existential interpretation of freedom. Two statements are presented to the interviewees, who are asked to say which alternative best corresponds to their own views:

(A) Both freedom and equality are important. But if I were forced to choose one or the other, I would judge personal freedom to be more important—i.e., that everyone may live in freedom and develop unhindered.

(B) Both freedom and equality are indeed important. But if I were to be forced to decide between the two I would choose equality as the more important—i.e., that no one is worse off than anyone else and that social class differences are not so great.

The question is problematic, since it relates to countries' political ideologies and class structures. In addition, *both* freedom *and* equality may be more important for people in one country than for people in another, but through the questions we only get to know how the interviewees relate the two to each other. Nevertheless, when attempting to illuminate the significance of independence in Swedish culture, the answers are noteworthy.

Among Swedes, 56 percent answered yes to the freedom alternative (A). The figure was higher for Finns (66 percent) and Norwegians (62 percent). Of the thirteen countries, freedom was assessed highest in Great Britain (69 percent). A number of other countries showed figures lower than Sweden, among them West Germany (37 percent) and Spain (36 percent).

Another side of the question of independence has to do with reliance on the opinions of others. According to the CMPS study Finnish people are more independent than Swedes in this regard and in their general attitudes toward life as well as within marriage. The European Values study indicates that 29 percent of the Swedes but only 14 percent of the Finns believe that to have a happy marriage it is important for the partners to share the same tastes and interests. The same applies to political sympathies. Most likely the explanation for this view lies in Swedes' strong desire for conflict-free relations.

More independence is suggested in Finns' answers to the CMPS question, "Do you have a feeling that your views and ideas nearly always agree with those of other people?" Only 20 percent of the Finns answered yes to this question, whereas 45 percent of the Swedes answered yes, a response that implies more conformist views.

Paradoxically, this does not prevent Swedes from demonstrating high degrees of "individuality." The assumption that their own views are "normal" gives Swedes strength and security in their attitudes. Swedes have a greater belief that they are right, and more Swedes than Finns therefore behave authoritatively and with self-assurance. That in the formation of their opinions Swedes appear more dependent upon notions mediated by their immediate surroundings is another matter (Daun, Mattlar, and Alanen 1989).

However, my immediate topic here is the need for social self-sufficiency, not dependence on opinion. One variant of the striving for social autonomy is the tendency to shield oneself from societal bonds and "loyalties," to emphasize instead one's private life. In the international youth study carried out in 1983, differences between countries cropped up in young people's answers to questions concerning their willingness to work for the best of society or for their own personal interests (Prime Minister's Office 1984).

Most of the Swedish youth were "personal-life oriented" (49.3 percent); a somewhat smaller portion were "socially oriented" (45.2 percent). Even more oriented to society were young people in the United States (55.3 percent) and the former Yugoslavia (72.0 percent), whereas youth in, for example, the former West Germany (27.9 percent), Great Britain (36.5 percent), and France (35.8 percent) were less.

Swedish Solitude

Many Swedes seem to prefer to be "left in peace"—even if not equally many go so far as to avoid sharing the elevator with their neighbors. In company with people they do not know, few Swedes feel "moved" to talk. Even normally loquacious Swedes may experience a slight discomfort at the pressure to say something when they share a narrow elevator with a superficial acquaintance. Many will chat about the weather, but would rather not have to.

Solitude offers ease and liberation. It provides a respite from the expectations of one's social surroundings. The satisfaction so many Swedes feel when they walk on their own in the woods, sit alone with a fishing rod, or take a long walk with the dog derives partly from an absence of social pressure to talk and adapt to others.

The desire to be alone has received critical comment from the Swedish ethnologist Gunnar Alsmark, who suspects "that much of present-day depictions of Swedish mentality bears strong traces of bourgeois self-indulgence":

> Swedes' putative love of solitude, for example, is probably most of all a highly valued upper-class virtue—namely, not to mix, but to choose exclusive leisure activities. These are very important. One lives in a somewhat secluded summer cottage; one goes on vacation with a few carefully selected people in a sailboat; one goes hiking in the mountains. And above all, one avoids crowded camping places and "holiday

villages," the loud, noisy presence of industrial workers vacationing on Öland [an island in the Baltic Sea], the endless
lines to the continental car ferries, where people pass the
time by drinking beer and playing cards.

It may very well be that because of particular work
or housing conditions, solitude is an observable phenomenon in Swedish society. But except for a relatively well-
off middle and upper class, it is no ideal state. When a while
ago I read interviews with shipyard workers in Landskrona,
collected in conjunction with the closing of the Öresund
Yard [in southern Sweden], it struck me how well developed many workers' social networks were. Not least the
family's great importance modified the heavily simplified
picture of the Swede as alone and unsociable. (Alsmark
1984, 146–47)

Alsmark shows how it is possible to postulate that Swedes' alleged
urge to be alone can be seen as contingent primarily on class.
Alsmark describes what he considers to be "exclusive leisure activities" (e.g., living in a "somewhat secluded summer cottage") and
contrasts this with the leisure activities of the working class, for
example, in "crowded camping places and 'holiday villages.' " He
assumes that workers prefer camping and more collective living arrangements, the desire for solitude being an "upper-class virtue."
However, behavior does not always indicate preference. In principle
it is possible that members of all social strata would prefer the more
secluded summer cottage to the "holiday village." Differences in
behavior may be due to differences in economic resources: those
with the lowest incomes are relegated to cheaper leisure activities.

An investigation of leisure homes (Larsson, Rönström, et al. 1979)
revealed that the desire to live in a "densely populated leisure area"
or "holiday village" pertained only among a minority of the respondents (8 percent and 7 percent respectively). Most preferred sparsely
populated areas, former farms, or farm cottages—that is, more secluded locations. The study included no figures for the different social strata, but the results are sufficiently clear in this respect, since
the desire for a more collective arrangement is generally insignificant. The conclusion is that even most Swedish workers want to live
off the beaten track.

However, comparatively more people within the working class prefer densely populated leisure or vacation areas. This is shown in the statistics covering desired locations of holiday homes in relation to where one's own summer cottage is presently situated (Larsson, Rönström, et.al. 1979, 162). One gets used to, and is also able to experience the positive sides of, the housing one can afford.

More people from the working class than from the highest social strata can find positive sides to the "crowded camping places." This is because workers more often have to crowd in with other families "of their own sort." The phenomenon is well known in housing research, which has documented that working-class households are often uncomfortable living in areas dominated by highly educated people (Ineichen 1975).

Several different sets of figures support both propositions. According to data from the 1976 Statistics Sweden survey of living conditions, 25.8 percent of all Swedes went for walks in the woods "alone" *at least* three times that year. It was somewhat more common for blue-collar workers to take walks alone (26.3 percent) than for white-collar workers to do so (23.1 percent), but the difference is obviously insignificant.

Answers to the 1970 CMPS survey in Stockholm county, however, tend to be much more diverse. To the question, "Can you endure being separated from your friends for quite a long time?" 73 percent of social group I, 71 percent of social group II, and 59 percent of social group III answered yes. Being together with friends was clearly more important in the working class.

Leaving aside the question of class differences, Swedish readiness to be alone, compared with that of Finns, is generally very marked. Seventy percent of Swedes but only 41 percent of the Finnish sample answered yes to the above question.

The CMPS survey also revealed that in addition to class differences there is a gender difference: 78 percent of the men but only 69 percent of the women said they could be apart from their friends without difficulty.

To the question, "Do you sometimes feel that it would be a relief to get away from your friends for some time?" 39 percent answered yes, which may indicate not only appreciation of solitude but also difficulty managing relations with friends. Very likely it is just that which is reflected in the positive charge that expressions such as *att få vara ifred* (to be left in peace), *slippa folk* (not have to be around people), and *att rå sig själv* (to be one's own master) have in Swedish—all expressions that are difficult to translate idiomatically into English.

The question of "Swedish solitude" is interesting in light of what has been said above about "social insecurity." Solitude frees the individual from feelings of social insecurity. Above I mentioned answers to questions about walking in the woods, not only to indicate how many preferred to do so alone, however forced the solitude was, but also to indicate the special significance of nature in this context. Gustav Sundbärg (1911) described Swedes' interest in nature as antithetical to interest in people, which he claimed Swedes lacked.

A good many Swedes probably feel that the human voice in nature should be subordinated to nature's own—the sounds of birds, the soughing of the wind through the trees. One should listen to nature in silence. When wandering in the countryside, picking wild berries, or sitting beside a lake with a fishing rod—on these and similar occasions people may converse, but it is primarily "nature that speaks." The individual conducts an inner dialogue with nature—or with his or her inner self with nature as a surrounding sanctuary. Experiences of nature affect the emotions, release memories. In nature these mental activities can go on without needing to take account of or adapt to the demands of other people. In nature many Swedes feel a freedom akin to the totally relaxed feeling they can experience in the company of a dog.

As long as it is not permanent or forced, solitude contains for many Swedes a sort of poetry—especially solitude in nature. There is a sweetness and a melancholy that are not difficult to find expressed in fiction and art (many would say music too, although the symbolic content of music is more difficult to translate). The Swedish poet and Nobel Prize winner (1916) Verner von Heidenstam's verse in "The Thoughts of Solitude" (from *Vallfart och vandringsår*, 1888, translated here by Jan Teeland) is well known:

> I have longed for home for eight long years.
> In my sleep I have known this longing—
> I long for home. I long where 'ere I go
> —but not for people! for the earth,
> the childhood stones I played among.

Independence as a Goal for Child-Rearing

The person who feels socially insecure mistrusts others' willingness to show interest and appreciation. In his book *Suicide and Scandinavia* (1964) Herbert Hendin writes that it was typical for the Swedish men he came in contact with not to share with their wives their worries over problems at work. The typical attitude was "She can't help me with it, so why tell her about it?" They seemed to consider a woman as someone to whom a man goes for praise and admiration for his success but not for understanding and consolation.

Hendin interviewed patients who had tried to commit suicide, but he found the same tendency among other Swedish men as well. He was surprised at this pattern, which contrasted with his findings in Denmark, where, as in the United States, men were much more prone to seek support from their wives in difficult situations. What the Swedish men were expressing may well have been a particular need for independence.

A similar reticence between spouses was also reported in a Swedish study of shyness (Skiöld 1975). In a Swedish research report on couple relations, 60 percent of the men admitted that they kept certain thoughts and feelings to themselves because they were afraid of "reactions" and because they were "so bad at communicating" (Nilsson-Schönnesson 1985). The same investigation also attempted to detect the degree to which individuals were emotionally engaged in their partners. The majority of respondents described a relationship involving clear boundaries and even a certain distance between partners. Only one woman claimed that she and her husband were "inseparable." Hendin interpreted the striving for independence—in his view, typical for Swedes—as a consequence of specific child-rearing, not a conscious application of a given traditional pedagogy but rather a largely unreflected behavioral pattern in the company of children. Hendin claimed that Swedish mothers, more than, for example, Danish and American, encourage independence and self-sufficiency in their children, that, in other words, children are encouraged to separate from their mothers early on, socially and psychologically. One consequence of this is that many Swedish men learn to think of dependence as something unacceptable, according to Hendin. They deny the existence of any such need and mask it behind an ostensible self-reliance. The Swedish male patients Hendin met, filled with anxiety about a problematic life situation, "tended to redouble [their] impossible demands on [themselves]" (Hendin 1964, 46). In this Hendin found one explanation for the high frequency of suicide in Sweden.

In a recent study, child psychiatrist Marianne Cederblad (1984) described the ambition to develop early independence for children as characteristic for Swedes. "In Sweden we have . . . extreme expectations from an early age regarding self-sufficiency in children, and parents see the defiance of children during their refractory periods as positive and desirable" (Cederblad 1984, 29).

Schools and preschools have a more pedagogically conscious praxis, but this too is carried out on the basis of the dominant culture. A proposal for a pedagogical program for children's after-school recreational centers, published by the National Board of Health and Welfare (Socialstyrelsen 1985), may serve as an example. One of the responsibilities of such a center is "to support the children in their release from close dependence upon adults." If this goal had not been considered especially important, it would never have been specifically mentioned, since such a liberation happens by itself, without support from any particular pedagogy, insofar as the child spends time outside the home. Further, the proposal states that "the development of social competence that strengthens children's ability to manage by themselves will become increasingly important" (Socialstyrelsen 1985, 9).

To Swedish ears, this is self-evident, and in Sweden it is viewed as something desirable for all children, not just Swedish children. Swedes, like other nationalities, suffer from an ethnocentric blindness to their own culture's peculiarities. In another culture—Greek, for example, or Mediterranean cultures generally—advocating early independence would need to be backed up by cogent arguments. It would not be considered self-evident. Even so, paradoxically enough, liberation from the home and from the adult generation is problematized in the Swedish debate. Children's striving for independence contributes to discipline problems, complicates the internalizing of adult norms, contributes to the early desire to form one's own household, and generally deepens the generation gap. An outsider would probably advocate countering this by retarding early independence, not urging it on.

Annick Sjögren (1985) has compared Swedish and southern European cultural patterns, noting that successful upbringing in Sweden "produces responsible, independent youth who in due course take their places in the collective." In the Swedish view, "each individual is independent, [and] it is mandatory that he or she direct his or her improvement and set his or her own boundaries." In southern Europe, especially in the countryside, children's happiness is instead said to consist of "adapting themselves in the best way possible to the family structure." An individual can only "become a whole person within the framework of a family, never by him- or herself" (Sjögren 1985, 40–41).

This is totally opposite to the Swedish view. Southern European parents wish to hinder their children's liberation from the adults in the family, not stimulate it. In southern European cultures it is both natural and desirable that the individual be dependent upon the small surrounding group. Though an underlying idea in Swedish culture is that the child will gradually take "his or her place in the collective," in southern Europe the state and its institutions are often seen as "an enemy that one nonetheless often uses for the benefit of one's family" (Sjögren 1985, 40).

Swedish culture can thus be presented as a contrast to the dominating values of southern Europe. But in central Europe and the United States, also, the family has a stronger position than it does in Sweden. Swedish authorities' taking children into care has received negative attention in the foreign press largely because of foreigners' different views of the family in relation to the state. The typically Swedish view does not perceive the family as an "inviolable entity."

Hendin found it typical that women in Sweden wanted to return to work after the birth of their children because it gave them greater satisfaction—even though going back to work was often explained in terms of "economic necessity." This subject is difficult to discuss objectively in Sweden, since it is such an emotional issue; Hendin's observation might be interpreted as calling into question motherly love among Swedish women. There is a self-stereotype depicting Swedes as especially concerned with their children's well-being, a thesis that can be underpinned by references to public arrangements for the care and protection of children, high staff-child ratios in public day-care facilities (reduced in the beginning of the 1990s because of cuts), an institution such as the Child Environment Council

(Barnmiljörådet), and much else. Love of children can, however, also be discussed in terms of strong emotional bonds, tenderness and emotional closeness/intimacy. In this regard, there may be support for Hendin's impression that Swedish mothers do not experience the same joy in being together with their children as mothers do in certain other cultures. "We do not place the same weight on emotional needs," observed the Swedish anthropologist Gudrun Dahl in an interview (*Barnen och vi* [We and the children], no. 1 [1988]: 18).

In his interpretation of the Swedish personality Hendin stated that this early enforced independence creates a separation anxiety among Swedish children. Indications of this include phobias like fear of the dark and fear of thunder, which often recurred in stories about themselves related to him by both patients and nonpatients. Also common was the fear of losing one's mother through her death. To Hendin these phenomena were the first signs of disturbance in the mother-child relationship; sleeping difficulties among small children pointed to a similar anxiety.

Twenty years after Hendin's study, the Swedish psychiatrist Johan Cullberg commented on the background and meaning of separation anxiety among Swedish children, and his comments may well be applicable to conditions in several other industrial countries:

> Our children are exposed to demands for adaptation that are often not on their terms but those of adults. All too often children are shuttled in and out of the collective by frustrated individualists—between other day-center children, the under-paid, over-worked day-care staff, and tired parents. Driven by our work, do we not make our children's earliest childhood too pressed—that time when children should be allowed total dependence on their parents? If it is true that a large portion of the younger generation feels deprived of some of its early intimacy, during the phase when the child builds up that which is called "individuation" and which provides the basis for a deep and durable self-esteem, then there will be an early and usually unconscious hatred within the child. . . . The boy who had to endure early separation all too rapidly, who had to suppress his oceanic need too early . . . that child as an adult will

associate his longing for intimacy with threats of being
abandoned. And the longing for intimacy is connected with
a "passive female element" within him that logically must
be denied. (Cullberg 1984, 10–11)

Children and Planned Independence

There is a rationalist streak among Swedes (discussed further in
a later chapter) that causes them to "plan" their independence.
This propensity "to plan" is encoded, as are the many other cultural
values, in Swedish linguistic expressions—for example, the Swedish
phrase *skaffa barn* (to get/acquire children). The expression suggests a goal-oriented act, committed after careful consideration,
like getting a new house. The concept of family planning has the
same significance, and family planning is something for which
Sweden (typically) has made itself known in its aid to developing
countries. Together a couple decides how many children they will
have and when, taking into account the family's economy and other
practical things.

The expression *skaffa barn* has, as far as I can tell, no counterpart in, for example, English. If one wants to say in English that
Tom and Ann *skaffat sig barn*, the translation would suggest a
slightly different meaning: "Tom and Ann had a baby." This means
simply that they had a child. Nor in French is there a corresponding
expression. "Children come from heaven, and they aren't anything
you 'get,' " commented my colleague Annick Sjögren, who grew up
in France.

For Swedes in general, family planning requires no particular
willpower or mulling over (even though in Sweden as elsewhere
many "unplanned" children are born). What is interesting is that
among native Swedes this way of thinking is entirely natural. One
plans without deciding to do so. However, children in many other
cultures are valued more highly and are considered absolutely fundamental. In many countries, when a man and a woman live together, they have children *without due consideration and discussion.*
This follows not from a lack of contraception techniques but from
another orientation to life.

Swedish family planning, however, need not mean that Swedish
mothers or parents "love" their children less, even if that love is

not entirely self-evident. On the other hand, because of the specially strong stress placed on gainful employment as a basis for identity and self-esteem in Sweden (which has been substantiated by international investigations, for example, the European Values System Study), Swedish women may award relatively great importance to education and work. If through his or her upbringing a person has incorporated independence as a central value, that person will likely also view his or her own children from a similar perspective, that is, as an "external quality" that the adult individual, after careful consideration, has decided to add to his or her life. This of course does not mean that this quality does not attract strongly positive feelings.

A Swedish expression like "One doesn't own one's children," in all its clarity, conveys the message that children are independent individuals outside oneself. The same message is contained in the not uncommon attitude that one shall not bind oneself too tightly to one's children. This attitude is bolstered by the argument that, among other things, it is difficult enough when the children move away from home.

Living Alone

No other country contains so many single-person households as Sweden. According to the census of 1990, 16 percent of the adult population (over fifteen years old) live alone and 36 percent of all households in the country are single-person households. In Stockholm, 32 percent of the adult population live alone; in the inner city, 44 percent.

This is partly explained by the high living and housing standards, but the origins of both Swedish housing policy and individual preferences lie in the special value generally awarded to independence. Young people want their own accommodation when they reach their twenties (or even earlier); old people do not want "to be a burden on their children"; newly married couples simply assume they will form their own households. Behind this is a need for independence/self-sufficiency, which the sociologist David Popenoe considers especially strong in Sweden (Popenoe 1985).

In conversations with me, Popenoe has pointed to a striking difference between American and Swedish students. In America students usually share accommodation with one or two friends, whereas in Sweden they almost always live alone. In both countries, students can usually afford to live on their own, so it is primarily attitude that separates them. Americans want a close friend; close friends help each other out and also lead to new social contacts.

In other parts of the world, with entirely different habits, having to live alone would be a terrifying thought for many. A Japanese student studying ethnology in Stockholm reported on her encounter with the *undantagsinstitutionen* in old Swedish rural society. She was shocked by the fact that often in conjunction with the transfer of the farm to the children, a contract was drawn up ensuring that the old people would be provided with the basic necessities and that the old people would build for themselves an *undantagsstuga*, or a separate cottage to live in when a married son took over the operation of the farm (Nakajima 1978).

High Divorce Frequency

Couples may break up their marriages or partnerships in order to achieve independence, and perhaps the high frequency of divorce in Sweden has some connection with such a goal. What is not mentioned in Swedish analyses of divorce is the emotional distance between the spouses that Hendin referred to, which might be one of many contributing factors.

Divorce is common in several otherwise differing countries, for instance, the United States and the former Soviet Union, but the causes most likely vary considerably. The high divorce rate in Sweden is a recent development, and one that has been accentuated since the 1960s. This does not mean that the positive experience of independence need be an equally recent phenomenon. Women's economic dependence on their husbands, and the generally acknowledged morality condemning divorce, previously accrued from obstacles that have now disappeared (Nilsson 1985). Other changes in culture and society have contributed to the divorce rate (Trost and Hultåker 1984).

The many circumstances colluding in divorce that are referred to in the literature are themselves sufficient to explain the high number of divorces in Sweden. Independence as a contributing factor is hypothetical—difficult to test empirically. Nevertheless, one can say that independence, "to be able to be one's own person," is experienced especially positively in Swedish culture. A divorce offers just that opportunity. Of those who later get involved in new relationships, there are comparatively many in Sweden who choose a freer "cohabiting partnership," since it at least gives a feeling of greater independence.

Many Cohabit (Without Marrying)

Sweden's very large portion of people cohabiting without being married is fairly unique, especially the number of partners who have children together. This development occurred dramatically fast. Over a short period the annual number of weddings fell from sixty-one thousand to thirty-seven thousand in 1966—a reduction of 39 percent. The frequency of marriage, specified by age group—for example, for unmarried women between twenty and twenty-four years of age—had fallen to a fourth of what it had been before this dramatic change (*Kvinnor och barn* [Women and children] 1982).

Nonmarital cohabitation had occurred earlier, around the turn of the century, especially in the northernmost districts (Norrland). The so-called Stockholm marriage became fashionable in the 1930s, particularly in antireligious circles. Nevertheless, the portion of nonmarried among cohabiting couples, from the 1950s to the beginning of the 1960s, is reckoned to have been not more than 1 percent (Nilsson 1985).

The causes of this incredible change are not altogether known. I think that positive experiences of self-sufficiency played a part. Self-sufficiency as a value may have existed for a long time, but because of a number of social changes it could be expressed concretely in the 1960s. The same kinds of social changes in other countries—for example, increased frequency of women wage earners, better birth-control measures, diminished power of church and tradition, less informal social control—have not had anything like the same impact in these countries. We may thus assume that Swedish couples, even before the 1960s—possibly long before—have related to each other with a greater emotional distance than have their counterparts in many other places in the world.

An alternative explanation is that some of the above-mentioned social changes occurred especially forcefully in Sweden: for example, the entry of married women onto the labor market, which made them economically independent, and, even more, the reduced role of tradition as the setter of norms—including secularization. Swedes' rationalistic, future- and change-oriented tendencies were especially potent during the 1960s. Regardless of what most actively produced the Swedish institution of cohabitation, its mark of independence is in line with the positive value ascribed to autonomy in many other Swedish contexts. (The rising number of weddings since the end of the 1980s suggests a general, culturally conservative tendency.)

The Border Between Private and Public

Swedes draw a relatively strict borderline between the private sphere and the rest of life. People can work side by side for years without socializing privately; many coworkers have never been to one another's homes. According to the study "Ensamhet och gemenskap" (Being alone and being together) (1976), more than 53 percent of employees never socialize with their colleagues in their free time. Many immigrants in Sweden have noticed that contacts with their Swedish coworkers never lead to meeting socially outside of work.

It is possible that a desire for independence also plays a role here. It need not be that work means so much less than private life and that as a consequence people prioritize acquaintances outside of work. Several studies indicate the contrary, among them the European Values System Study, which shows that, in comparison with other nationalities, very few Swedes "regret having to go back to work after the weekend."

The need for independence is expressed also in relationships with neighbors. In the study "Ensamhet och gemenskap" (Being alone and being together) (1976), 50 percent of the respondents picked the alternative "In this area most people keep to themselves," though there was great variation between different types of residential areas, for instance, between single-family and multi-family housing areas. Swedes primarily socialize with close relatives. In my own research on housing questions, I have consistently encountered among the people I interviewed a cautious attitude toward socializing with neighbors. This attitude may have to do with the need for independence as opposed to the fear of being "drawn into" a circle of neighbors that will curtail one's privacy, one's maneuvering room.

Jean Phillips-Martinsson (1981) has pointed out that the inclination to draw a sharp demarcation line between working life and private life handicaps many Swedish businesspersons in their dealings with foreign contacts. Swedes often keep strictly to negotiations and are reticent about themselves as private persons. They seldom initiate business discussions with "small talk" about their children and family, their hobbies, and other private everyday subjects.

One function of this protective boundary around private life may be that it safeguards integrity and ensures the individual of a feeling of independence from the outside world. By not "letting in just anybody," one's private life remains intact as a breathing space or zone where one does not have to rise to others' expectations.

Seemingly meaningless aspects of Swedish culture can be seen in light of this border between private and public: for example, the custom of thanking the hosts for a nice evening *before one dons one's coat and hat*—something that astonishes many foreigners. As long as the guests do not have their coats on, they are totally within the hosts' private sphere. It is with intimacy—a quality of the private sphere—that farewells should be exchanged. Outer garments—hats, coats, and so forth—are symbols of the public space in which they are used.

Another emphasis on independence is the Swedish habit—very remarkable in many foreigners' eyes—of taking along sheets when staying overnight with friends. The usual argument has to do with "showing consideration to the hosts." The effective, that is, not conscious or intentional, reason probably concerns maintaining symmetry in social relations—that is, mutual social autonomy. In addition, it is not unusual in Sweden (or in Norway) to ask to "buy" a cigarette from a workmate and to "divide the bill" (go dutch) at restaurants (Klausen 1984).

Foreigners in Sweden may take this seemingly systematic assertion of independence negatively—as ignorance and aloofness. A young American woman I interviewed said, "In Sweden one is invisible"—of no interest to strangers.

On one occasion, when visiting Ireland, her husband's home country, she and her husband had been out for a walk and had started arguing.

We ran into a man who commented, "She's very independent, isn't she?" He was referring to what he'd heard us say.
That would never happen in Sweden, where people would,
on the contrary, pretend they hadn't heard a thing. It's something existential; it's not only more pleasant when people
come and see you—I miss that a lot—but it's also as if you
live through other people, not just on your own, like in a
vacuum. Once I traveled through Sweden on the train and
started to bleed heavily and had to lie down on a seat in a
first-class carriage. There was only one woman there, and
she saw of course that I was ill but didn't comment on that,
only said that I shouldn't put my feet up on the seat. In
America or Ireland, she would have said, "Oh, my dear, are
you alright? Can I help you with anything?" Instead, [this
woman] simply stared out the window. Later, when I got
worse, I asked her if she would ask the conductor to come
and arrange for an ambulance at the next station when we
arrived, but she wouldn't go out in the corridor and find a
conductor. She said, no, he would certainly be coming anyway in a few minutes.

Not all Swedes would behave like the woman in this episode, but I
would say that the course of events described above reflects something typical in the Swedish mentality. The probability that the
American would have had a similar experience with another Swedish
passenger is not insignificant. What may be interpreted as heartless-
ness by readers should instead be classified as a culturally given
shielding-off of the "surrounding world"—the public sphere and its
people and events. What the episode in the train reveals is a kind of
threshold of discomfort, which is connected with being thrust out into
an alien drama, something entirely outside of one's own private life.

At a lecture I held for local employees in a large Swedish company abroad, I was contacted by a young Italian. He wished to hear
what I thought of his experiences of his Swedish workmates. One
thing had especially bewildered him, and his question illustrated
just this theme, the border between private and public. He said that
he had done a Swedish workmate a favor; had helped him with
something in his work. What the Italian did not understand was that
the Swede never reciprocated and seemed to take the favor for

granted, something that was part of the job. I told the Italian that Swedes see things like that: working life in Sweden is, much more than in Latin countries, a formalized system where one does not expect to do and receive favors but simply "does what one should."

Avoidance of Conflict

In the present context, avoidance of conflict refers to the inclination to eschew direct confrontation with people with whom one is deeply at odds. It is typical of many Swedes to avoid emotionally charged topics of conversation and topics over which opinions divide. In a conversation between friends at work, for instance, or between guests at a dinner, it is common for Swedes to try to change the subject or to respond evasively or noncommittally to questions (to the degree that they respond at all)—simply to avoid exposing a serious difference of opinion.

Of course, this does not mean that conflicts do not arise between Swedes or in Swedish society. What I am referring to is a *tendency*, a significant personality trait; there are a considerable number of Swedes who do not hesitate to say what they think.

Fifty-five percent of the population involved in the CMPS survey from Stockholm county (26–65 years of age) answered no to the question, "Do you readily attack opinions and attitudes that are contrary to your own?"—fewer men (46 percent) than women (63 percent) and somewhat fewer in social group I than the other social groups. However, it is important to note the general, flexible nature of the question. It could refer to discussions between two people or in a group, where contrasting opinions are part of the given conditions—for instance, in a trade union meeting. Particularly in situations where friendliness and sympathy are desired—for instance, workplaces or private social circles—many Swedes experience open disagreements as uncomfortable (see Ehn 1981).

However, it should be recalled that what are measured in the CMPS are personality traits, not how people behave in real situations, where who is present, what is actually talked about, and the general nature of the situation are important. Moreover, every society contains structural or inbuilt conflicts arising from the incompatible interests of different groups. It is, nevertheless, a reasonable hypothesis that the tendency to avoid contention also has a dampening effect on such inbuilt conflicts, something that everyone with an international perspective who regularly follows political debates in Sweden can confirm. Another hypothesis is that this personality trait has become more palpable over recent years, partly as a consequence of the postwar ideology of consensus and harmonizing.

"Particularly difficult for them was the open expression of anger or a frank criticism of anyone in their immediate surroundings," writes Herbert Hendin (1964, 44) of Swedish men. Since restraint of aggressive impulses characterizes shy people, it would seem obvious to apply Hendin's theory of early separation to Swedish shyness. Ulla Holm too (1978) states that shy people "do not dare to confront points of view they do not share."

Geert Hofstede's 1984 study of masculinity in forty countries (as measured among staff at IBM) is in accord with these observations. His study showed that Swedes generally appear to be dependent upon surrounding views and attitudes and upon having good relations. Swedes place on the extreme end of Hofstede's scale as the most "feminine," that is, as those who most emphasize the social surroundings and a friendly atmosphere.

As I have already mentioned, the situation is also important, not only the personality (see Magnusson 1982). This means that a cultural norm that prescribes harmony and amicability can make an aggressive person rein in his or her feelings in certain situations.

In his study based on participant observation in a factory, *Arbetets flytande gränser* (The shifting limits of work) (1981), Billy Ehn mentions conflict avoidance practiced as "peaceful coexistence." There are lots of potential sources of conflict in mixing together immigrants and Swedes, but differences in cultural background and, for example, political attitudes were played down, and instead, certain similar interests were highlighted: drinking, women, cars, and a coarse, male camaraderie. The foreign workers were motivated to adapt to Swedish circumstances on the general terms of immigrants—subordination and anticipated conformity. But the circumstances were also influenced by the Swedish workers' culturally influenced personalities and norms: in sum, "to avoid trouble" whenever possible.

In his later study of life in children's public day care, Ehn noted a parallel between conflict avoidance among day-care staff and the relations between factory workers. In order not to complicate their necessary coexistence, the foreign factory workers also eschewed "touching upon their major differences. Striving after harmony was the rule" (Ehn 1983, 145). Ehn encountered the same value orientation in the written guidelines for preschool pedagogy:

> The official preschool pedagogy is representative in the sense that it almost entirely disregards conflict, aggression, and violence. The picture painted by the state Child Day-Care Enquiry and its successors places mutual understanding in the center and leaves out the disputes that actually occur in daily life. Conflict avoidance should perhaps therefore be interpreted as a kind of Swedish "self-understanding," a symbolic construction of one's own cultural identity, in opposition to the malevolence [occurring] in other parts of the world. (Ehn 1983, 145)

There is a great deal to suggest that, as Ehn says, conflict avoidance expresses among Swedes a common image of a national identity, but such a self-image would not flourish in a totally opposite social reality. Conflict avoidance is also a norm in child-rearing. "The staff value quiet, orderly and tranquil children." The day-care staff implant this orderliness with the help of nonaggressive, impersonal exhortations: "Whatever stupid things [the children] do, the staff do nothing other than try to correct them by talking to them," even if the staff's "fingers are itching" (Ehn 1983, 96–97). According to the Child Day-Care Enquiry, children are allowed to "channel their aggressions" in outings in the forest.

Examples of conflict-avoiding behavior can also be found in encounters between staff and parents. According to Ehn, these meetings "can often be rather tense," and he refers to a critical observation: "One chooses silence or talking generally about safe subjects instead of talking about acute problems" (Ehn 1983, 71). The parents' self-restraint, especially as observed by nursery staff, is illustrated in the following:

> In the day-care center, the sisters Karin and Anna are calm and good-natured. But when their parents arrive in the evening, they change completely: Karin howls and Anna throws

herself on the floor. At first, the parents smile and try by hook or crook to get the girls to put their coats on, but the girls refuse. Karin kicks and hits; Anna takes off the clothes her mother has just put on her. Both run away. The parents start sweating and look pained, but they maintain their dignity. They don't shout or become visibly angry, and they don't say anything harsh to the children. (Ehn 1983, 68)

The parents are here in the presence of day-care staff, and Ehn interprets their high degree of emotional control to be a consequence of their acting "in front of a public." The situation demonstrates the significance of the *cultural norm* that dictates avoidance of aggression and conflict. It exemplifies not only a culturally given personality trait but also the border between the private and the public in Swedish culture. In short, it is often disgraceful to expose "private" behavior publicly.

Even so, emotional control probably exists, albeit weaker, also within the family. Hendin noted that "[n]either boys nor girls are allowed to express anger toward parents and siblings as openly as are American children" (1964, 67). (This phenomenon has most likely changed somewhat since the 1960s, when Hendin made his investigation.)

The preschool children Anna and Karin, in the episode described above, were then still so small that they could express their anger toward parents. However, with restrained parents and day-care staff as their models, they would learn in due course to control their feelings—or channel them in another direction.

It would be wrong to present Swedes as nonaggressive in a deeper sense, partly because aggression exists naturally in all people, partly because, if Hendin is correct, the early separation from parents itself creates anxiety and rage. H. Lewinski (1941) has pointed out that several characteristics of shy people reflect suppressed aggression. However, aggression can find outlets in, for instance, sports, driving a car, and drinking and, as Hendin has observed, can be sublimated in performance at work.

The Swedish psychologist Martin Johnsson of the University of Utrecht concurs with the identification of Swedes with inhibited aggression (circumscribing the expressions of aggression). He has compared the results of DMT (Defense Mechanism Test) upon the selection of military pilots in Sweden, Holland, Iceland, and the

United States. At least compared with test subjects in these other countries, Swedes appear relatively more inhibited.

Thus, generally speaking, Swedes deplore and reject "aggressiveness." In an international comparison of traffic safety in nine countries, Sweden occupied a special place with regard to opinions of the significance of the "human factor" in traffic accidents (L'Hoste 1978). From the alternatives "lack of attention," "aggressiveness," "tiredness," and "inexperience," the (1669) Swedes alone placed "aggressiveness" in the fourth and last place; they believed that aggression, because it was seldom manifest in Swedish behavior, seldom caused traffic accidents. Those interviewed in France, Japan, the former Yugoslavia, the former Soviet Union, Great Britain, Spain, South Africa, and West Germany all placed "aggressiveness" in second place; 7.7 percent of the Swedes mentioned aggression, a small figure compared with, for example, the 26.4 percent of the British respondents. The very term "aggressiveness" has a negative clang in the Swedish language, in contrast with the positive connotations it has in, for example, the United States.

Swedes have learned neither to criticize nor to contradict publicly, according to Phillips-Martinsson, in her book *Swedes, As Others See Them*. "Whereas an Englishman can very well criticize a proposal which has been presented at a meeting by saying 'Bloody nonsense!' a Swede would probably take the criticism personally" (Phillips-Martinsson 1981, 45; cf. Jenkins 1968, 259). In many countries strong feelings are normal; resistance to strong feelings, an eccentricity.

"We have very strong feelings and are used to conflicts—something we have every day," noted a Kurd (now a Swedish municipal employee) in an interview with me. "It can be disturbing for many [Swedish] authorities when one is like that. When at my job I comment on others' work, then I am disturbing the order. I think, if you do it this way, it will be better, but they take it as interference."

An immigrant Finnish home-language teacher in Sweden, whom I interviewed, told me about a conference whose theme was immigrants. She described a discussion that had arisen in the afternoon session. The two Turkish so-called cultural advisors (a newly established post)

> started to argue with each other, which led to irritation among the Swedes, perhaps mainly because [the Turks] got

so loud. [The Swedes] tried to hush up the one who was most obstinate, but then he got so angry that he left. The Swedes applauded. I was so disappointed. He left, okay, but they didn't need to react—*that* was the biggest mistake. I had thought that we could understand each other and meet each other halfway, but now I don't believe that. They [the Swedes] don't see how they themselves behave, and then they demand that we [the immigrants] should be exemplary and refined! They thought they were ever such good people.

The Swedes in the audience seemed to have experienced what happened as a victory for mutual understanding: the pushy, obstinate person was forced to leave; virtue won the day. The applause released their repressed ire. Was this how it was? In any case, it was how the Finnish woman comprehended the incident.

The Indian anthropologist H. S. Dhillon, who was preparing a research project in Sweden in the beginning of the 1970s, reported from his preliminary notes that in Sweden it was a matter of "being polite, not aggressive and stubborn. Thus anyone who gets heated in a discussion is taken to be an anxious and neurotic figure. . . . So very much weight is placed, strangely enough, on being in accord" (Dhillon 1976, 46). The example is not meant as an argument for greater obstinacy among Swedes but as an illustration of how someone from another cultural perspective can relate in a totally opposite way to what is a fundamental value in Swedish culture: namely, mutual understanding.

In a debate article in the national newspaper, *Dagens Nyheter* (29 June 1985), Modji Mortazavi, an Iranian psychologist working in Sweden, noted that a "Swede suffers from being in conflict with his surroundings, whether alone or in a group. He cannot bear long-lasting conflicts"—a mentality that otherwise "entails certain psychosocial, economic, and bureaucratic difficulties." Comments like this one deserve to be discussed in more detail than space permits here. Nevertheless, it should be said that people in most cultures likely "suffer" from being in conflict with their surroundings. However, if, as in Sweden, the conflicts are not allowed to be openly expressed—released—and anger is repressed, it is generally damaging or painful to the individual. In addition, to Swedes, disputes in the family or with friends or workmates involve a deep discomfort, since these are experienced as alien elements that everyone should try to circumvent or stop as quickly as possible.

In a collection of comments by foreigners, social anthropologist Ulf Hannerz (1983) addresses the question of how conflict-confronting behavior is comprehended by Swedes. Many Swedes think that conflicts lead nowhere.

> A fairly typical response is "It doesn't matter whether we discuss this, because we have such different views." That is the very reason something should be worth discussing; after all, a discussion is not a choir of voices. The expression "I think so in any case—and you can think what you want, and that's that" is pertinent here; [the expression implies that] if people cannot agree, they can at least keep quiet. There is an obvious contrast with what we here in the North tend to label as generally "Southern": the propensity to seek differences of opinion—indeed, construct them when they do not exist. (Hannerz 1983, 11)

One of the CMPS questions illuminates the degree of disinclination to promote conflicts: "Do you frequently say things you don't really mean, only because you are fond of teasing people?" Of the interviewed (aged 26–65 years), 19 percent answered yes—more men (24 percent) than women (15 percent). Young men deviated strongly: of those eighteen to twenty-five years old, half answered yes; the girls deviated very little from the adult women (21 percent). That the phenomenon is clearly a cultural one is demonstrated by a comparison with the Finnish CMPS material: 41 percent of the Finnish men but only 24 percent of the Swedish men answered yes to the same question. The answers given by American and Swedish students to a similar question, "Do you sometimes enjoy making fun of other people?" show an interesting difference: 74 percent of the Americans but only 35 percent of the Swedish students answered yes.

Among the management of Swedish companies there is also a clear tendency to avoid confrontation and open conflict (Forss, Hawk, and Hedlund 1984). "This can be expressed as shunning corrective actions against an underperforming subsidiary manager, avoiding embarrassing or difficult decisions, or avoiding strong enforcement of decisions taken," according to Hedlund and Aman (1984, 15) from the Institute of International Business in Stockholm.

Striving to achieve harmonious relations also appears as a topic in sociologist Roger Bernow's national study (1985) of subjective welfare, carried out in cooperation with Swedish Radio. The interview subjects were asked for their views on the following three statements, which were taken from the Crowne-Marlow scale, designed to measure the incidence of a positive bias in interview surveys. The aim was thus to investigate individuals' inclination to suit, or "comply with," the interviewer, but the responses shed light on the issue of conflict avoidance as well.

	True	False
I have never intentionally said anything to hurt anyone.	45%	55%
It doesn't matter who I'm talking to; I'm always a good listener.	51%	49%
I am always nice and friendly, even toward people I dislike.	36%	64%

The categorical tone of these statements ("never intentionally," "always a good listener") renders it even more remarkable that so many of the interviewees thought the statements suited them. It is of course possible that among the others interviewed were people who generally shunned conflict but who were not prepared to answer equally categorically "never" or "always."

In the comparative CMPS study involving American university students that I administered in 1987, the Swedish avoidance of conflict was very apparent in the answers to questions measuring degrees of aggressiveness. To the question, "Does it amuse you to ridicule your antagonists?" 53 percent of the Americans and only 11 percent of the Swedes answered yes.

Susan Sontag (1969): "The Swedish avoidance of conflict is little short of pathological"

Not only secretiveness makes the Swedes silent: it's a whole system of anxieties, a perception of the world as extremely dangerous, treacherous. The source of treachery is, one must surmise, themselves as much as the Other—though it's anyone's guess which has psychological priority, the fear of another's aggression or of one's own. In this taboo-ridden country perhaps the most notable taboo is raised against the signs of aggressiveness. . . . Their marked avoidance of aggression, even in its minimal forms, comes through in the Swedes' mild voices, and in the low noise level in public places. . . . One hardly ever hears people quarreling, and there is a strong aversion to disagreement as such. The Swedish avoidance of antagonism sometimes goes to really supersonic extremes. I remember one evening last autumn after a day's shooting out in the suburbs returning to town with my assistant, production manager, and a script girl; we were heading for a new restaurant to have dinner, but nobody was sure exactly where it was. Someone said, "I think you continue two more blocks and turn right." The driver of the car said, "No, we go three blocks and turn left." In an entirely pleasant tone the first person said, "No, go two blocks and turn right." After which the third Swede in the car intervened quickly with "No, now, let's not quarrel."

Do you understand what I found sad in this ludicrous moment, and in many similar micro-dramas? There are few qualities I admire more than reasonableness; and I'm far from admonishing the Swedes for not embodying some lush standard of Mediterranean temperament and volatility which is not my own either. Still I'm convinced that the Swedish reasonableness is deeply defective, owing far too much to inhibition and anxiety and emotional dissociation. To repress anger as extensively as people do here greatly exceeds the demands of justice and rational self-control; I find it little short of pathological.

The demand for repression seems to arise from some naive misunderstanding or simplification of what goes on between human beings: it's simply not true that strong feelings escalate so inevitably into violence. And to avoid confrontation and to repress disapproval to the extent the Swedes do shades, rather often, into passivity and indifferentism. For instance, I'm sure that it isn't only because of the chronic shortage of labor that people rarely get fired here, no matter how they bungle their jobs. It's also true that most Swedes would prefer to continue operating some activity with incompetent personnel than face the unpleasantness of speaking severely to someone, hurting their feelings and incurring their hostility. (Sontag 1969, 26)

Sontag's last assertion, which must have been for her more or less an intelligent guess, has been confirmed by the previously mentioned Swedish management researchers Forss, Hawk, and Hedlund (1984).

Sontag's description of Swedes is heavily negative, with expressions like "sad," "absurd," "defective," "pathological," "naive misunderstanding," and so forth. Her critical stance is, for her as well as for many other foreigners in Sweden, a consequence of a subjectively experienced encounter with a foreign culture, a confrontation resembling that of Swedes' meeting contrary immigrants, and similarly, the reaction is one of irritation. Through the criticism, the encounter—the culture "shock"—is dramatized, and it becomes a defense of one's own (in this case, American) culture, which therefore is taken to be the only correct and sound culture.

What Sontag sees as an absurd reasonableness, passivity, or indifference, Swedes consider politeness, friendliness, conciliation, not always putting oneself first—basically encapsulating the Christian commandment to love one's neighbor. That this can exact a price, for instance, in the form of incompetent personnel whom the management keeps on out of fear of hurting them, does not exclude possible positive consequences in other contexts.

A Reverse Interpretation: The Desire for Reward

The avoidance of conflict is illuminated inadvertently through Elfstadius and Pressner's reference to O. Fenichel (1945, 520). Fenichel discusses the connection of the "heterogeneous superego" with social anxiety and sees such a "superego pathology" as induced by an extremely inconsistent upbringing. What is interesting is that inconsistency in upbringing is said to make the child uncertain of what behavior will ensure the parents' love. "Instead of being able to internalize the parent into a permanent norm, [the child] is forced continually to adapt to what temporarily prevails in external reality" (Elfstadius and Pressner 1984, 51).

This means that if his or her upbringing does not infuse security into the child, the adult individual will become especially dependent upon affirmation of his or her value from others (on varying grounds). Ehn's study of public day-care (1983) reveals an element of inconsistency in Swedish child-rearing, namely, the "hesitation" about how one should best treat children.

What I have so far described as conflict avoidance, the fear of social penalties, could from this perspective and in certain contexts be described as the opposite—as the desire for reward, to have one's social ego confirmed. The wish of the individual then becomes to "comply" or "accommodate"—to talk and behave in order to be liked.

Can Divorce Be a Consequence of Conflict Avoidance?

It is part and parcel of modern Swedish life that many marriages end in divorce and that many unmarried partnerships break up. The same is true for many other countries, but the background causes differ. As the need for independence might be one factor behind divorce, the avoidance of conflict might be a "specifically Swedish" other.

My point of departure for this hypothesis is an interview with a nurse in a suburban children's health center. Through her work the nurse had gained some insight into young marriages. She said, "It is as if people had the wrong expectations—I don't know. But if neither is used to talking about their relationship with each other, they just quarrel. One word follows another, and people don't take back what they've said. So they split up" (Daun 1980, 85–86).

What she is basically saying is that the conflict provoking the quarrel is experienced so strongly that it prevents the couple from continuing to live together. Such is probably the case in those marriages where the partners' life together is generally characterized by shunning conflict and repressing aggressions. Given these sorts of preconditions, an open, emotional quarrel is experienced as a shock.

This line of reasoning is supported by Richard Lynn's (1971) data on a lower degree of anxiety or emotionality among Swedes, which indicates weaker emotional reactions: one does not become livid when angry, or ecstatic when happy, or beside oneself with grief when sad. The lack of experience of such strong feelings—in any case, of the negative ones—can produce shock when they suddenly explode.

Clearly, Swedes in general are brought up to restrain their aggressions and to avoid *bråk* (roughly "trouble," but the particular negative tenor of the word is difficult to translate), although strong feelings are more easily accepted inside the family than outside. But attitudes toward quarreling are negative, and the memory of mother and dad quarreling is assuredly experienced by many Swedes as a sign that their parents' marriage was not all that happy—an experience that contrasts with reactions to the same thing in many other countries. When the newly married couple, having imbibed such attitudes, have their first major quarrel, there is a risk that both partners will interpret the event as proof of having "chosen the wrong person": each is shown to be another sort of person.

However, there are cultures in which face-to-face conflicts are not, as in Sweden, heavy with angst but are considered an integral part of one's social life: quarrels with one's subordinates, with loud neighbors, with the butcher who sold tough meat, with the waiter who served cold soup, with the busybody mother-in-law. With such attitudes, one's first quarrel with one's spouse is not experienced as a catastrophe. Perhaps quarreling is not even considered relevant to matrimonial happiness. The borderline between love and hate is paper thin, so the saying goes, but how many Swedes agree with that?

The prevailing view in Sweden is that relations between people should be ruled by mutual understanding, amicability, and a "civilized control of emotions." People should talk to one another in a "normal way." It is possible that this places particular demands on marital harmony as well. In one's marriage—or so the Swede typically hopes—one can find some respite from the stresses resulting from unavoidable conflicts at work and elsewhere outside one's own walls.

Swedish Versus Finnish Aggressiveness

More Finnish women and men are openly and demonstratively aggressive than Swedish women and men (Daun, Mattlar, and Alanen

1989). Swedish men stifle—and perhaps try to repress—their feelings when they are angry. They are also more prone to take revenge than Finnish men, which of course is another way of channeling aggression. Swedish women, however, express a *desire* to fight back when attacked.

In addition to the tendency to suppress aggressiveness, Swedes are also likely to *feel* less aggressive. More Finns than Swedes flare up when they do not get what they want; more Finns easily become irritated and riled at other people. Finns can be beside themselves with rage. The differences here lie on the 10 to 15 percentage-point level, but the percentage levels per se are not especially high. Only 31 percent of the Finns and 19 percent of the Swedes said they easily lose their temper.

The greatest difference between Finns and Swedes has to do with being provoked. Forty-seven percentage points more Finnish women and 42 percentage points more Finnish men felt immediate feelings of hate.

Finns' greater aggressiveness is confirmed by Geert Hofstede's index of masculinity (which in part measures aggressiveness). As has already been mentioned, Sweden landed at the bottom of forty nations—even when controlling for women in the sample (i.e., calculating the index one would have had if the proportion of women was equal in the samples of all the countries). Sweden then has 6 index points and Finland 51(Denmark has 22, Norway 10, the United States 62, and Japan 87) (Hofstede 1984, 189).

Avoiding Conflict in Political Contexts

In political assemblies and debates, conflicts are institutional; that is, differences of opinion *are supposed to* come forth and not be circumvented. However, the conventions, unwritten rules, and attitudes in political interaction reflect general cultural norms. Compared with many other countries, Sweden (and to a degree Scandinavia in general) has the reputation of having a political culture in which sharp conflicts are generally avoided whenever possible.

This means that even in political circles, conformity is preferred. In a critical interview, a former local Swedish politician who had grown up in Spain remarked to me that "[t]here are people in Sweden with good ideas, but it is often said of them that 'he [or she] is so controversial,' as if it were detrimental to provoke controversy, to question what is said. What is interesting is that within the parties, people are voted in on the basis of their contacts—not primarily because of their ideas. In this Sweden has much in common with Mexico."

The absence of rancor and wrath in the Nordic parliaments has been described by the political scientist Herbert Tingsten, in his essay "Folkstyret i Norden" (Popular rule in the Nordic countries) from 1940. For purposes of contrast, he chooses to compare Sweden with France, where

> astuteness combined with an impassioned presentation is common; cheers and protests egg on and confuse the speaker. On important occasions, the discussion becomes a dramatic battle of wits between fundamental ideas. In strong contrast stand the parliamentary debates in the Nordic countries. . . . At least in Sweden, it is considered somewhat inappropriate to present with fervor a general political point of view or philosophy; the environment is perceived by all as unsuitable, and the impression would be similar to that rendered by someone making an elaborate thank-you speech at a simple dinner. . . . Applause is rare and feeble. . . . Shouts and protests are well nigh unknown. . . . The total impression is one of an everyday calm in which boredom is assuaged by a pleasant and convivial comradeship.

What Tingsten is describing is the absence of open aggressiveness.

> As has already been implied, the debate is based on facts; that is, one fairly rigorously keeps to the subject in question. . . . On no occasion has it happened that a party or member of a group has tried to exploit having the floor in order to render a decision impossible in a given issue or to force the majority into concessions [filibustering]. . . . It is also remarkable that Swedish legal praxis knows of no intervention against a speaker who loses his head other than a warning from the Speaker of the House.

Things are very different in the Israeli Knesset, where members are frequently sent out of the plenary, or in the West German

Bundestag, where speakers often have to endure aggressive comments from opponents sitting in the benches. Foot stomping and scuffles also occur in the British Parliament. In the Bundestag minutes published in *Das Parlament* (21 September 1985) the secretary noted all interruptions, shouts, applause, laughter, and so forth—an illustrative contrast to the reigning style of the Swedish parliamentary debates.

Conflict Avoidance as Lack of Civic Courage

A letter to the editor published in the newspaper *Expressen* (21 March 1983) under the headline "Why Are Decent Swedish Men Cowards?" may serve to illustrate a tendency that is often explained by the anonymity of modern society. People do not dare to intervene, or "poke their noses into other people's business," as it is so negatively put in Swedish parlance. But the tendency not to intervene certainly gives rise to other, possibly more debatable attitudes as well.

Is our civic courage hereditary, or have we been schooled to cowardice? The husband in a Danish family I know has told me that one of the things that surprised him the most when he was first in Sweden was that Swedish men can stand looking on without intervening when a policeman or another respectable citizen is being beaten up by thugs.

By way of explanation I said that we have laws making it risky to intervene on behalf of the victim. Such help can be taken to be an assault on the attacker.

My friend didn't believe me—we're surely not that crazy. In Denmark, it's just the opposite, he said. The person who doesn't help someone in need can be taken to court for not intervening.

This issue was highlighted for me by an experience I had last Saturday. Together with a colleague and his wife, I and my other half were traveling home after vacationing together in the mountains.

In a town in central Sweden we stopped for a meal in an ordinary gas station café. It was fairly full of people like us, lots of families with children and at least 40 heads of families.

Unfortunately, also present were a couple of members of that all too accepted mob who seek every occasion to provoke that despicable drudge, Svensson [roughly the equivalent of the faceless "Smith" in English].

Two such people in their 20s amused themselves by throwing sugar cubes around at other customers. The female employees couldn't do anything for obvious physical reasons. Everyone except my colleague and I pretended not to notice; however, neither one of us was prepared to go along with being terrorized by such riffraff. We told them to behave themselves.

My friend went off to buy gas. I sensed more trouble in the wind and asked the ladies to leave first. They managed to leave the place only chased by a few taunts. When I proceeded to follow I was attacked by both men. In a fairly violent fist fight I was left on my own by around 40 large, strong, 100 percent Swedish men, who gazed up at the ceiling or down at the floor or at their coffee cups—in any case, gave no sign that they either heard or saw that one of the other customers was being treated in such a way.

Only after a while did two more-valiant men come to my assistance, so that two were pitted against three. Then the thugs went off, and we needed to fear no more from them.

Why is it that normal Swedish men are so cowardly? Do they reckon on help, I wonder, when they themselves are assaulted for no reason? I have related this incident to an Iranian I know. He laughed, and said that in his country (which in Sweden is described as barbaric) it [the situation] would be inconceivable.

Among the reasons behind the described incident was first and foremost a fear of violence, but does this not also exist in other countries? The information I have been able to gather suggests that such fear is not everywhere so strong that it prevents strangers from assisting people in distress, or that the impulses (rage, annoyance) spurring on action are stronger in these other cultures.

Another factor behind such incidents is indifference concerning what happens outside one's own "sphere of relevance," what is usually called lack of informal social control. Apathy is part of urban culture and as such is not specifically Swedish. However, there is a generally widespread Swedish attitude, summed up in the idiomatic expression "One should not poke one's nose into other people's business." There is no corresponding expression in, for example, the German language. In Germany, the opposite prevails: one should get involved; it is tantamount to a moral precept. Astrid Stedje claims that this could be the psychological trait that most blatantly distinguishes German mentality from Swedish.

A third factor is people's knowledge of general patterns of behavior. There may have been several people in the café who would have intervened had they not been so certain that no one else would.

A fourth factor is social insecurity, which has already been discussed as typical for many Swedes: the shame associated with failure, "cutting a poor figure," fear of the judgment of others—in essence, shyness. In the situation described above, the brave intervention sought by the writer was complicated by the fact that it would have occurred *in public*, not merely in front of friends and acquaintances. Such "stage fright" is one of the most common expressions of shyness (McCroskey 1984).

The incident also illustrates the specifically Swedish difficulty of giving vent to aggression. Aggressive impulses are curtailed by social insecurity. It is not impossible that some of the passive men in the café pondered later what they would have said or done had they not been so pacified by the drama—the phenomenon encapsulated by the concept of *esprit de l'escalier*. Regardless of the hypothesis concerning the effect of shyness, the issue is one of temperament. The degree of emotionality or anxiety, as Richard Lynn prefers to call it, is constituted by the intensity with which the individual reacts to different stimulae (Lynn 1971). The upshot is that Swedes, who are citizens of one of the "low-anxiety countries," react comparatively weakly to all kinds of experience. Consequently, they become less angry and annoyed than people in "high-anxiety countries." In the incident in the gas station café, part of the explanation is that despite the anger many doubtless felt, they did not become furious enough to overcome restraint and rush in to help—which is precisely what would have happened in many other cultures. When people become angry they react emotionally and act without stopping to think.

Aversion to Violence

Physical violence is the strongest expression of conflict. We should therefore expect that aversion to violent actions is especially prominent in Swedish culture. Inhibited aggressiveness is itself a restraining factor, "even if the fingers itch."

This does not mean that physical violence against children or adults does not occur in Sweden. We all know it does. However, it does mean that the cultural norm very firmly rejects physical violence. This norm has also been sanctioned by legislation, of which the most remarked outside of Sweden is the law against corporal punishment. In the *Children and Parent's Code*, chapter 6:3 (from 1 July 1979) it says, "The guardian shall exercise that control over the child which is required with regard to the child's age and other considerations. The child may not be exposed to physical punishment or any other abusive treatment." Officially, the child's right to avoid punishment should in principle take precedence over the parents' right to their child.

The idea of totally forbidding corporal punishment has existed for a long time in Sweden. The psychologist Ake W. Edfeldt relates that the subject was discussed on several occasions after the Second World War and that corporal punishment in school was prohibited in 1952, after changes in the school regulations. In 1957, the regulations covering the penal code were altered "so that in principle it became as punishable to hit one's own children as to physically attack another person" (Edfeldt 1985, 29). But an out-and-out prohibition against corporal punishment in the home did not arrive until 1979. Edfeldt also describes the changes in public opinion: in a survey in the early 1960s only every third person asked was against corporal punishment in any form; almost twenty years later, three out of four were against it.

For purposes of comparison, Edfeldt mentions that in the United States there is evidence of a return to an earlier positive attitude toward corporal punishment as an instrument in child-rearing. "The tendency in the United States during the 1970s has been that more municipalities have approved corporal punishment in the schools than have forbidden it" (Edfeldt 1985, 33).

Regarding the actual implementation of corporal punishment, Edfeldt found that the frequency of severe corporal punishment (with clear risks of physical damage) is equally great in Sweden and in the United States (4.1 percent and 3.6 percent respectively). Heavy physical punishment, however, contrary to what one might think, is not integral to extreme situations, nor is it associated to a psychologically special group of parents among whom culturally inculcated norms are less powerful. This is true for both Sweden and the United States, and thus severe corporal punishment is as interesting a mirror of culture as the less heavy variant.

In the United States quite a few cases involving "a blow with some sort of instrument" (Edfeldt 1985, 44)—for example, a rod or cane—have been registered, whereas in Sweden parents generally only use their hands. In Anglo-American culture, with its British legacy of integrating corporal punishment into the system of child-rearing, punishment is usually meted out after calmly considering the child's wrongdoing and then deciding suitable punishment—even though spontaneous, undeliberated punishment does also occur in these countries. However, in the Nordic countries, according to one investigation, it is thought despicable to hit children deliberately, but understandable if one does it when provoked and very riled (Edfeldt 1979). Thus in Sweden one would expect spontaneous punishment generally carried out with the hands. Interesting for its illumination of norm formation is Edfeldt's observation (1985) that among parents the incidence of lighter physical punishment declined substantially in the first year of the anti-corporal punishment law—not because of fear of penalties but because the effect of the law was to change social norms.

The figures for actual violence between men and women in Sweden and the United States are quite similar, although armed violence is more common in the United States. Also similar are figures for violence between children and for teenager violence against their parents (mainly mothers). About every fifth seventeen-year-old in the Swedish study had at some point during 1980 hit one of his or her parents, and every third case amounted to assault and battery.

The Swedish avoidance of conflict is a behavioral tendency. It becomes anchored in the personality through culture, but it is not any sort of all-powerful controlling factor. In this respect, Sweden and the United States differ in their legislation and in their attitudes toward violent acts. However, deviations from norms occur in all countries, either because the individual cannot incorporate the ideas of

the dominating culture or because the situation itself elicits deviation. Strong feelings of frustration can be bound up with a situation
and provoke violence. It may even be that the pent-up aggression
present among many Swedes gives rise under certain circumstances
to all the greater outbursts of fury.

The psychiatrist Clarence Blomquist has an interesting notion that
associates inhibiting aggression with pacifism and resistance to box-
ing, physical punishment, the death penalty, violent methods of co-
ercion within mental health care, and so forth. "As children, those
people whose aggression is inhibited have not been allowed to
show their aggressiveness. As adults, they can no longer express it
in an adequate way. It is often suppressed, and a reaction formation
helps to keep it out of consciousness. The aggressiveness such people
can exhibit when they fight aggressiveness in others often reveals a
conflict between their own pent-up aggression and the superego."
Blomquist emphasizes that suppressed rage can consequently express itself in violent actions as well as "be sublimated and made to
serve constructive purposes" (Blomquist [1969] 1975, 79).

According to the psychologist Barbro Lennéer-Axelson (1981),
part of the explanation for men's physical maltreatment of their
wives is the release of pent-up aggression they take home from
work. Anger is not displayed at the workplace not only because the
individual "for purposes of self-preservation" refrains from telling
off his or her boss. The norm precluding conflict also applies
between workmates or colleagues on the same level, for example,
between teachers in a school, where as a consequence certain political, ideological, and even pedagogic questions become tabooed
subjects in the teachers' room.

Let me repeat here that this negative attitude toward violence
should not be exclusively interpreted in a narrow psychological way
as a sublimated inhibition of aggression. Sweden's peaceful history—
over many generations and with regard to both domestic and foreign relations—undoubtedly plays a part. It has had psychological
consequences, and it has promoted a certain mentality. Modern
Swedish history has been marked by a stable social and economic
development that has extended to and provided opportunities for
the entire population. In contrast to the living conditions in many
more-populous countries, for example, Italy (see Daun 1992), com-
petition among citizens in Sweden has been relatively slight (at least

up to the dramatic changes and the depression in the early 1990s). Swedes have not needed in the same way as others "to sharpen their elbows." This side of social development has had its historical consequences for Swedish mentality too.

Any explanation of Swedish avoidance of conflict must be multi-factorial. Like all other explanations of national cultural traits, its causes must be sought in many different conditions.

Honesty

Swedes think of themselves as honest. According to a national survey, honesty is a typical Swedish trait (Zetterberg 1985). However, this national stereotype has lately become somewhat tarnished, which explains why, in the same survey, other respondents described Swedes as "chiselers." Weapon smuggling, the "Ebbe Carlsson affair" (a political scandal linked to the investigation of the murder of Prime Minister Olof Palme), financial crimes in the upper social strata, and many other scandals and "affairs" over the last decade have reinforced the impression that the Swedes are no longer honest, no longer "the good ones."

The picture of Swedes as honest has a long ancestry and seems to be shared by non-Swedes. "The Swedes have such a reputation for honesty that when the Commissioner of Police for Foreign Immigration was arrested for spying, it made headlines as far away as Kuwait!" notes Jean Phillips-Martinsson in her book (1981, 43).

In the United States, the image of honesty coupled with naiveté is part of the folklore about Swedish Americans. When I was growing up in Sweden in the 1940s and 1950s, there was a staunch belief in Swedish honesty. It was said that in Stockholm one could lose one's wallet on Kungsgatan (Main Street) and later go and fetch it at the nearest police station. This was meant to contrast with what would happen in other countries.

However, to many foreigners, Swedish honesty can be naive, blue-eyed, principle-bound, wooden, and remote from the conditions of real life. The phrase *die dumme Schweden* articulates this view, even though the phrase is actually Swedish, not German, and thus denotes a Swedish self-image. In many countries bribery, flattery, and exaggeration are thought to be an integral part of "real life," but they are repudiated by most Swedes as dishonest and false. If one gives a compliment, it should be truly meant. However, in the eyes of others, it may look as if we Swedes actually believe that principles can transform reality.

A Swede would not tell a colleague whose home he has visited that his house was "exceptionally tasteful," his wife "incredibly beautiful and charming," his children "wonderful," and the dinner "unforgettable." To an honest Swede such exaggerations are all too easy to see through.

The question is again whether the stereotype has any empirical basis and, if so, how and to what extent. Crime statistics and contentious popular views complicate the issue. CMPS sheds a certain empirical light (but gives no clear-cut answer). For example, to the question "Can you tell a white lie without feeling guilty?" 43 percent of the Swedes responding answered no. Other questions dealing with conscience and right and wrong show a similar line of response—but age and gender-related variations are significant. Seventy-one percent of young men between eighteen and twenty-five but only 56 percent of the young women said they could lie without pangs of conscience. The question is as much about having a bad conscience as lying.

The concept of honesty has different areas of application: for example, not stealing, and telling the truth (the seventh and eighth commandments). The Swedes in the European Values System Study appear to value both these virtues especially highly. To the question whether one thought most people followed the eighth commandment, "Thou shalt not bear false witness against thy neighbor," 60 percent of the Swedes answered yes. Differences here between the Swedes and other cultures—for instance, Danes (13 percent), Finns (22 percent), Norwegians (38 percent)—are striking. The average positive response for the Latin countries in Europe was 26 percent, and for northern Europe, 25 percent, although there were great differences between countries. Of the nine non-Nordic countries, none had a higher frequency of yes answers than 35 percent (Great Britain)—much lower than Sweden's. There was a comparatively large number of individuals who obeyed the commandment in the United States (38 percent) and in Japan (43 percent), where surveys have also been carried out.

The response to the commandment "Thou shalt not steal" was similar: 65 percent of the Swedes thought most people obeyed the commandment, with smaller portions of Danes (13 percent), Finns (26 percent), and Norwegians (52 percent). Nor in this instance did other European countries attain such high figures as Sweden; the closest was Great Britain (38 percent). The figures for the United States and Japan were 39 percent and 55 percent respectively.

These figures should not be interpreted to indicate that honest behavior follows norms. Differences between attitude and behavior is another topic. Nevertheless, the Swedish attitude toward lying probably influences behavior in a way that seems odd to many foreigners. This very likely coheres with the homogeneity of Swedish culture. It is worth noting that the difference between the degree of honesty ascribed to oneself and that which is ascribed to other people is much smaller among Swedes than among other nationalities. This may be so because many Swedes believe themselves to conform to a greater degree than do people in other countries or because particularly many Swedes think people are basically good. I return to homogeneity in the next chapter, but want first to present the views of two immigrants: a Finnish Gypsy and a young American woman. Their stories complicate Swedes' stereotyping of themselves as honest.

The Gypsy answered my question whether one could trust what a Swede said in the following way:

> Let's take as an example workmates who've known each other many years. You think you've got mates you can trust, but then one day. . . . We had two girls, pretty young, at work who were on sick leave. When we were all together, people said, how can [the girls] be sick so long? What have they got? Then one day they came back to work. The boss said, "Are you okay now?" Everybody began to laugh. Then I said, "It doesn't have anything to do with your wages whether the girls are sick. But now, let's hear all the crap you've been saying since they've been gone." When they are together they have fun, but when one leaves, then they talk a load of shit about that person. That's hard for me to understand. . . . Where I work now, Hasse and I arrive first in the morning and he always likes to talk about all the bad

things that happen in the world. And he usually talks about mates who aren't around. I'm quiet and he thinks maybe I agree, but I'm too tired to deal with his talk. He bad-mouths everybody, but when they all come in, he laughs and claps everybody on the shoulder. So you think they're false, the Swedes. In Finland people think you should be honest.

In the American's story, the similarities to the Finnish Gypsy's experiences are striking:

Already in the first weeks (of the course at *Filmhuset*), small groups were formed that stayed together. You always sat together with the same people at lunch, kept to your group—sitting with others was not approved. There were lots of intrigues too. I sat together with four other women and had to get into very intimate subjects with them. It felt like something very personal (confided to you) that should not go any further—something to exclude others with. It was a struggle to get friends, and it felt like that was the idea, that you should fight for friendship, and when you finally became friends, you should be so incredibly close. . . .

But when I met them on their own, they talked about the others. It was as if you should always criticize people outside—to emphasize the togetherness between those talking to each other.

My own interpretation of this Swedish pattern is that many Swedes have difficulties lying to others "straight in the face"; nor do they "make things up." To that extent they are honest. But they also want positive relations and a feeling of mutual understanding when they talk to people in a personal way. So they do not openly criticize the person they are talking to, even if they are in fact critical. They swallow their tongues and choose other subjects of conversation. Criticism is instead communicated to others who are willing to listen and agree. The "backbiting" is then used as a way of finding accord (what the American intimated in her remarks about the conversation "not going any further, something to exclude others with").

The desire not to lie stands counter to the desire to achieve mutual understanding. The opposition is dissolved through silence and the selective avoidance of sensitive subjects. What one says is true, honest, but need not be the whole truth.

The question does arise whether the pressure to conform among Swedes cannot lead some to lie about their personal views when they think that such lying would promote neighborliness or a good atmosphere at work. Perhaps one uses a white lie to avoid quarreling with one's mother-in-law? In any case, there are grounds for the hypothesis that Swedes are more prone to avail themselves of a white lie than Italians, for instance, and people in cultures with less pressure to conform and agree and more inclination to quarrel and argue face to face.

This hypothesis is supported by the answers to the CMPS question, "Can you tell a white lie without feeling guilty?"—answers provided by a sample of students from Verona, Italy, and a sample from Umeå, Sweden. Of the Italian students 39 percent answered yes; of the Swedes, 58 percent—considerably more.

But to the same question 69 percent of a sample of American students answered yes. Why this difference?

Homogeneity

A homogeneous culture is an integrated culture; people are close ethnically, linguistically, religiously, and morally. Swedish culture is homogeneous, though this does not mean that the culture has historically been free of external influences. Furthermore, the degree of homogeneity has varied with different periods. In the Middle Ages, for example, a culturally influential German population resided in Stockholm, and indeed the Swedish language is still full of German (and other) loan words. The foreign and the Swedish have over time gradually melded together, so that new elements are experienced as genuinely Swedish: they have been incorporated. What homogeneity entails is a "horizontal" unanimity, a substantial shared mentality among the native Swedish population over the same period of time.

This means that as a member of this Swedish culture one need not develop—as one would in a heterogeneous or disintegrated culture—a more thoroughgoing ability to interpret other people, their thoughts, views, and intentions. It is true that people in all cultures use many codes other than words—for example, intonation, mimicry, body language, clothes. In a homogeneous culture, however, these other codes are used in a relatively simple way, leading one to think one can classify people adequately. In general, Swedes (like Norwegians) assume that people mean what they say. The belief that ordinary people are "honest" is fundamental.

In a newspaper interview, a Swede who had been living in Greece for fifteen years commented on differences in customs between the two countries. The contrast between the "straight," or honest, communication in Sweden and communication fraught with many ramifications is evident in her remarks. "To compare [the Swedish] with the Greek art of conversation, where double meanings and ambiguities are a part of the linguistic playfulness—'Don't you understand? You are so naive!' Ann Kristin's workmates (in Greece) tell her. 'To you we have to say exactly what we mean.' "

Such a presumption contrasts with the preconditions in heterogeneous cultures in which the context has to be taken much more into account with all interpretations. This is because interpretation is much more demanding when communicating with people who are different from oneself and because one expects less "loyalty" from strangers. Caution is to be observed.

Gustav Sundbärg, in his book published in 1911 on the Swedish psyche, commented that Swedes are no psychologists—that is, no experts on human nature. His judgment still holds fairly true:

> Swedes never interest themselves in *studying* people. Try in company not to slander a person who is not liked—that would do the trick; nor to raise artlessly a popular person to the skies—that will be followed by an equally artless agreement. But try calmly and impartially and somewhat more deeply to *analyze* the character of a person whom everyone in the company knows, try to discover both his good and less good sides and explain how they relate to each other. The result will inevitably be—general silence. And after a few moments, someone in the company will pursue another topic of conversion.

It is by "reading between the lines" and perceiving the small "signals" that people interpret the unsaid. This is also how people become

curious about others' personalities, but the more an individual rec-
ognizes him- or herself in other people's code systems the more
passive in this respect he or she tends to become.

Susan Sontag (1969) observed that instead of psychological insights, Swedes fill their conversations with quantifications—a rough
generalization but a telling one. How many hours of sunlight there
were last month, when one went to bed last night, how much rent
one pays. According to Sontag, figures are emotionally neutral;
with them one can make impersonal even what is intimate.

Hannerz (1983, 21) has some interesting references:

> This being so bound to facts extends from everyday life
> to scholarship. The prominent American sociologist Alvin
> Gouldner (1975, 310–12) has described how he discovered
> this trait among his Swedish colleagues. Hardly anywhere
> else in international sociology can one find such an ex-
> plicit, formalistic method morality as among the Swedes. It
> seems as if they have declared war against insecurity. But it
> also means that they hesitate to play with ideas and that
> they feel uncomfortable with what is unclear by nature.
> When Gouldner posed broad and open questions—prima-
> rily to keep the conversation going—even about matters he
> thought the others had experienced personally, he received
> the answer that they "did not have any information on these
> things." And when they occasionally tried to respond with
> the guesses and speculations his questions required, he
> thought they seemed tense.

To illuminate the preconditions for the growth of an entirely
different culture, more pervaded by the imagination, Hannerz recalls many of the thinkers who have influenced our view of society had their roots in Jewish minority existence: Marx, Freud,
Simmel, Durkheim, Levi-Strauss. According to Hannerz, they all liberated themselves from the conventions of everyday thought. He
finds a parallel in many outstanding contemporary American come-
dians—Lenny Bruce, Woody Allen, Mort Sahl, Dick Gregory—who
all belong to ethnic minorities and consequently have been forced
into a double consciousness. "Humor is subversive, it is an anti-
ritual. It jars the prevailing ideas and perceptions of reality. But in

Sweden, with few exceptions, we lack a comic tradition" (Hannerz 1983, 21).

In a culture like the Swedish, in which, because of cultural homogeneity, communication between people does not require much flexibility and rapid accommodation, it is easier for people to adhere to a system of rules. Independent ideas, personal judgment, rest on uncertain ground compared with given rules, regulations—"facts." This goes some way to explain what seems to foreigners a marked rigidity in Swedish society.

In a 1987 article in the newspaper *Expressen*, a reporter related some events that took place in Kulturhuset in Stockholm in conjunction with a reading by the Nobel Prize winner Joseph Brodsky. The reporter did not get in, because the hall was full and all the tickets (costing KR 40) were sold.

> At the door of the hall stood a young guard in uniform. He was not to let anyone in without a ticket, and he stood there with his arms crossed over his chest, tall and blond, young and strong. The reading started at 1:00 p.m., and after an hour, the first of the audience left the hall, one by one or in small groups. Then some of the people waiting outside began to appeal to the guard, saying that there were now places free. He said he had his orders. Throughout, members of the public continued to leave, either because they couldn't stay any longer or thought they'd got enough poetry for their 40 kronor or because they'd satisfied their objective of being there and seeing the Nobel Prize winner in person.
>
> But the people outside still were not let in, despite all their entreaties, arguments, and occasional agitation. One of the employees of Kulturhuset entered into various discussions with people, always referring to the management. When an older woman with a Danish accent told him that he should learn to follow his own common sense, he went and rang his boss, who said no once again.

The lack of compromise demonstrated by this incident should not be taken as a sign that Swedes' reputation for compromise is mistaken. Compromises are resorted to sometimes for the pragmatic purpose of getting on with things without major delays, of coming to decisions quickly. In other contexts, the compromise may be a way of avoiding the difficult feelings aroused by dispute. In the example from Kulturhuset, the guard had nothing to gain by being flexible, no overweening goal to achieve. Not compromising was, on the contrary, wholly compatible with his duties and the social role ascribed to Swedish public employees, who are assumed to treat everyone the same.

Given the well-integrated Swedish culture ("everything hangs together"), it follows that everything is associated with a larger context. Compared with people in a heterogeneous culture, Swedes have more reason to think that they know, understand, comprehend, and command their own culture. The same has been said of Norwegian culture. All arguments for a point of view are considered in Norway to function as a sign of group affiliation, which is why they are not fully valued as arguments "but rather diagnosed as symptoms of a superior common identity that we already have clear views about" (Larsen 1984, 23). The tendency to "pigeonhole" people, to classify them on the basis of their views, certainly exists in much less homogeneous cultures than the Swedish and Norwegian. What is interesting is that in our part of the world this tendency appears to constitute a distinct pattern.

It explains a great deal about the Swedish pattern of communication: the reluctance to voice opinions about loaded questions in front of people one does not know well, the cautious, somewhat passive position taken when one does not know where the opposite party stands.

Of course, even a relatively homogeneous culture contains divergent opinions and controversial issues; and beyond that culture, in encounters with foreigners, Swedish homogeneity provides little of the security felt with good friends. On the contrary, homogeneity can easily lead one to overestimate one's ability to interpret, to understand, the behavior of others. This makes it risky to give off the "wrong" signals: for example, wearing expensive, elegant clothes when one holds socialist views. By affiliating oneself with an established code system, one lessens the risk of being misinterpreted. Before expressing one's views on a controversial issue, one tries to detect the position of the opposite party.

What Swedes say to each other is thus interpreted to a significant degree as signs or symbols of a personal identity or group affiliation. However, the more culturally mixed a society, the more risky or complicated is such interpreting. The individual's overall perspective and knowledge of other groups are much too limited, and therefore opinions, ideas, and experiences are considered separate and distinct more often than they are in homogeneous cultures. One in fact often does not know if people are what they seem.

In England, for example, it often happens that one of the participants in a meeting assumes the role of "opponent" and criticizes the presented proposal, tries to find its faults and weaknesses. He or she may actually be very much in favor of the proposal but consider it important to have it thoroughly scrutinized. This playing the role of "devil's advocate" occurs more seldom in Sweden, where the others would likely associate the advocate with his or her critical opinions. Afterward, they can say, "What a pain, we won't include him in the future." Critical opinions are taken as "honest" expressions of a dismissive stance.

Individualism Versus Collectivism

In the United States, Sweden is often referred to as a "socialist country," partly because Americans identify socialism with social democracy but also because of the Swedish emphasis on collective and uniform solutions in the public sector—from day care for preschool children to higher education, health care, care for the elderly, and the pension system. As a consequence of the dramatic economic and political changes in the beginning of the 1990s, this picture of Sweden has lost a great deal of its validity. On the other hand, as the American sociologist David Popenoe has pointed out (1985), in the United States there is an inclination to exaggerate the theme of individualism in American social history. Since varying degrees of individualistic and collectivistic tendencies coexist in many countries, how to best examine the question of individualism versus collectivism depends very much on how one defines individualism.

Some data would indicate an individualistic tendency in Sweden. In his book *Culture's Consequences* (1984), Geert Hofstede presents an individualism index for forty countries. The index is composed of six work goals (see also Daun 1991). On this index scale, Sweden scores 71 points, thereby landing in the tenth place among the most individualistic countries—the United States being first with 91 points, and Venezuela last with 12.

This result is supported by what I have already presented in the section on independence: the stress on social autonomy, not being dependent on others, whether neighbors, relatives, employers, or whoever. The law also views the individual as an independent unit. "Family" and "kin" are vague and legally rather irrelevant categories. For example, if a Swedish family put an apartment at the disposal of the family matriarch, the mother would be taxed for the apartment as "a residential benefit." This is a *Swedish* point of view, even though many Swedes may be upset about the consequences of it. The intervention of the authorities to the disadvantage of the individual is not popular in any country. However, legislation always has cultural roots: certain ideas can only arise in a certain climate.

A similar case would be that of a condominium owner who sublets his condominium to a son or daughter. The owner may be liable for back taxes if he only charges the amount of his own costs, in the form of monthly fees to the residents' association, when these are lower than the general rent levels in the district where he lives. He should charge the market rent. If he charges no rent at all, then it is a gift in kind and has to be declared as a housing benefit. Grown children and old parents are formally not part of the family.

Another expression of independence among Swedes is the practice—very widespread by international standards—of cohabiting without being married. Interestingly enough, autonomy in this situation was abridged by the 1987 cohabitation law, which in part places cohabitation on an equal footing with marriage. The measure was a response to the fact that cohabitation without marriage had become so common.

Swedish people tend to be cautious in their relations with their neighbors, to a much greater degree than are Americans, for example. Many Swedes fear being drawn into a relationship with a neighbor that they later might regret and that might prove difficult to quit. This is especially tricky because Swedes have difficulties "saying no" and setting boundaries when there is the risk of hurting someone. Newly arrived in the neighborhood, Swedes do not go around and introduce themselves to their neighbors, and the neighbors in turn do not organize any welcoming parties.

Swedes draw a relatively strict borderline between the private
sphere, consisting of their families and very close friends, and the
public sphere, which includes all other contacts—neighbors, workmates, and more distant relatives.

The individualistic efforts to be independent coexist, paradoxically
enough, with collectivistic elements in Swedish society. The same
characteristics have been attributed to Norway: "Norwegian men and
women are individualists by being independent and self-sufficient. In
this way individualism and conformity are brought together. While
Norway (like the other Scandinavian countries) is undergoing extensive social and cultural changes, the ideas of equality defined as
sameness and of individualism defined as independence seem to be
reinforced" (Gullestad 1989).

Like the Norwegian, Swedish culture stresses sameness and conformity and plays down differences in encounters with others. When
Swedes meet, they generally try to establish mutual understanding,
accord, consensus, and friendliness. They seek topics of conversation that allow them to express similar views and experiences.
They each want "to play the same melody" with the same rhythm
and in the same key. This intention or desire is unconscious and
only occasionally tactical. Consequently, Swedes are never eager to
express what they think about controversial issues if they have no
idea what others' views are on the subject. As has already been
mentioned, Swedes avoid face-to-face disputes.

In Swedish society people stress similarities and disregard dis-
similarities. It is the custom, for example, to ensure that guests at a
dinner party are placed next to others with whom they "have something in common." This contrasts with the custom in many more
heterogeneous countries, where people enjoy being with others
very different from themselves: divergent opinions and experiences
guarantee lively conversation.

Clubs, voluntary associations, and study groups have the same
function of emphasizing harmony and cohesion. In no other country is such a large portion of the population involved in voluntary
activities. In no other country does such a large portion of the population attend courses, not primarily to educate themselves but for
social and leisure purposes—for example, courses in bookbinding,
pottery, Chinese cooking, personal development, foreign languages,
local history. In all these contexts people's similarities have drawn

them together. The group is largely structured by the shared activity—in the course or in the club. Participants discuss bookbinding
techniques or whatever it is they are doing. The differences that
always exist between people only rarely surface, which is why their
sameness feels much greater or clearer than it actually is. The same
applies to the leisure activities, bingo and choir singing, so popular
in Sweden. In these cases, the gathering is even more structured,
and the feeling of togetherness reinforced by the collective activity.

These kinds of formalized collective interaction have a long tradition in Sweden. For hundreds of years, the *byalag* (village board, or
committee), composed of independent landowning farmers—whose
activities and pronouncements followed certain rules (*byordning*,
roughly "village ordinances")—governed in rural Sweden rather
like a parliament on a micro level. Nineteenth-century popular movements, the free church movement, the temperance movement, and
later the labor movement served as models for collective activities
in general. The organization of meetings with agendas, minutes,
and chairpersons who determine the strict order of speakers became firmly anchored in popular movements and is now considered self-evident.

Popular movements have had an enormous impact on Swedish
society, where formal groups and organizations tend to be strong
and influential—in contrast with individuals, who are considered
weak and are often ignored except when representing an organization. Individual opinions are more likely to attract public notice if
they are conveyed by a well-known person or popular television
personality. Nevertheless, in Sweden as elsewhere, largely through
the increased impact of the mass media, the individual is more and
more becoming an object of interest, not least in political propaganda. However, Sweden is still far from straightforward personal
elections, and the political personalities who are seen at home on
television have their respective organizations as their indispensable
bases. In Sweden, the individual is still largely legitimated by representing a collective. Charisma and rhetoric and the power of persuasive speaking are gaining in importance but do not suffice in the
long run; a leader is not primarily an individual but above all a
member of a group.

Non-Swedish observers have described national politics in Sweden
as a small world in which decisions are made in small groups, very

much based on informal contacts, where people represent different political parties, labor unions, and so forth, and where these public decision makers know each other personally (see Heclo and Madsen 1987). Individualism in southern Europe and Latin America could be brought in for purposes of contrast. In these parts of the world, few people belong to formal groups. Not even socialist parties were or are based in popular movements. Political leaders are mainly given leadership on the grounds of their putative individual capacities and their charisma. They hardly "represent"; they lead.

Consequently, Swedes are ambivalent about their "stars" (the more neutral term "celebrity" is seldom used), whether in sports, show business, or culture. The stars' successes may be admired, but their exclusiveness and out-of-the-ordinary achievements often give rise to envy and therefore to malicious pleasure when the stars "fall." The high value awarded to *sameness* makes all personal success problematic.

In Sweden eccentrics are not regarded with the same positive interest that they allegedly are in Great Britain (Weeks and Ward 1988). Rather, all deviance from group norms and common group patterns is potentially threatening to the individual. The individual should fit in with coworkers and neighbors. Group pressure makes it especially difficult for immigrants with an academic education to obtain employment consonant with their qualifications. "Personal chemistry" is particularly important, since academically trained professionals cooperate with colleagues to a great extent on the basis of individual initiative and intuition and not according to prescribed routines. The psychological condition and capabilities of the professional group have greater influence on results than do, generally, those of manual workers (this is true for many other countries as well). But since the group pressure for sameness is especially strong among Swedes—associating along the same lines, laughing at the same jokes—immigrants are assumed not to fit in. This stereotyping may explain why so many foreign university students, graduates from technical universities in Sweden, have had such difficulties finding an employer—even when their skills are demanded on the labor market.

The ability to cooperate is highly valued in Sweden, especially in the recruitment of high-level staff. Training children to cooperate is one of the items on the pedagogical program in Swedish day-care centers, even though group orientation is already so deeply ingrained that perhaps what needs to be inculcated is rather the opposite capacity, that is, the ability to act as an individual.

The emphasis on sameness, the desire not to deviate, is also indicated in the responses given by Swedish youth in an international survey (Prime Minister's Office 1984). One of the questions concerned "desired lifestyle" ("I want to live as I please"; "I want to be rich"; "I want high social status"; "I want to contribute to society"). Of eleven nationalities (the others were Filipinos, Japanese, South Koreans, Brazilians, West Germans, British, Yugoslavs, French, Americans, and Swiss) the Swedes desired high social status least of all: only 1.8 percent, an insignificant figure when compared with, for example, 20.8 percent of the French and 25 percent of the young Germans. Among the Americans this goal was chosen by 7.2 percent, a low figure but still much higher than that for the Swedes. What young Swedes wanted, comparatively speaking, more than young people in other countries was "to live as [they] pleased"— the goal of 86.8 percent of the Swedish respondents. This would seem to reflect the need for autonomy, but it is an autonomy that nevertheless subordinates itself to the "invisible" conformity of the collective.

Given the above, we may conclude that Swedes often try to enter formal groups where they interact with others largely on the basis of their group membership. The formal group serves as a necessary resource for those striving for power and influence; in relation to power, the collective is always superior to the individual in the Nordic countries. Such commitment to the collective also makes it necessary to adapt to the views and values of the group in question, and therefore collective entities tend to be very well integrated and homogeneous in Sweden.

The much sought-after feeling of sameness, which in Swedish is encapsulated in the word *gemenskap* (difficult, if not impossible, to translate adequately into English, since its lexical meaning, "sense of community or togetherness," lacks the exceedingly strong positive ramifications of the Swedish word), can be achieved in two different ways. One is to confine private relationships to one's immediate family and a few very close friends. Extreme cases, which are not all that exceptional among Swedes, seek to be alone. (To exemplify this linguistically, one should note the positive value in

Swedish of the expression *att slippa folk*—to avoid [encountering] people.) The second way is to organize every interaction with others around shared participation in some group or club: such shared activities might include working together, participating in a course, singing in a choir, dancing in a folkdance ensemble, and enjoying the benefits of membership in a yacht club. In such contexts differences between people are confined to the margins, and interaction is limited to the "level of sameness." Thus individualism (defined as an emphasis on independence/autonomy) and collectivism (defined as affiliation with common points of view and patterns of behavior) are two ways of dealing with one and the same dilemma—that of uniformity in a differentiated world.

Feelings

Immigrants to Sweden sometimes discuss "Swedish coldness," whether Swedes really are as "cold" as they seem (Daun 1989). Some claim that indeed they are; others say their patterns of behavior only make them seem that way. Swedes do not express very clearly the warm feelings they actually possess; one simply has to know them well. In this regard, Swedes' own views of themselves, reflected in their next most common self-stereotype, is as "stiff" (Zetterberg 1985; Freund 1980).

This is not merely a dinner-table conversation topic, it is also a scientific question. It seems to be a fairly common point of view also among culture researchers that "cold behavior" is only a form, a language; Swedes show emotion other than with hugs and kisses and torrents of words. It is often said that even within families, Swedes touch each other less than do people in some other cultures.

It is easy to disprove empirically the extreme interpretation that Swedes lack feelings. However, if Swedes are comparatively cold, does this only refer to ways or forms of expressing themselves, or is it also representative of a relatively low degree of emotional intensity?

Naturally, there are also lively and emotional Swedes who are occasionally reminded that they are too loud, too loquacious, too ardent. When necessary, such people can restrain themselves so as not to make a bad impression in a job interview, for instance, or when meeting their future parents-in-law for the first time.

By way of illustration, let me relate an encounter with an elderly professor of sociology I met at the University of Minnesota. His father had emigrated from Sweden to the United States as a young man. I asked the professor what he recalled from his childhood as being particularly Swedish; he answered, first and foremost being admonished to control his feelings.

In her book *Of Swedish Ways*, the Swedish American Lilly Lorénzen claims that many Americans of Swedish extraction have described how frustrated they felt during their childhood: "I cannot remember that my father or mother at any time made any visible display of affection for me, and sometimes I ached inside for a little love" (1978, 88–89).

A Swede, married and living in Greece for fifteen years, related in a newspaper article that when at home in Sweden she was "more discreet. The first thing I notice when I come home on a visit is that people are never angry" (*Dagens Nyheter*, 29 February 1988).

It is easier to take note of *expressions* of feelings than it is to observe the feelings themselves. This dilemma explains the discrepancy in interpretations of Swedish behavior referred to at the beginning of this chapter. How do you measure feelings? One way is to register physiological expressions like pulse, reddening of the skin, and so forth. Such studies show that individuals differ in their physiological reactions to different stimuli. This probably means that they also feel differently. But these differences in physiological reaction very likely also have a cultural basis; that is, they are influenced by "internalised norms concerning the kinds of emotions that it is appropriate to experience in specific situations, these extending to physiological arousal as well as to subjective feeling states" (Scherer 1986, 10). Thus, the intensity of feelings depends not only on individual personality differences but also on culture, that is, feelings culturally defined as appropriate.

Interestingly enough, most people agree that there are individual differences in "temperament." Many of us know people who easily lose their temper or are extremely talkative and loud. But when it comes to "national character," the question often presented is whether Swedes—that is, all Swedes—are quiet and emotionally disciplined. Hence everyone can dispute the "idea of national character" and give examples from their own experiences of people who deviate from the description. However, the question is not to what extent Swedes react less strongly than other people, except in a statistical sense. The question is whether temperamental individuals constitute a smaller proportion of the Swedish population than they do in, for example, Finland or Italy. The answer is yes; although there are Italians whose personalities could be described as "typically Swedish," these Italians constitute a minority in Italy.

There are individuals in every country whose personalities would fit in better in another country. There are Swedes who "act out" and who feel liberated after moving abroad—I have met some like that— as there are immigrants who to a degree feel more at home in Sweden than in their native countries. An American colleague who tried but failed to get a university position in Sweden has found during his periods as guest researcher that he feels more at home with Swedes and their low-key profile (than with his compatriots). A Greek author resident in Sweden told me that he enjoyed not having to talk to people so much, which he would be expected to do in Greece. Among Swedes there are some dominant personalities who succeed as directors in Swedish subsidiary companies abroad but whose "bossy" style gives them problems at home.

Variations in personality are biologically limited. An individual can be an introvert or extrovert, aggressive, shy, neurotic, depressive, or whatever (see Allport and Odbert 1936). Whether an individual characteristic is biologically inherited or originates in the surrounding system of norms, there are a limited number of possibilities.

No culture, no society, is able to create unique personality *traits* among its members, traits that for instance only Swedes possess. However, a sociocultural environment may foster the development of certain personality characteristics among the people in that environment, while other environments encourage other characteristics. For example, a particular method of child-rearing that is especially common in one country may affect the statistical distribution of a certain personality trait (Perris et al. 1985). However, it is extremely difficult to predict specific personality traits issuing from specific childhood experiences or methods of child-rearing (see Shweder 1991). Consequently, what is typical for one nation is its specific distribution of personality traits and the percentage of individuals who may be said to share a particular personality profile (Terhune 1970). What may be considered a unique national characteristic is the dominating combination (or combinations) of personality traits.

Not even a very homogeneous culture shapes everyone in the same mold. Even if all the children in a socioculturally homogeneous society were brought up in exactly the same way, they would still possess different personalities. This is because personality is not only anchored in the environment but is also biologically inherited. This is clearly demonstrated in studies of identical twins.

Hans and M. W. Eysenck have roughly estimated that more than half of all personality variations are due to biologically inherited factors. They have also studied the putative connections between extroversion and neuroticism on the one hand and blood-group distribution on the other. The data emerging from this study "appear to support at least to some extent the possibility that differences in personality between countries and cultures may be genetically determined" (Eysenck and Eysenck 1985, 111).

However, as Hans Eysenck and his coauthor point out, "a great deal of work remains to be done as regards the question of genetic background factors in personality traits and comparisons between different countries and cultures." Richard Lynn (1971) made a similar attempt to find analytical connections between "race" and "anxiety," but with poor results. These research efforts stand in glaring contrast to early physical-anthropological research, especially the German, which claimed to be able to describe people's "character traits" through their physical-anthropological characteristics. Modern genetic research has been more successful. We now know, for instance, that certain personality variables correlate to enzyme activity in the blood, which in turn is more or less exclusively genetically determined (see Klinteberg, Oreland, et al. 1990–91).

In any case, expressions of personality can be read and measured. Lynn's book (1971) contains data concerning degrees of "anxiety" (which could be translated as "emotionality") in various countries, that is, the emotional intensity of reactions to different stimuli. Anxiety is not the same as "angst," although an intensive form of anxiety can be neurotic.

A person with high anxiety has stronger reactions; a person with low anxiety has weaker reactions. If these two people are placed in the same conflict situation, all other things being equal, the former will become the most angry. In ordinary language, we would say that they have different temperaments. As implied, this difference may be in part genetic, but it may also be related to internalized norms for *how one is supposed to feel* in certain situations. As has been mentioned, differences in patterns of reaction not only distinguish individuals but also cultures.

Lynn classifies thirteen countries in three groups. Sweden is placed in the group with low anxiety, together with The Netherlands, Great Britain, and Ireland. The middle group contains Denmark, Switzerland, Norway, and Finland. The high-anxiety group includes Austria, West Germany, France, Italy, and Belgium. This classification is based on psychological investigations in each country and is, for my purposes, the most interesting of Lynn's results. He also describes several stringent methodological, but nevertheless unsuccessful, attempts to explain personality differences between countries with sociological, climatic, and physical-anthropological variables. Lynn reports certain positive indications, but all are rather weak.

In any case, what is interesting here, beyond the potential explanations for shifts in anxiety, is not only that weak emotional expressions—like those Swedes are known for—constitute a cultural form that can be given different significance in different countries, but also that the Swedish expressions of feelings may directly reflect a lower degree of emotionality, that is, lower emotional intensity. In other words, Swedes seem not to "feel as strongly" as certain other people.

When a Yugoslav immigrant admits that his hand lands on the child's rear before he has a chance to ponder the matter or consider what sort of punishment would be best under the circumstances, it not only reflects a child-raising praxis different from that adopted by most Swedes (Ehn and Arnstberg 1980), it also indicates a higher degree of emotional intensity, even if cultural precepts for how one ought to behave conspire to shape emotional expressions. This is an important difference between feelings and emotional expressions, although it seems that feelings too are somewhat culturally inculcated.

In many respects, Swedes tend to deride strong, spontaneous expressions of feelings. They are considered stupid and childish—among some Swedish men, even feminine. There is a generally embraced opinion that adults should be clearly conscious of what they do, and this is considered specially important when raising children. Symptomatically, there is no counterpart to the French *crime passionnel* in Swedish law. Powerful feelings can be accepted as extenuating circumstances in criminal cases, but such considerations are generally very restricted.

Consequently, Swedish courts show comparatively greater restraint in awarding compensation for "mental suffering" than for economic loss, for example. This is evident in a comment by the attorney general regarding the case of an inventor who for *seven years* remained under indictment for tax evasion. When the indictment was lifted, the inventor sued for KR 100,000 in damages on the grounds of mental suffering, but was awarded only KR 10,000. His lawyer claimed that he had suffered permanent damage, but the lawyer's assertion did not convince the attorney general, who concluded that "it is difficult to assess suffering in monetary terms, and the level of compensation for suffering in Swedish law is low" (*Svenska Dagbladet*, 28 December 1986).

The social anthropologist Tord Larsen (1984) has described similar Norwegian attitudes toward emotions. *Föleri*, or "emotional drivel," is a common Norwegian insult. Larsen's reference material comes primarily from the United States, which offers illustrative contrasts. The similarities between Sweden and Norway do not preclude emotions' being disparaged more in Sweden.

Swedes, Finns, Italians, and Koreans

One method of accessing the feelings of others is to use questionnaires and people's own assessments. The CMPS survey of Finnish and Swedish personalities sheds light on the role of emotions—or how strongly people usually react—in the two cultures (Daun, Mattlar, and Alanen 1989).

To the CMPS question, "Do you easily lose your temper if you don't get what you want?" 19 percent of the Swedes and 31 percent of the Finns answered yes (the difference between Swedish and Finnish men was even greater). To the question, "Do you easily get annoyed with other people?" 14 percent of the Swedes but almost twice as many Finns (26 percent) answered yes. A third CMPS question was, "Does it sometimes happen that you get frantic with anger?" and here 47 percent of the Swedes and 59 percent of the Finns answered yes. To judge by these responses, fewer Swedes by their own admission experience intensive hate or rage. That Swedes have lower "anxiety" than Finns is evident in Lynn's data.

Other comparative CMPS material has been obtained through cooperation with professors Pyun Kwang-soo and Rafal Gozdzik at Hankuk University for Foreign Studies in Seoul. The sample there contained 370 Korean students of foreign languages. To the first question mentioned above—about losing one's temper—27 percent of the young Swedes (18–24 years old) answered yes (only 16 percent of a sample of students at the northern Swedish university of Umeå). However, 51 percent of the Koreans answered in the affirmative, and even more Italian students (60 percent) at the University of Verona. The proportion of temperamental people—to use an everyday idiom—seems greater in Korea and Italy than in Sweden.

One might object that the Italian and Korean responses only reflect a cultural form (i.e., not content), "to lose one's temper," and that Swedes thus need not have different feelings—that only the "customary" emotional expression differs. The difference could then be explained by the negative Swedish attitude toward aggressive behavior, which fosters a greater degree of control over one's feelings.

But how then does one explain the expressiveness of those temperamental individuals who deviate from their own social surroundings? Such expressiveness cannot be dismissed as superficial, since it cannot be identified as an imitation of normal Swedish behavior. On the contrary, it is clearly an inevitable expression of a specific set of feelings.

An extreme example of this is the case described by the anthropologist Jean Briggs in her book *Never in Anger* (1970). The Utku Eskimos she studied never became angry or irritated: "It is not just that they do not express anger; they 'feel' no anger." Nor do they have any terms or conceptual nuances for anger (cited in Solomon 1984, 244).

To sum up: the two groups of immigrants in Sweden who interpreted Swedes' "chilly behavior" totally differently are both right. On the one hand, there is a generally accepted norm that in part regulates Swedes' *emotional expressions* (especially outside of the private sphere), with the result that Swedes seem less emotional than other nationalities. On the other, fewer Swedes get angry, so their feelings actually appear cooler. But feelings are also influenced by norms, particularly the norm prescribing which feelings are appropriate to any given situation (Scherer 1986). But this is still a question of feelings—not expressions of feelings.

Grief After the Murder of Olof Palme

About three weeks after the murder of the prime minister a poll was conducted by the political scientist Gunnel Gustafsson in collaboration with colleagues at the University of Umeå. The poll was distributed among around 2500 school children and adults in Luleå, Södertälje, and Umeå. The respondents were representative of the total Swedish population with regard to gender, social background, age, party sympathies, and so forth. A similar investigation was carried out in the United States by Professor Roberta S. Sigel in Chicago after the assassination of President John F. Kennedy. The Swedish survey was drawn up so that the results would be comparable to the American (Gustafsson 1987).

The Swedish mass media noted (as did individuals) that after the murder of Olof Palme Swedes wept openly, for instance, when they came to lay flowers on the place where he was shot. This was noteworthy because Swedes' crying in public was considered so exceptional. Even so, comparison between the Swedish and American reactions—and even with those of immigrants in Sweden—shows that the native Swedes still reacted less emotionally.

Of native adult Swedes, 24 percent admitted to crying. Among the adult first-generation immigrants in Sweden, 44 percent admitted to crying, and 53 percent of adult Americans said the same. To the statement "I was so upset and confused I didn't know what I felt," only 11 percent of the adult native-born Swedes, but 35 percent of the adult first-generation immigrants, and 38 percent of the Americans agreed. Also, the children resident in Sweden but born abroad reacted more strongly than the native-born Swedish children (21 percent and 7 percent respectively admitted to crying).

Norms for Being Quiet and Taciturn

In Sweden loudness is often associated with having a lively temperament. Lively people mostly do not talk in low voices. Being quiet is seen as an expression of the opposite emotional stance. I have already mentioned that in addition to the feelings themselves, the explanation for emotionally related behavior lies partly in norms denoting how one *should feel* in a given situation, partly in norms for how one *should behave* in a given situation.

There are different ways of being taciturn. One way, according to many immigrants, makes close contact with Swedes difficult; this way of being taciturn can sometimes be due to communication anxiety. Another sort may be due to lack of social training, imagination, or the ability to find something to say. Related to this is the sort demonstrated in lengthy pauses and generous silences, which are evident even among Swedes who in fact find it easy to discover subjects for conversation. A fourth variant is the low voice.

All of them can in part be explained by cultural norms. A sample of Chileans interviewed mentioned reticence as a typical Swedish trait (Thörnberg 1985). "It is so quiet on the train. In Chile we say 'hello' even when we don't know the other passengers." Contact with neighbors was described similarly: "You greet each other in Sweden with a reserved 'hello' and a nod; no conversation arises. . . . To go in an elevator and 'be completely silent and only stare at the buttons' also feels very strange" (Thörnberg 1985, 11). Regardless of the power of feelings in an individual, there are norms that essentially determine how quiet or talkative that individual is to be in the country where he or she lives. When immigrants, raised with other norms, encounter Swedish behavior, they may be surprised, or they may find previously obtained stereotypes to be confirmed.

Even communication anxiety has a normative background, since it arises in response to the expectations, demands, and critical judgment of others: the less I say, the less the risk of making a fool of myself. The ethnologist Annick Sjögren, who was raised in France, has described the contrasting attitude, where the spoken word "weighs lightly." Words disappear, "vanish into thin air," so one need not watch one's words, be careful of what one says (Daun 1984). In Sweden being reticent derives from the tendency to think before one speaks, to formulate one's statements in one's mind before saying them.

The notion of *kallprata* ("small talk," literally "cold talk"), which predictably has no counterpart in French, reflects the Swedish disparagement of talking for the sake of talking. It follows that particularly talkative Swedes are described as *pratsjuka* (garrulous), *pratkvarnar* (chatterboxes), *pladdermajor* (babblers), *frasmakare* (phrasemongers); there are many negative vernacular expressions for people who talk "too much." However, this Swedish pattern also has parallels in other countries. The Spanish-born Swedish ethnologist Julio Ferrer has described the Castilian view that one should not talk too much and not talk unnecessarily. Similar norms, which can be confirmed by many aphorisms, apply in northern Spain, but not in southern Spain. Nevertheless, words are more "flighty" in Spanish, and Spaniards place less weight on the spoken word than do Swedes.

Talking at the same time, interrupting, and putting words in another person's mouth are accepted in both Germany and France, whereas in Sweden many children are taught that interrupting is rude. Among neither the Germans nor the French is it considered impolite to raise one's voice in order to gain the floor.

Herbert Hendin (1964) notes that language reveals norms and values, as, for example, in the expression *att tiga ihjäl* (to kill by silence). He finds it significant that Swedes, who are so quiet, choose extreme reticence as a means of communication. However, silence in Sweden may contain a positive message as well as a negative one.

Silence can be a positive attribute in several ways. The Swedish phrase *tyst och fin* (literally "quiet and refined") has no equivalent in French. Swedes will, for instance, describe a child as a *tyst och fin liten pojke* ("fine, quiet little boy"), and everyone knows what is meant—that being quiet is positive. Such a remark would be incomprehensible to a French person. To Swedes, the opposite behavior—being loud—is pretentious, ostentatious, overbearing, sometimes upsetting and vulgar, depending on how the person is generally. Low-status immigrants are often subjected to negative comments when they talk with loud voices (Öhlund 1982).

The Swedish folklorist Bengt af Klintberg related to me the following about a visit to a pizzeria in Stockholm:

> As in so many other pizzerias, in Lilla Bussola the customer places an order and then gets a number. When your pizza or spaghetti or whatever is ready, the waiter calls out the number. Then you are supposed to shout and wave, whereupon the waiter comes to the table with your food. While I sat and waited for my "Cappriciosa," I watched the customers who had ordered just before me. When the waiter called out their numbers, none of them answered with as loud a voice as his [the waiter's]. One of them said "Here" in such a low voice that it hardly reached the counter. Or they

waved their hands in silence. A couple of them clearly were
so distressed by the situation that . . . they got up and went
up to the waiter and took their plates!

Behind Swedish silence lies the strict boundary line drawn in
Sweden between the public and the private. To raise one's voice
sufficiently for others to hear is tantamount to a declaration of "intimacy." Even to call out somebody's name across the street is a private matter.

Signaling in traffic is often considered an undesirable expression
of aggression in Sweden. According to the traffic regulations, one
should only signal in order to "avoid danger." Cultures differ even in
this matter.

The Kurdish writer Mahmut Baksi (1976, 26) has compared the
silence in Sweden with noise levels in his homeland in Turkey.

> I am in the Central Station in Stockholm. Not a sound to be
> heard. What a calm and quiet place! It feels very strange.
> For as long as I can remember I've hated silence. *I love up-
> heaval and noise.* Maybe this comes from my background.
> It's no exaggeration that when two people meet on the
> street at home in my village, the whole block can hear
> what they're saying. We who come from the Middle East
> like sounds, noise, etc. Silence frightens and confuses us.
> We think it's boring.

The Bulgarian writer Jordan Raditjkov (1980) has written an account of his travels in Sweden, which has been translated into Swedish. He has related the following about a visit to a Swedish family in
their summer cottage:

> After breakfast most of the guests stayed outside on the
> lawn to sunbathe. Without saying a word they placed their
> colorful chairs so that they all sat with their faces toward
> the sun. Swedes are good at being silent. I do not know
> if they are united in their silence—as lovers often are—
> or if each has learned to cut himself off from the others.
> (Raditjkov 1980, 104)

Silence, taciturnity, quietness, and stillness prevail to a much greater extent in Sweden than in many other places in the world, and this gives rise to norms, expectations, dictates, decrees. The norms that help to shape Swedish silence are expressed with particular clarity in the following quotes from interviews taken from an essay on Swedes' attitudes toward immigrants: "Then there was lots of trouble and conflict because they like come with their languages and ways and they shout and scream and are loud. Swedes are quiet." And then this from another interview: "I think it's crucial if the immigrants are noisy and if they're seen out on the streets, coming with large families, so there's lots of noise. Then people don't like them. We're not used to that. You see it yourself when they come along in the subways, like fifteen of them, yakking away. You don't get mad, but it's like you sigh and think, god, what a pain—can't they keep quiet?" (Öhlund 1982, 41).

Norms for Being Temperamental

Immigrants who have largely adapted to Swedish norms try to avoid exposing themselves to criticism from Swedes. The following remarks are from a Yugoslav interviewed by Billy Ehn (Ehn and Arnstberg 1980, 60):

> If I'm offended at work, I get angry; I swear and want to tell people to go to hell. Then they [the Swedes] look at me so strangely. . . . I've stopped myself from blowing up and making a big thing out of what happened. I wouldn't have in Yugoslavia: if someone did something dumb to me, I would have slugged him. In Yugoslavia I wouldn't have stopped to think. Here you restrain yourself.

Swedes generally think that immigrants get angry more easily than Swedes. It is less well known that the Swedish norms prescribing emotional control also apply to expressions of joy. Ehn interviewed a Yugoslav woman who had lived in Sweden for fifteen years. She had the following to say about her workplace (Ehn and Arnstberg 1980, 146):

There is a Norwegian girl at work, and though Norway and Sweden are alike, she feels far away from home. She told me that she had trouble controlling her temper, but she had to here. I've had the same experience. I've had a lot of trouble putting a damper on my feelings—they're not as excitable as the Norwegian's but they're open. I show it when I'm sad and when I'm glad. It's easy for me to laugh and say, "Well, what a lovely day it is today!" But you're not supposed to say that in the personnel room. Once I felt really happy and bright at work. I don't remember exactly what I said, but one of my workmates wondered what was wrong with me, if I was sick or something. Sick!? I was happy! After that I was more on my guard.

A Lapp student from northern Sweden told me of similar experiences when she began to study at the University of Umeå. She felt she had to adopt another manner—not be so eager, cheerful, and quick—in order to fit in among the Swedish students.

It is not feelings per se that are dismissed or derided in Swedish culture. It is the strong, openly exposed feelings of rage, joy, or sorrow, which are relegated to private life, although even privately these emotions are not as legitimate as they are in many other cultures. As the Swedish psychotherapist Christina Skogsberg has pointed out, feelings that are either rarely or never expressed verbally are appreciated—for example, feelings for nature and feelings of contentment. What Swedes defend themselves against is the force and power of certain emotions:

> Feelings are difficult and dangerous. Feelings disturb the design, they threaten our rational lives. Feelings should be isolated, channeled, and hidden away. I believe this is related to the qualities of feelings' being like a motor (emotion). It applies to movement (excitement), reaction (reacting and counteracting movement, pressure, and force). But also to giving signals. . . . (Other types of feelings are considered desirable—contentment, for instance.) (Skogsberg 1985, 150)

Christina Skogsberg herself encountered the desire to hide despair, when she was operated on for breast cancer and placed in a ward with other patients who had had the same operation. In her posthumously published book, *Jaget och omvärlden* (The self and the surrounding world), she writes that she was "forced to go out" to cry, even though crying is an important part of grieving:

> I neither saw nor heard anyone else cry in the ward. With very small, sometimes cheerful means, the staff quenched the tears. I should think that this was seldom even conscious on their part. They were friendly, considerate, pleasant. When I was released from hospital, I spoke with a doctor I admire about the climate on the ward, which was so hostile to tears. His response was clear and immediate: "But what would it be like if everyone lay there crying?" (Skogsberg 1985, 151)

Another example of restrained emotional display can be found on maternity wards. When giving birth, many Swedish women try to moan as little as possible, and they often ask, when it is all over, whether they screamed very much. They are very pleased to be told they did not. A midwife interviewed on a television program in 1982 said, "I am often asked the question—'Did I scream a lot . . . did I make a fool of myself?' Why? Because it is forbidden to express strong feelings, and giving birth is a situation in which it is natural to give vent to strong feelings." In many cultures, it is perfectly natural to respond to pain loudly—for instance, when giving birth (Weibust 1988).

In public debates in Sweden latitude is given for a certain amount of pathos, but still little in comparison with other countries, such as Germany, England, and the United States. In Sweden, feeling very negative about something—for instance, free abortion—is not countenanced as an argument; only facts are recognized. A debater who shows too much emotional engagement in an issue has in principle lost the debate on those grounds (which does not preclude the debater's also attracting a certain amount of sympathy). A Swedish politician must keep a cool head and calmly and collectedly weigh the facts. This special emphasis on rationality can seem very cold to strangers.

It is significant that the Swedish language has no counterpart to the American "pep talk"—"a usually brief, high-pressure, and emotional talk designed to influence or encourage an audience"

(*Webster's* 1977). Both the form and the function are comparatively alien to Swedes.

For the observations of a non-Swede about the sphere of politics, consider the German journalist Hans Magnus Enzensberger's report on the Swedish elections in 1982. He found himself in a group that he depicted as a cross-section of the country's power elite—highly placed bureaucrats, journalists, and so forth. He described reactions to reports from various electoral districts, illustrating what was to him an alien mentality:

> [T]he first results attracted only the occasional acknowledgment by those present. Not a trace of tension, excitement, "election fever." Already in the days before the election I had been struck by the incredible equanimity with which Swedes conducted their election campaign and by the speakers' stoical politeness.
>
> In most democratic countries, election campaigns provide the opportunity to transform the grey routines of ordinary party politics into theater. Elections are spectacles, rites of passage, carnival—a sort of rhetorical football championship where pent-up aggressions and suppressed passions are released, an outlet for all aggressions, failures, and disappointments in the everyday life of politics. (Enzensberger 1982, 10)

Behind generational conflicts in Sweden as well as in many other countries lies the difference in temperament between youth and older people. Adult Swedes generally dislike young people's "unruliness and loudness" and dislike immigrants for the same reason. These attitudes also constitute the official measure of normal Swedish behavior. As aggression in children and youth is disapproved of in the schools, so aggression in clients of the social services is disapproved of in any context. Swedish interpretation of aggressiveness confirms such clients as "social cases." In custody disputes, when one party keeps calm and the other in frustration erupts in anger, the latter's strong feelings do not work in his or her favor. Outbursts of rage are not thought to attest to "stability and maturity." Equally, prisoners and mental patients demonstrating calm and collected behavior are rewarded by having an easier time getting leave.

Indeed, as in many other countries, in Sweden, the person who behaves calmly has the advantage over the person who reacts and acts strongly in various situations. However, discrimination against the latter seems especially marked in Sweden. Swedish child-rearing emphasizes the child's ability to be reasonable and unemotional, even in difficult situations, according to Herbert Hendin (1964, 67): "To be *tyst och lugn*, that is, quiet and calm, is something of a Swedish ideal, particularly for the boy and the adult man."

Differences Between Swedes Regarding Feelings

Here, as elsewhere in this study of Swedish mentality, I deal mainly with a level of abstraction in which differences between categories of the population are not taken into account. What I am pursuing is Swedishness as a general disposition, not variations on a theme. These systematic differences exist in the realm of feelings as they do in other areas of the personality; for example, Swedish women are less emotionally controlling than are men. Gender differences between young people are particularly great: to the CMPS question, "Do you easily lose your temper if you don't get what you want?" 15 percent of the boys between eighteen and twenty-five years old but 31 percent of the girls answered yes.

With regard to class differences, we know that disciplining one's feelings is stressed more in bourgeois circles than in the working class (see Frykman and Löfgren 1987). Among workers, certain groups—for instance, construction workers—are known to be especially outspoken, unafraid of confrontations, to be "bold" or "rude" (Forslin and Hansson 1978). According to James Peabody, certain stereotypes of the English working class—for example, the comic book figure Andy Capp—signify "an impulse-expressiveness that is very different from the traditional self-controlled English national character" (Peabody 1985, 92).

Possibly, workers experience anger more often because they find themselves more often in situations that elicit such feelings. To the CMPS question, "Does it sometimes happen that you get frantic with anger?" more people in social group III (i.e., the working class) answered yes—especially men (43 percent)—than in social group II (37 percent) or social group I (33 percent).

Similarly, there are generational differences. Young people are more demonstrative than adults in their displays of anger and joy, but the differences are smaller than one might think. To the CMPS question, "Do you find it difficult to get angry and irritated?" 45 percent of the respondents between twenty-six and sixty-five years answered yes, but among youth between eighteen and twenty-five only slightly less (40 percent) gave the same response. We know from other investigations that emotional receptiveness, or ability to react, decreases with years (Lynn 1971).

Social Causes Behind Swedes' Calmness

Dominant patterns of behavior are established when one is very young, and the conditions under which one lives at that time are partly determined by the social structure, for example, by the prevailing political and economic situation. From a similar point of departure, differences between anxiety levels in different countries can be explained; hence the total political-economic environment can cause stress, which in turn affects the general psychic status of the population. A similar phenomenon has been documented in research on working life: people who work under stress and have problems with their work tend to take their stress and irritation home—to their families and their private lives.

Stress in a society may be caused by political, social, or economic instability. Richard Lynn elaborates this theme in the book he has edited, *Dimensions of Personality* (1981, 278): "The presently most reasonable conclusion seems to be that differences between countries as regards neuroticism are mainly due to the varying degrees of stress the population is exposed to. The most common stress factors are clearly military failure and occupation, political instability and possibly economic problems caused by rapid economic development and industrialism." Lynn also points out that certain climates may be more stressful than others (see Eysenck and Eysenck 1983, 59).

The theory of political instability and the like is bolstered by data concerning neuroticism in advanced Western countries in comparison with Arab countries, which Lynn discusses on the basis of Eysenck's survey (1981, cited in Eysenck and Eysenck 1983, 59). Even clearer is Hofstede's data on neuroticism, also included in Lynn 1981, in which fifteen Western industrial countries are compared with seven Latin American republics—"notoriously turbulent societies characterized by high degrees of political conflict, revolutions and counterrevolutions, high inflation, guerrilla activity, etc." (Eysenck and Eysenck 1983, 60).

This index of neuroticism confirms the above-mentioned difference in aggression between Finns and Swedes. In Hofstede's data covering forty countries, Finland appears very different from Sweden (and the other Nordic countries) by having a higher degree of neuroticism. The Finnish sociologist Erik Allardt has made comparisons between Finland, Sweden, Norway, and Denmark that show considerably higher levels of stress symptoms in Finland. By way of explanation he mentions the unusually rapid changes in Finnish society that have occurred over the last two decades. Between 1960 and 1975 Finland underwent one of the swiftest structural transformations in the whole of Europe. As recently as 1960, 32 percent of all Finns supported themselves through agriculture and related industries. By 1975, the percentage had decreased to 12 percent, and in 1980 it had dropped to under 10 percent (Allardt 1986).

This data has been confirmed by interviews in the European Values System Study, where more Finns than Swedes, Danes, or Norwegians admitted to being "often aggressive"—even if the differences were slight. A larger proportion of "often aggressive" persons reside in continental Europe, especially in Italy and West Germany.

Some of the data in the European Values System Study might be thought to dispute what has so far been noted regarding emotional control among Swedes. These data show that Swedes do not consider "self-control" so important to teach children (16 percent of the Swedes, 28 percent of the southern Europeans, 31 percent of northern Europeans). However, the same stress theory tells us that such child-rearing principles are less important to Swedes, since stress factors are weaker in Swedish society. The more difficult the living conditions, the stronger the neuroticism; the more "nervy" the personalities, the greater the risk of powerful outbursts of feelings and the greater the grounds for teaching self-control. Significantly enough, twice as many Finns as Swedes voice the need to inculcate self-control (31 percent and 16 percent respectively).

Moreover, in Scandinavia many consider it unmodern and an obstacle to natural personality development to inculcate self-control, whereas elsewhere in Europe people maintain a more traditional view of child-rearing. Even so, Swedes are particularly controlled in comparison with what is generally the case on the Continent.

Let me illustrate by relating some of what an elderly lady from southern Germany told me of her experiences during her first trip to Scandinavia. During the journey through Sweden, the train unexpectedly stopped at a small station, where a message was related through loudspeakers. As if the passengers had being doing so all their lives, they all got up, put on their coats and hats, took their bags, and left the train. They did this calmly, methodically, and in well-nigh total silence. "*Ganz ruhig,*" remarked the German lady with feeling. Someone who knew German told her that there was a fault on the line and that buses had been arranged for part of the rest of the journey. According to my informant, in Germany such an occurrence would have given rise to very noisy discussions and loud expressions of dissatisfaction.

Emotional Expressions: The Language of Culture

Considering the Swedish norm proscribing strong expressions of feelings, it would be interesting to know *how* Swedes communicate their emotions. That many people restrain their feelings does not mean that they lack them or that they are never exposed.

Since strong, open, emotional expressions are often avoided, many Swedes convey the same thing more weakly or more "trivially." Instead of saying "I love you," which to Swedish ears sounds artificially romantic—as in a cheap romantic novel—one says "I like you." Similarly, translations of foreign films are often "Swedified." (Tord Larsen [1984] has described this sort of "trivialization" in the Norwegian language.)

The German-born writer Peter Weiss has addressed the Swedish fear of strong feelings. From the perspective of an outsider in Sweden, he described his relationship with the Swedish actress "Cora," who was able to act out strong feelings on stage, but in private was dependent, uncertain, distrustful, frightened of the passion he showed her (Weiss 1964).

Rituals offer another way to express feelings. In Sweden embarrassing "naked" feelings are covered up by ritual—for example, the convention of celebrating "name days" or birthdays. For the sake of comparison, it should be noted that turning fifty in the United States attracts nothing like the attention that it does in Sweden. Since all people are not equally observant or concerned to keep track of special days, individual congratulations function very much as certificates of friendship.

Another ritual aid is clothing, especially in recent times when etiquette does not rule as strictly as it once did, and especially in contexts where a certain dress is not formally prescribed. In Sweden, to dress better than usual for a private dinner party (in contrast with practice in the United States, where people often dress less formally than they do at work) is a sign of respect for the hosts, a method of tacitly showing regard. This does not mean that such communicative means are lacking in those parts of the world where verbal expressions of feelings are common. What it does mean is that "indirect" means of communicating emotions are particularly adequate in cultures such as the Swedish.

I suggest that ritualistic modes of communication have an especially prominent place in Sweden, as, for example, the dinner speech. Again, the United States is useful for purposes of contrast. In Sweden, someone taps a wine glass, rises, and speaks. Normally the speech ends with a toast to the object of the speech, the host or hostess or whomever—sometimes there are "three cheers" too. The speech may be serious, but wit is appreciated. Unwritten rules also dictate when speeches from different speakers are in order. The more detailed the rules, the greater the "security" they offer. In the United States, dinner-party speeches are much rarer.

The very form the speaker chooses in dinner-party addresses carries a message. Warm feelings for the object of the speech are conveyed via the great pains taken by the speaker in his preparation. A long and elaborate speech, perhaps even in verse, attests to the amount of time and commitment the speaker has devoted to his friend (see Nott 1961, 151). Thus, written speeches that are read aloud should not necessarily be taken to indicate communication anxiety. Reading a speech can also be interpreted as clear proof of friendship, whereas spontaneous speeches reveal less effort—comparable to a much too simple gift.

Foreigners in Sweden often note the care with which, for example, tables are set—everything contributing to a "perfect" arrangement. This is hardly typical of the working class, but it is not restricted to the upper social strata. The practical function of the arrangements is clear with regard to choice of guests and their placement at the table—taking care that they fit in with one another. The efforts expended on preparations such as cleaning and, of course, cooking communicate a great deal. Escorting the hostess to table is considered a great honor.

For their part, the guests express regard by arriving on time: not too late, not too early. They have flowers or something else with them to present to the hostess (even the selection of flowers or of another gift is significant), and finally, at a later date, they *tackar för senast*—thank the hosts for their hospitality (literally, "thanks for the last time," which could very well be a glass of wine three years ago)—a unique Swedish custom.

In addition to the ritual framework around the giving of gifts, other circumstances can function as *pretexts*, to ensure that the receiver is not embarrassed by direct indications of friendship. For instance, you can take fruit from your own garden to friends or to work and say that you "want help getting rid" of it. You can offer your services or lend tools; "Just say if you need a hand."

Other gestures include sending postcards from trips, or Christmas cards (in no way exclusively Swedish but very much in line with the tendency to use highly formalized means of expressing friendship). Nothing explicit need be said in these missives about feelings or friendship; loyalty is conveyed through regular written communication. A completely different "tacit" expression of friendship is the firm handshake. Looking someone straight in the eye while shaking his hand is a way to reinforce the communicative function, especially since it is not common to look people straight in the eye other than a second or two when greeting someone or saying goodbye. Akin to this is the more serious meeting of glances during the traditional Swedish toast.

Bowing is a universal symbol for humility (regardless of the actual attitude of the person bowing), and to show humility is a way of showing respect. Related to this is the bourgeois custom in Sweden of dinner guests' taking the hosts' hands immediately after the meal and thanking them for the food. The situation is dramatized further when, after rising from the table, the guests stand in pairs in a queue to thank their hostess for the meal. Another way to pay homage is not to drink before the host has raised a welcome toast (see Lorénzen [1964] 1978).

These elaborate dinner rituals only apply to a limited degree to the working class. Exceptions may also be made for young people to the degree that they break with the traditions of their parents. However, compared with corresponding population categories in other countries, the pattern described above is typically Swedish.

The different ways men and women express regard are the focus of a study of twenty-eight Swedish couples—a small sample, but the message it conveys is supported by other studies. One question put to the couples was, in what way did they express affection for their partners?—how much through words, and how much through actions? The results were as follows: "About the same numbers of women showed affection through their actions as through words *and* actions. The majority of the men, however, expressed their affection only through actions" (Nilsson-Schönnesson 1985, 43).

The same study revealed a similar tendency among men and women to use different means of communication in conflicts. "In quarrels having to do with feeling badly treated or hurt, most of the men demonstrated a withdrawal tactic. The women, on the other hand, openly demonstrated their emotions, for instance, by being sad, sour, angry. Even when the dispute had to do with division of work, the men tended to withdraw, while the women 'complained, shouted and screamed' " (Nilsson-Schönnesson 1985, 51).

Feelings between friends, expressed even indirectly, have different degrees of intensity. Such differences may be wider and clearer in countries other than Sweden. Despite the implications of the above, indirect means of expression are not generally more common in Sweden than elsewhere. It is the particular importance of the indirect means—as symbolic actions and gestures rife with implicit meaning—in contrast with the open and immediate, the explicitly verbal and tactile (except for shaking hands), that is specifically Swedish.

It seems that in other countries friendship expresses itself as "a helping hand"—that is, giving help to friends who are ill or in need—more frequently than it does in Sweden. This can be partly explained by the extensive public care in Sweden, and by Swedes' having the economic means to pay for help.

Especially strong bonds of friendship are said to exist in the former Soviet Union, and these bonds may in part be a consequence of the lack of care and social services (Smith 1976). In Sweden, people are not prepared to do as much for their friends, possibly because of the need for independence and self-sufficiency and the sharp boundary between the private and the public that characterizes Swedish social patterns.

A Swede whose sister married an Italian and moved to Italy told me what happened when one of her female in-laws was seriously hurt in a car accident. The situation was critical, so the Swede went to the in-law's Italian sister. When she arrived at the hospital waiting room she found a large number of people, friends as well as relatives. No one was allowed to visit the badly injured woman, but they stayed in the hospital anyway, assaulting the doctors with questions every time the doctors made an appearance. Visitors came and went, day and night, to an extent my informant had never experienced in Sweden.

Rage and sorrow in Swedish culture are also expressed more indirectly than in many other countries. Antipathy is most often "expressed" through avoidance of contact (the previously mentioned expression "to kill by silence" comes to mind here). One pretends not to see the person on the street; sometimes, if a meeting is unavoidable, one apologizes for not getting in contact, but then drops the contact anyway. Of course, this inclination to avoid confrontation does not necessarily pertain to professional publicists, who maintain the tradition, in Sweden as they do elsewhere, of defaming each other in papers and journals. However, here too the public debate in Sweden is comparatively restrained.

The same is true of pain and sorrow. At funerals Swedes predictably try to keep back their tears, and under no conditions allow themselves to fall into loud expressions of grief. Should their emotions overpower their control, they turn their faces away to hide their tears. Drying one's tears and sniffling are accepted, especially for women, but cries of despair are embarrassing and are remembered long afterward.

Childbirth pain has already been discussed. Women are allowed to cry in pain, even though self-control here too is the ideal. A study of visits to the dentist shows that more "immigrants" than Swedes demonstrate "exaggerated expressions of pain" (Widström 1983, 245).

Swedes avoid contacting people suffering grief, partly because Swedes worry about their ability to control their feelings, not because they necessarily believe, as is frequently mentioned, that leaving sorrowing people alone is "considerate." Conceivably, some people actually think the best course of action would be to contact the friend or workmate, for example, whose wife recently died of cancer, and say something appropriate—"but what do you say in such a situation?" The very idea of placing oneself in an emotionally upsetting situation can be a further restraint.

In a workplace where people from several countries are employed (Swedish Radio International), I heard the following. One of the employees, a non-Swedish woman, was grieving for the death of someone close to her. When this became known, she was given immediate sympathy and condolences from many of her non-Swedish colleagues, who hugged her and wept with her. None of her Swedish workmates approached her. They kept themselves "considerately" at a distance. That there most likely are situations and contexts in Sweden where this sort of reaction is less common, where even the opposite would occur, does not prevent its demonstrating a significant Swedish pattern. In this regard Philip Zimbardo (1977, 51) mentions the behaviorist view, "that shyness is an automatic reaction in certain types of social events," that shyness comes from (a) never having learned the "correct" social skills, which would help in such situations, and (b) assuming that one will behave inappropriately and thus landing in a state of anxiety about one's behavior.

Consequently, passivity in the face of friends' grief should not be interpreted to mean that Swedes disregard feelings or lack sympathy. Rather, they lack the skills to deal with strong feelings and are afraid of doing the wrong thing, of behaving clumsily. Furthermore, in Sweden, individual grief is considered part of the absolutely most private sphere, where outsiders are expected to keep themselves at a distance and thereby to show respect.

Rationality

Gustav Sundbärg, who in the beginning of this century was commissioned by the Swedish government to study Swedish emigration to America, was rather critical of Swedes' practical talents: "And therefore we have so many 'practical' men—even at the top of society, on boards, in management—whose 'practicality' actually consists of an ability to perceive insignificant things clearly and obscure large questions" (1911, 36).

However, Sundbärg did praise Swedes' "organizational abilities." Value judgments aside, both of his observations basically refer to the same personality syndrome characterized by a strong emphasis on rationality, common sense, matter-of-factness, orderliness.

"In Sweden, rationalism has long dominated the climate of opinion," writes the sociologist Hans L. Zetterberg in *The Rational Humanitarians* (1984, 84):

> A pious Swede is often ashamed of admitting his allegiance to God, while a rationalist Swede is not at all shy about admitting his to Reason. Irrational expressions, ranging from official Church doctrine about hell to the private mysticism of Dag Hammarskjöld's diaries, are often looked upon with scepticism and even suspicion. Rationalism permeates the content of radio and television programs and the editorial and opinion pages of the large newspapers. Political discourse often resembles seminars on economics, political science, and sociology. Political debate in Sweden deals primarily with technical questions.

In his book on Sweden (1968) David Jenkins has devoted one whole chapter to "The Practical Swede." As proof of Swedes' practical inclinations, he reminds the reader that Swedish population statistics go all the way back to 1749. Jenkins confirms Swedes' early reputation for practicality by quoting statements from Joseph Marshall and J. T. James, English travelers in Sweden in 1769 and 1819 respectively.

Cultures may be described according to where they lay heaviest emphasis on a scale between strict rationality and strong displays of emotion, even though reality rarely fits such simple schemes. French culture is well known for having both a "Latin temperament" and a rational intellectualism (de Gramont 1969). Intellectualism is said to be characteristic of French pictorial art—for instance, cubism and fauvism—as well as of French horticulture and French literature. The antithesis of the geometrical order of the French garden is the English garden, modeled after nature itself, and the antithesis of French intellectual painting is German expressionism.

Where does Sweden stand between these poles? Sundbärg notes the dominance of nature in Swedish art and poetry in lieu of any truly developed depictions of people. The descriptions of nature, like the feelings for nature, are seldom dramatic, tending instead to be lyrical, reflective, calm. More typical is Carl von Linné's enthusiasm for natural science classifications. The influential historian of Swedish literature Henrik Schück has discussed the Swedish romantic writer Georg Stiernhielm's "almost alarmingly sober view of love," which, according to Schück, indicates Stiernhielm's "thoroughly Swedish psyche" (cited in Gustafsson 1984, 26).

In a review of the book *Schweden*, written by the Swedish art historian Rudolf Zeitler (who grew up in Germany), Ulf Hård af Segerstad quotes Zeitler's pronouncement on Swedish medieval churches and estates from the seventeenth and eighteenth centuries: "They are, so to speak, examples of practical art and seldom creations of any note." To this Hård adds, "[Zeitler] has thus described a characteristic of our practical/pragmatic architecture that holds true even today" (*Svenska Dagbladet*, 17 September 1985).

The translator and critic C. G. Bjurström (1984, 166), describing "the Swedish" from a French perspective, remarks that French readers of Swedish poetry are often amazed to find "such concrete language, such exact observations." The same applies to depictions of nature.

The development of the public sector in Sweden has increased the opportunities for applying rationality. Social life is more and more influenced by experts, a development that has parallels in many other countries. Even so, there is a Swedish version of this rationality, which, according to Hans Zetterberg, lacks the French version's "pure stringency" or the British "pragmatic" orientation or the German emphasis on "perfect solutions." Swedish rationality "is marked more by moderation than by logic driven to its final conclusion. Its key word is (the untranslatable) *lagom* which means both 'reasonable' and 'middle-road.' This stance is akin to the British commonsense rationalism that views abstractions as something foreign" (Zetterberg 1984, 85). The departures from Swedish commonsense rationality noted by Zetterberg—for example, the 1970s anti-intellectualism, New Age astrology, and oriental mysticism—do not invalidate the description of Sweden as a nation whose culture is permeated by rationalism.

"In Sweden practicality is king, and when there is a conflict between practicality and other values, the other values give way." This assertion comes from the American journalist David Jenkins, who lived three years in Sweden. He goes on to say that "[o]ne of the great advantages of this cool, unemotional approach to problems is that it saves a lot of arguments. When intelligent people get together to make decisions with their minds firmly on the objective, there is no particular reason to disagree" (Jenkins 1968, 23–24). In fact, this description is exaggerated, but it is useful for purposes of contrast with Jenkins's experiences in the United States and elsewhere.

Public expressions of a practical disposition have been noted by many foreign observers. "[Everything follows] the planners' logic, whether thirteenth or twentieth century," reports the British travel writer Jan Morris (1984, 129) from a visit to Stockholm. According to David Popenoe, "In no other Western society have government planners been granted the amount of authority they have in Sweden" (1985, 99). The "philosophy of planning" entails that one believe in the possibilities of arranging social conditions for the best of all citizens by means of rational thinking. The idea that central rule and organization can guarantee satisfactory living conditions exists of course in many other European countries besides Sweden. But planning philosophy remains especially vital in Sweden, perhaps even more so than in socialist states, in the sense of extending to more social sectors and areas of life. Indeed, Sweden is often classified by Americans as socialistic just because of its detailed regulations. Many have considered this to be a totalitarian tendency (Huntford 1971). Like many other non-Swedes, the Finnish-Swedish writer Marianne Alopaeus (1983, 148) has wondered, "Why don't people say no? Why do they submit? In the end it is *their* country, not the state's or the tax authorities'."

Of importance here historically is the fact that the Swedish Social Democratic party governed for such a long time. Social democratic ideology set its stamp on society in Sweden for a longer period than in any other country. The conviction that "collective" decision making—that is, decision making by the central authorities—guarantees the greatest justice has had an enormous impact. But this view of the state and public authorities seems to have been bolstered by the Swedish belief in factualness and rationality, which allow little room for individual feelings. This "making politics scientific" is most notable in Sweden. "The main current in Swedish radicalism has contained a belief in progress, a passion for knowledge, and it has been modernistic, rationalistic, and reformist," according to the historian of ideas Kjell Jonsson (1987, 2), who also points out that this radicalism emerged simultaneously with the so-called breakthrough of the modern era in the 1880s.

The American political scientist Thomas Anton (1975), who in the beginning of the 1970s studied Swedish city planning, states that a Swedish "government" or "board" will disregard expressions of opinion not based on facts. Anton's basic attitude toward the Swedish planning model is positive and thereby resembles to a degree that of David Popenoe in the latter's study of the suburb of Vällingby (1977), and of Marquis W. Childs in his classic *Sweden, the Middle Way* (1936).

However, Swedish organizational ability was mentioned already by Sundbärg in 1911, and others have traced it further back in history. The formation of the centralist state by King Gustav Vasa in the sixteenth century is often held up as an early illustration. And it does not seem to me too speculative to claim that the weight and influence exerted by the public authorities has been part of Swedish cultural patterns for a long time. Given this background, it is hardly incomprehensible that Swedes "do not say no."

However, this does not mean that the opposite tendencies do not exist. A debate in the newspaper *Dagens Nyheter* in the fall of 1982, headlined "Is Sweden Totalitarian?" illustrates one inflamed political issue of the time. The freedom of the individual and "civil society" were pitted against the collective and the public authorities, not only in bourgeois political propaganda but also in the somewhat freer academic debate. This "debate on freedom" cannot be discussed in depth here. However, regarding questions of Swedish mentality, it is important to recall that the cultural patterns presented in this book as typically Swedish are criticized by Swedes themselves, not only by foreigners (belief in planning, "lack of feelings," avoidance of conflict, lack of imagination, etc.). Such criticism is itself proof that these cultural traits are vital, since they are experienced as all too dominant. They also show that "Swedishness" is not a simple, clear-cut phenomenon but a complex reality. There are counterforces in Swedish society, within the women's movement, for instance, and within alternative movements that oppose a great many significant aspects of Swedish social and cultural traditions. Also, since the present book was written and first published (1989), neoliberal political forces in Sweden have been further weakening the largely social democratic exercise of public authority.

Factualness

People who stress common sense instead of feelings appreciate matter-of-factness. They strive to keep to the facts: they are rather reluctant to speculate or fantasize. They decline to express themselves if they are the least uncertain of their facts. They like statistics and scientific investigations and are happy to use them for purposes of discussion. Such persons typically feel more comfortable with experimental psychology than with psychoanalysis. This inclination toward the quantitative, nonspeculative, concretely detailed, and artless dominates Swedish scholarship (cf. Austin 1968).

Susan Sontag (1969, 24–26) found Swedes to be "notably unpsychological." She claimed that the schools of psychiatry derived from Freud never took root in Sweden and that Swedes generally were psychologically insensitive. Her statements about psychoanalysis are not so valid today, two decades later, but the pattern she describes still applies.

> Swedes show a strong aversion to reflecting about motives and character. The remarks people pass about each other at work and after social encounters are terse and flat. The usual thing one hears a Swede say about someone is that he or she is "nice": Less often, "not nice": a great effort is made to find people nice. Any extended scrutiny of someone's character, that staple of everyday middle-class conversation in the United States, gets little response here—as if Swedes can't fathom the reason behind the expenditure of *that* kind of intellectual effort. Generally, I've noticed, Swedes are not given to puzzling over things. Whenever possible, situations and words are taken at face value.

Matter-of-factness is apparent in conversations between Swedes, in what they talk about, which is dominated by exchange of facts that are elaborated and evaluated. In the following, Sontag describes a typical Swedish conversation. Her tone is light, but what she brings up rings a bell.

> Favored topics are: the weather (Swedes never stop suffering from the cold, the lack of sun); money (they are shameless about telling or asking how much something costs); liquor . . . ; and plans of action (from saying "I'm going to pee" when leaving the room for a minute to announcing a vacation). Once underway, dialogue tends to have a certain pedantry; people balk if you skip steps in explaining something or jump around from one topic to another. And conversations are always in danger of running out of gas, both from the imperative of secretiveness and from the positive lure of silence.

Rational Orientation

All societies contain an order based on reason, *ratio*, although the Western world is sometimes considered to be steered too much

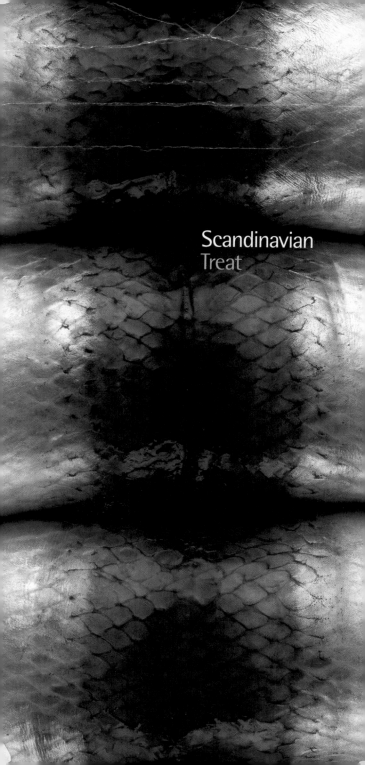

Scandinavian
Treat

menu

We are delighted to welcome you on board this flight. We will
shortly be offering you a selection of beverages. This will be
followed by the main meal.
The first course is smoked turkey, lettuce and Havarti cheese.
For the main dish you can choose between either ground beef
patties with parsley butter and Lyonnaise potatoes or chicken
teriyaki with stir-fried noodles.
For dessert strawberry cheesecake.
Coffee and tea with cognac or liqueur.
After the meal you can relax and enjoy today's movie.
Between the meals we are happy to serve you movie snacks.
Please do not hesitate to ask the flight attendant if you need
anything during the flight.
Breakfast will be served close to our arrival and consists of
cold cuts, yoghurt, hot rolls and marmalade, coffee or tea and
orange juice. Enjoy your flight.

Velkommen om bord. Om kort tid kommer vi rundt med et
udvalg af drikkevarer, inden vi serverer Deres hovedmåltid.
Forretten består af røget kalkun, hovedsalat og havartiost.
Som hovedret kan De vælge enten små hakkebøffer med
persillesmør og lyonnaise-kartofler eller teriyakikylling med
lynstegte nudler.
Til dessert serverer vi jordbærostekage. Kaffe eller te med avec.
Efter måltidet kan De slappe af til dagens film.
Mellem måltiderne kan vi byde på filmsnacks.
Hvis der er noget, De ønsker under rejsen, bedes De henvende
Dem til flypersonalet.
Morgenmad vil blive serveret, kort tid inden vi lander, og den
består af pålæg, yoghurt, varmt brød og marmelade, kaffe eller
te og appelsinjuice. God rejse.

Välkommen ombord. Vi kommer snart att erbjuda Er något att
dricka för att sedan fortsätta med den stora måltiden.
Förrätten består av rökt kalkon, sallad och havartiost.
Till huvudrätt kan Ni välja antingen pannbiff med persiljesmör
och lyonnaisepotatis eller teriyakikyckling med wokade nudlar.
Till dessert serverar vi jorgubbs-cheescake.
Kaffe eller te med avec.
Efter måltiden kan Ni koppla av och titta på dagens
filmföreställning.
Mellan måltiderna serverar vi gärna filmsnacks.
Ta gärna kontakt med kabinpersonalen om Ni önskar någonting
under resan.
Frukost kommer att serveras när vi börjar närma oss vår
destination. Den består av kallskuret, yoghurt, varmt bröd och
marmelad samt kaffe eller te och apelsinjuice. Trevlig resa.

Please accept our apology if your choice is not available

E-SEA-H1-04/00-ds

by common sense, rationality, science, and too little by feelings and "human considerations." Humanitarianism can "lose its heart" (Zetterberg 1984). Judged by other standards, Western civilization may be highly unreasonable and short-sighted, for example, when it consciously goes about destroying the natural resources on which human beings are dependent. Clearly the words "reason" and "sensible" can acquire a range of different meanings.

By the Swedish stress on rationality I am essentially referring to a general emphasis on practical objectives. James Peabody (1985) has suggested the term "practicality/empiricism" for the corresponding tendency in English culture, which is expressed in the practical, problem-solving orientation of scholarship. Perhaps as a state of mind this is best described as the antithesis of irrationality, joy, instinct, grief, rage, dreaminess, imagination, intuition. Swedish rationality contains a good portion of that common sense which Zetterberg found to resemble the British. Compared with floods of feelings, this common sense seems "dry," narrow. It is possible that it contains the seeds of that *tråkighet*, that particular "dullness," many foreigners discover in Sweden, even if they cannot always put their finger on what it is.

Common sense is easily combined with the Lutheran puritanism that permeates certain aspects of Swedish culture. To counter misuse of alcohol, for example, the reintroduction of alcohol rationing, which Sweden had between 1914 and 1955, has been suggested. In the public debates on alcohol, it would be as unthinkable to mention that alcohol also gives pleasure as it would be in Norway to claim that the population drinks itself into the intimacy that Norwegian mentality does not naturally contain (see Larsen 1984).

"Pleasure is a very serious matter in Sweden," notes the Danish journalist Mogens Berendt (1983, 123), and recalls that before noon restaurants are not allowed to serve drinks stronger than light beer, that spirits cannot be served in hotel rooms, that a bar may only be a small space connected to a restaurant, that drinks cannot be served in sidewalk cafés, that company expense accounts cannot include alcohol.

Swedes are very familiar with these and other regulations; that they are ridiculed by many foreigners is also well known. I do not mean to join in that critical chorus grumbling about "Big Brother Society," even if occasionally it may seem as if I am. Many Swedes indulge in such complaints, as do many foreigners; but aside from the critics, many foreign commentators admire the Swedish social order.

The study of Swedish mentality offers many interesting examples of detailed regulations with which Swedes, on the basis of certain values, try to give a specific shape to life in Sweden. What is remarkable is the weight Swedish culture attaches to "orderliness." It should not be surprising that the vast majority of Swedes submit to this system of rules, since they "breathe the same air" as those drafting the regulations. The authors of the French book *Suède, la reforme permanente* (1977) subscribe to the notion of Sweden as a country in which social development is a process of constant reform guided by rationality and justice. Arne Ruth, cultural editor of the newspaper *Dagens Nyheter*, has recalled the importance ascribed by other countries to the so-called "Swedish model" as a "persuasive radical argument." Sweden's pragmatic implementation of new solutions within extremely diverse areas is well known and discussed. Two of the more remarkable Swedish reforms are mandatory dimmed headlights—to be on whenever driving a vehicle, day as well as night—and paternal leave. Changing to right-hand traffic in 1967 was little short of an organizational triumph.

One of the points of departure for Swedish reforms lies in a particular cultural orientation: the humanitarianism that developed early in the Nordic countries (Zetterberg 1984). Even if this humanitarianism was rooted in Christianity, according to Zetterberg (1984, 89), "[t]he most elaborate manifestation of the welfare state—the one we find in Sweden—is a product of Leftists in a rather secular state." It is understandable that reform is the Social Democrats' method for realizing their socialistic ideology, but reform policies would fall on deaf ears if their goals and intentions were not consonant with the Swedish pattern of culture.

Another precondition of reform may have been the prevalent view of change as an indication of progress, a view that prepared people for the risks involved with what is new. This basically positive attitude toward change is expressed in the concept of "social development" to denote all changes in society. In Geert Hofstede's "Uncertainty Avoidance Index" (1984), which measures the tendency to avoid uncertainty, Sweden landed at the bottom of forty countries—assuming age was held constant (Japan was highest).

This indicates that Swedes are very willing to accept change—as long as it does not threaten security. Typical of societies at the bottom of this scale is that, as in Sweden, they give a great deal of responsibility to young people.

As in other Nordic countries, among the most fundamental principles in Swedish reform politics are *equality* and *justice*. Adherence to these principles has brought about, among other things, the world's most equalizing tax laws (which as of 1991 have become less so because of an adjustment in the tax scales). These principles may be detected in the generously broad qualifications for higher education, local-authority adult education, and other educational reforms; in reforms favoring the physically and mentally handicapped; in the institution of ombudsman; in the particularly restrictive legislation against bribery and corruption; and in the world's most humane criminal policies. The Danish professor of economics Bert Rold Andersen (1984) describes certain political peculiarities in the Nordic countries as evincing a "passion for equality" long before the advent of the welfare state.

Another principle pertains to *life and limb*, which has led to especially thorough traffic legislation and enters into specific building requirements and measures to ensure child safety.

A third important principle in Swedish reform policies concerns the *enlightenment of the people*—the will to educate and inform the citizens of the country. This has resulted in obligatory sex education in the schools, promotion of consumer interests through the establishment of the National Board for Consumer Policies (with a consumer ombudsman), and state support for adult educational associations as well as other cultural subsidies. This principle can be discerned in the Swedish radio and television's pedagogical ambitions, which range from the formation of a special company—Educational Radio—to television programs devoted to the spread of public information.

A fourth principle concerns practical purposefulness, which has led to, for example, binding regulations stipulating the "function-determined planning and design" of dwellings built with state loans. The architect Peter Adler claims that trust in the public authorities is necessary if the complicated system of building norms is to function (see Adler 1977). And according to the historian of ideas Kjell Jonsson (1987, 5–6), "Swedes have experienced the good state, which molds people for their own good. The Swedish *state* has given us a better society and a better life. The authorities have rarely encroached upon civil rights, and thus we approach them with trust and confidence."

Hans Magnus Enzensberger (1982, 12–13) has also pointed to the emphasis on common sense and solidarity in Swedish politics:

> Everything I heard during the election campaign indicated that I had landed in the realm of sense, insight, solidarity, consideration. I had witnessed a noble contest during the course of which all participants were only concerned with one question: how can we assist the pensioners, the unemployed, the disabled, and the outcasts of society? No one appealed to the low, selfish instincts that other societies were obsessed with. When I thought of my own country, the Republic of West Germany, a nasty feeling welled up in me—envy. My own countrymen seemed an egotistic and asocial horde, who devoted themselves to extravagance, boasting, and all sorts of aggression.

Orderliness

People who place greater weight on rational thinking than on emotions are presumably also orderly, and thus responses to questions measuring this personality trait should be of interest in the present context. One CMPS question was, "Do you get annoyed with people who are not well behaved and punctual?"

Analysis of the answers given by a sample of Swedes (26–35 years old) and one of Finns (29–71 years old) confirms the hypothesis that emotional discipline and orderliness are interconnected. Eighty percent of the Swedes and 74 percent of the Finns answered yes to the CMPS question. This is backed by data indicating that a larger proportion of Finns than Swedes are emotional, sentimental, aggressive. However, the comparison is complicated methodologically in two ways, which is evident in the comparison of Swedish students in Umeå with Italian students in Verona. According to Richard Lynn (1971), Swedes and Italians demonstrate predictable differences with regard to "anxiety," but the responses given to the question mentioned above show no significant difference: 57 percent of the Swedes and 59 percent of the Italians admitted to being irritated.

Apparently, the same question is often understood differently depending on society or culture, which means that the answers are not always comparable. The extent to which a comparison of responses is misleading depends largely on how the question is formulated. However, regarding punctuality and good behavior, it is clear that the meaning of these qualities varies culturally. For example, it is entirely possible that an Italian in Italy who regularly arrives twenty minutes late can feel irritated with people who are not "punctual," that is, who arrive much later than he does. However, a person in Sweden who tends to arrive twenty minutes late is quickly labeled someone with difficulties being on time—and is made aware of this.

Another methodological complication has to do with our lack of knowledge of the sample Lynn (1971) used when he classified Italy as a "high-anxiety country." On the other hand, we know that the majority of the students at the University of Verona come from northern Italy and that the more emotional and less disciplined behavioral patterns are associated with southern Italy. Thus we do not know whether the students in Verona differ significantly from students in Umeå with regard to punctuality—or, in other words, to what degree punctuality is part of a more general cultural difference between North and South.

A third source of error is the widespread negative (almost "racist") attitude toward southern Italians that exists in northern Italy. Northern Italians hold southern Italians in contempt for what they consider lack of work discipline and a general lack of personality traits associated with modernity. Hence northern Italian students should hypothetically have been particularly sensitive to the question of behavior and punctuality; they should have been anxious not to be associated with heavily derided characteristics. On the contrary, they probably wished to "distinguish" themselves, to underline the difference between their own orderliness and punctuality and the southern Italian lack thereof—regardless of their own actual performance.

Because of these methodological conundrums, perhaps the responses to this CMPS question cannot be used. Irrespective of the answers, it is possible that orderliness and punctuality are interpreted much more strictly among Swedes than among Italians. Qualitative data point in this direction. An acquaintance of mine from Milan whom I consider punctual and orderly once jokingly suggested that he benefited from Italians' reputation in northern Europe. At a pinch he could allow himself to arrive late in Sweden, since he would only be living up to the general stereotype of Italians. However, there is little doubt that most Swedes usually prefer to plan their time rather than allow themselves to be governed by impulse and spontaneity. The different descriptions the film directors Ingmar Bergman and Frederico Fellini have given of their respective compatriots are pertinent here.

A Swede I interviewed, who lives with her family in Florence, has vividly related how she—in contrast with her Italian colleagues in a medical laboratory—was always careful to put everything back in its place at the end of the day. She also was sure to wear a clean smock, while the others went around in their "blood-stained smocks." The habits and routines she had adopted in a university lab in the Swedish university town of Lund remained her norm and basis for comparison.

Further *qualitative* material supporting my contention is the Swedish habit of planning meetings—both private and nonprivate—well in advance. One decides the time for the meeting, when it should start and when it should end. In this way, one can schedule one meeting between 1:00 and 3:00 P.M. and another between 3:30 and 5:00 P.M. This is considered efficient and an expression of "organizational ability." However, people from other cultures may find deciding in advance when a meeting will end—regardless of what is discussed or what crops up in the meeting—inconsiderate and ineffective. The meeting may need to continue—how can one exclude that possibility from the start? It is also impolite to those who are prevented from expressing their opinions and inconsiderate toward the person who is forced to "round off" what he or she is saying when the time is up.

A significant portion of Swedish leisure is organized—in clubs and associations, study circles, and other educational activities. In 1981, about one-third of all Swedes took part in study circles, and a little more than that (37 percent) were active in clubs and associations. All this is planned, scheduled, and placed into routines, not a matter of spontaneous or improvised activity. The same applies to Swedish formal meetings, with their "agendas" and lists of speakers. Time spent on other popular leisure occupations—for instance, singing in choirs—is also highly scheduled. All these activities tend to follow a given pattern: requesting permission to speak, writing minutes, carrying out prescribed tasks, following instructions, singing from written music, and so forth. The popularity of these leisure activities cannot be "explained" by particular personality traits, but running throughout Swedish culture there seems to be a certain consistency that can be observed in a variety of other contexts.

As has been mentioned, Swedes want to plan even private activities. A young American woman who had been living in Stockholm for five years related in an interview with me that she and her Irish boyfriend once visited Swedish relatives in southern Sweden.

> We wanted to hitchhike, and we called [the relatives] and said which week we'd arrive, but couldn't say exactly which day. When we finally came, they were very upset that we arrived without their being told beforehand exactly when. I first thought they were upset because we wanted to stay in the same room even though we weren't married—people would be upset about that in the States. But no, we realized they didn't mind that at all, but what was still upsetting them was that we hadn't planned our visit. That was a "moral lesson."

The Theory of the Politically Indoctrinated Swedes

It seems impossible to avoid the often-brandished thesis of Swedes' political indoctrination (Jenkins 1968; Huntford 1971). According to Enzensberger, the Swedish Social Democrats, in contrast with many other governing parties with similar ambitions, have actually succeeded in "taming people." Enzensberger goes on to say that "I inquired about the price of this peace, the political costs of this re-education, and everywhere I began to get wind of a widespread repression and its revival—the musty odor of a mild, inexorable, ubiquitous pedagogy" (1982, 13).

Three interrelated conditions may explain Swedes' propensity to "endure." One is related to rational thinking. Many Swedes have a pronounced pragmatic attitude, which leads to their asking themselves: What do I get out of the welfare state's arrangements in terms of subsidies, benefits, and various kinds of public service? And though I may dislike high taxes, can it not be contended that these taxes give me equivalent benefits? Moreover, what would it serve if I were to protest? And how would I go about it—write letters to the editor, agitate among my workmates? No, politics are determined so much through democratic elections that I should simply let things be. And how would another government drastically reduce taxes—and thereby the "package of benefits"—without losing political power already by the next election? Swedish order has been gradually introduced through decades of social development, and major changes cannot be expected through a change of government—in any case not in anything but the very long term—after my time! (It should be mentioned that since this book was published in Swedish in 1989, considerable cuts have been made in welfare programs, for financial reasons.)

Another explanation is Swedes' low degree of "anxiety," or emotionality. Fewer Swedes get very emotionally upset by conditions they do not like than do the Germans and the French (Lynn 1971). Their antipathy can be quite strong without it giving rise to powerful aggressions or resistance; in other words, this "cool" reaction pattern need not be synonymous with a lack of firm criticism.

A third explanation is that all culture is indoctrinating. Even the most energetic opponents of Swedish alcohol regulations or tax policies invariably view these things from a generally Swedish point of view (which is of course not unequivocal, but all its variants originate in Swedish social realities).

The need to conform is also part of Swedish culture, and this need counteracts protests not supported by a large number of people. Peabody (1985, 87) has pointed out that "the Protestant ethic, while fostering individual achievement may tend to suppress 'individuality' in favor of social conformity." To socially insecure individuals—that is, many Swedes—the group offers security; being able to express one's opinions under the aegis of the collective feels safe.

Compared with Finns, Swedes are less independent with regard to "their opinions and views and in their general attitudes" (Daun, Mattlar, and Alanen 1989). Swedes and Finns differ strikingly in their response to the CMPS question, "Do you have a feeling that your views and ideas nearly always agree with those of other people?" Only 20 percent of the Finns but 45 percent of the Swedes answered in the affirmative. This response reveals the Swedes to be significantly more dependent than Finns on the group or norm for their opinions.

David Jenkins (1968) has commented that "[i]f there is widespread conformity in Sweden, it is because there is a will to conform, not because of pressure." But this should not be confused with my statements on all culture being indoctrinating and consequently leading to conformity. Cultures differ in degree of integration and degree of the universal need to be like most other people. This difference in degree appears clearly in the comparisons with American and Italian students. On the CMPS scale of *exhibition* (need to be noticed, need to deviate from the majority), Swedes are the least independent.

Seriousness and Its Kinship with Rational Thinking

Foreigners often describe Swedes as serious or earnest. This may be due in part to a kind of practical sense, a simple matter-of-factness that seems "dry," since there is no intention of adding to the pleasure of the moment.

A woman I interviewed told me of an experience at the day-care center her little boy attended. The parents had been invited to a party with the children, and it was decided that both parents and staff would paint their faces and dress up as clowns. The children played and had a good time, while the staff and parents sat and watched in their clown makeup.

However, Swedish culture contains particular contexts—for instance, crayfish parties, bachelor parties, hen parties and showers, certain sporting events—that in their rituals stimulate, even enjoin, adults to the sort of elation that is otherwise the province of children.

In his book on children's public day care (1983), Billy Ehn writes that staff seldom participate in the children's play and that they seem afraid of making fools of themselves. Seriousness seems to be a more psychologically motivated condition than gaiety, more in line with the somewhat introverted personality traits of many Swedes (Daun, Burroughs, and McCroskey 1988). Passive observation feels more "adult." It also seems reasonable to interpret the adults' passivity as shyness, an anxiety over one's own performance and a fear of making a fool of oneself.

Practical sense and adult seriousness provide a desired security. Uncertainty in informal contacts and interaction is recompensed by *duktighet*. Time-saving behavior governs business dealings to the detriment of a more sociable "small talk" and sometimes to the detriment of relations with foreign contacts. In sports contexts, greater weight is placed on physical performance than on social interaction and playfulness—in contrast with Denmark, for example.

The earnestness when toasting someone, which involves "a silent speech for the object of the toast" (Wingårdh 1958, 152), is a sort of replacement for the conversational talents many wish they had. "Many prefer to keep quiet if they find nothing worth saying, and suffer in silence while others compete for the floor" (Phillips-Martinsson 1981, 45).

Jens Allwood has commented on the mass media presentation of bad conditions or states of affairs, both domestic and foreign. Swedish media coverage, whether in the press, on radio, or on television, almost always lacks the cynical levity with which similar subjects are often treated in other countries. "Rather, the tone is naive and grave" (Allwood 1981, 43; cf. Nott 1960). That most Swedes would probably consider such cynical levity as off-putting underlines their heavy emphasis on seriousness. In Sweden, joking about tragedy is frowned upon, since one would then seem indifferent to others' unhappiness. "[The Swede] is very sensitive, sometimes too sensitive. He feels sad about others' problems and wants to help," according to an immigrant Iranian psychologist, Modji Mortazavi, writing in *Dagens Nyheter* (29 June 1985). One of the characteristics of Protestant ethics is the tendency to introduce moral values in all situations, which tendency is, according to Peabody, a sort of systematic "rationality."

What I have discussed in this chapter is a psychological tendency (the stress on rationality) in relation to a way of behaving (serious-

ness). It is not difficult to find empirical proof of these two phenomena; it is more difficult to get a grip on their causes and putative connections. Seriousness may stem from the strict Lutheran Church—a
commonly made connection. Seriousness can also be a trait of the
socially uncertain and introvert personality, often the Swedish personality, possibly more often in big-city contexts (but not in big cities
universally) than in smaller, well-integrated communities.

I can do no more than sketch the subjects of seriousness and rationality in the present book. However, it has crossed my mind that
we are approaching the core, or the point of gravitation, in the
modal Swedish personality. A special study of these matters would
probably help to illuminate Swedes' way of evaluating and judging
their surroundings, social conditions in other countries, and immigrants in Sweden.

To many Swedes common sense and rationality seem to be strongly
linked to technical and economic development. This means that
technically and economically advanced countries are thought to
contain a higher degree of rationality than less developed countries. From this point of view it should follow that the concept of
common sense would include a notion of intellectual prowess, "the
ability to work out things," pragmatism, effectiveness—in other
words, capacities that are considered necessary to realize this desired high technical and economic level. Southern countries are associated more with emotional values—folklore, souvenirs, good
food, songs and music, lovely weather—all the things that go to
make up Swedes' main impressions when they travel south.

The vitality that in the eyes of Swedes seems to emanate even
from southern Europeans who have heavy and repetitive work—
whether true or just a Swedish myth about southerners—contrasts
with the overall gravity, the earnestness prevailing at home in
Sweden. Another aspect of this contrast is the moral conflict between
play and seriousness. Seriousness carries a moral weight: it is "grave";
it symbolizes responsibility. Play, superficial gaiety, and sensuous
pleasure are naturally not rejected, but are nevertheless awarded a
clearly subordinate position. They are generally relegated to the
world of childhood, to poetry and art, possibly to holidays, leisure,
and family life late at night, "when everything else has been done."

Such an attitude can be self-critical, but it still prepares the
way for belittling "southerners," which in turn provides grounds for

discriminating against immigrants. But the phenomenon not only pertains to immigrants, who can be viewed more or less positively as a result of personal acquaintance, for example; it also concerns a general view of other countries and societies.

Such an extremely prejudicial attitude toward people was aired on a program in the radio series *Öppet Forum* (Open forum), on the local Stockholm station in 1982. The program was reported to the attorney general's office, where it was found guilty of (racial/ethnic) contempt. However, what was most interesting were the interviewer's opinions on technology and economy. A broadcast interview with an African woman on the program provided an opportunity for the reporter to air what he thought were the prerequisites for development:

> As you just heard, she couldn't answer this. What would Mozambique be like if there were only Swedes there? She knows in her heart of hearts that there'd be big fancy houses, each with its own swimming pool. We'd have it good down there, with large farms and plantations. What's it like now? Well? Sand and such like, the odd plant and seed here and there and some god-awful elephant clumping past. . . . Mud huts! And more mud huts and then those old metal tubs they got from the war. Gas barrels. Gas barrels and all the rest of the crap. For they're lazy; they don't want to work down there. They just dance all day and all night long and drink that slop they call drink down there. That's what they do. (Hedman 1985, 48)

According to established Swedish opinion, with rational planning one can make use of existing resources and create something good. Rational planning began as early as the 1860s within the housing sector in Sweden (Thörn 1986). However, as in other countries, housing conditions in Sweden are based on a variety of economic—but also historical—circumstances. This means that even "Swedes" born and brought up in Mozambique could very well have lived in mud huts. Swedish residential building is connected not only to the level of technology and economy; in no other country has rational housing planning been conducted so extensively and decisively as in Sweden. However, this comparison is actually impossible, or, rather, "unhistorical."

One expression of the special value awarded to so-called modern society may be discerned in the answers given by the nationally representative sample of Swedish young people (18–25 years old) in the third international survey of youth in eleven countries (1983). One of the questions had to do with what they could be proud of in their respective countries. The Swedes mentioned first and fore-most conditions relating to Sweden's welfare standards ("living stan-dard," 66 percent; "welfare system," 62 percent; "level of educa-tion," 49 percent; and also "success in sports," 55 percent; and "nature and natural resources," 71 percent). Among the five topping the list, "history and the cultural heritage" (mentioned by eight countries) and "culture and art" (mentioned by seven) were men-tioned by youth in other countries *but not in Sweden* (Prime Minis-ter's Office 1984). The response would probably not surprise most Swedes, to whom it would seem natural and satisfactory to stress welfare standards over history and art. To Swedes—though this thinking is in no way peculiarly Swedish—what is remarkable is that other people do not think as Swedes do, not that others think the way they do.

Modernity as a National Self-Image

If it is possible at all to discuss the core of national Swedish identity, that core would be this notion of modernity, of being part of mod-ern Sweden, part of an advanced, highly developed, rationally orga-nized country whose leading principles include justice and social welfare.

Regardless of how adequate this self-image is, it should be clear that many Swedes' perspectives on the world are heavily tinged by the idea that most countries—at least outside Scandinavia—are less advanced in these respects. They are not as modern. In a survey of Swedish school children, 57 percent characterized Swedes as "mod-ern." When a group of businesspeople were asked to give a corre-sponding characterization, several of the answers suggested the same self-image. Swedes were said to be well organized, rational, effective, punctual, well educated, socially aware, materialistic. The emphasis on welfare and justice has already received comment. What warrants special reflection is the question of identity: "Who am I in my capacity as a Swede? What is my particular profile?"

One self-stereotype associated with modernity is that Swedes have no particular culture at all. This does not mean that they lack a cultural heritage—Swedes refer to Walpurgis Night fires, Midsummer celebrations, crayfish and herring feasts, and other *folklore*. All this is considered picturesque, pleasant but superficial, without any deep meaning. However popular crayfish are, their cultural significance is obviously extremely limited—they are not "indispensable." The old peasant society—with all its attendant preserved customs—is definitely part of the past, and much of the charm of these customs lies in their contrast with the modern. Swedes have, or are generally presumed to have, a relaxed relation to the past. Midsummer Eve is "fun"; it is also rather meaningless. "We're no longer dependent on traditional thinking; we no longer believe in superstitions; we don't go to church; we're not ruled by irrational ideas." So might a fairly common Swedish self-image be formulated. However, many Swedes have just the opposite image of immigrants, who are held to be traditional, religious, irrational. Part and parcel of this world of beliefs are Swedes' critical attitudes toward religious fanaticism and fundamentalism as well as toward wholehearted nationalism, chauvinism, and the alleged willingness among some people to sacrifice their lives "to achieve paradise" or "for their leader."

Gender equality is also part of Swedish national self-understanding: that Swedish teenage girls go dancing without adult supervision, that girls choose their mates, that child-rearing is not strict—in contrast with child-rearing praxis among immigrant families from, for example, the former Yugoslavia, Turkey, or Iran.

Swedes' perception of themselves as "modern"—in contrast with their perception of immigrants—emerges clearly in the so-called immigrant jokes in which a main theme is immigrants' primitivism and their lack of experience of modern housing. There are jokes about immigrants who break up the parquet flooring and raise potatoes in the subfloor, or who wash their feet in the toilet bowl. These stories do not generally relate "immigrants' " actual patterns of behavior; they relate Swedes' notions of themselves as especially modern. Swedish self-awareness is based upon the idea that a Swede is a child of an urban, technological society where even in one's wildest imagination one could not entertain the idea of accommodating a pig on one's balcony.

It is significant that the Norwegian jokes told among Swedes do not present Norwegians as primitive peasants but as dense or amazingly stupid. These jokes are remarkably similar to Norwegians' "Swedish jokes" and to Polish jokes in the United States. "Immigrants" generally refers not to immigrants from Scandinavian countries or to those from other northern Western countries but to immigrants from the South: southern Europe, Latin America, the Middle East, and Africa.

Many Swedes think that immigrants are like Swedes were "before," when men neither helped with the dishes nor changed diapers, and teachers disciplined their pupils with the rod and by sending them to stand in the corner. This *traditional* society was also found in Sweden "once upon a time," but it is still a reality in other countries known for their dogmatism, injustice, lack of humanity and of scientific discipline. This is one *Swedish* perspective on foreign cultures.

Part of the Swedish self-image is also a readiness to compromise, which in Sweden is considered a prerequisite for civilized relations between people with conflicting interests. Compromise is seen as the only acceptable way of settling conflicts. If each of the parties gives and takes, they both stand to gain more than if they refuse to budge. Confrontations marked by intractability get nowhere, according to many Swedes, who view the inability to compromise and the "senseless aggression" in many places as signs of primitiveness and lack of reason and human development. Again, the national Swedish self-image expands in meaning when contrasted with other cultures as Swedes interpret them. In this *discourse* an unwillingness to compromise, or intractability, may conceivably be explained in several ways, for example, with reference to religious faith or general primitiveness. However, what is not included in the discourse is that a willingness to compromise presumes that the areas of dispute are not so great that they cannot be bridged without the parties losing face and self-respect. Conflicts or divisions have never been so deep in Sweden; Swedes lack historical experience of such things. In some countries, the basic emotional attitude is that "you don't deal with the devil." One simply does not negotiate with evil: one fights it.

This conceptual world, which associates modernity and reason and accommodation, is integrated into the general attitude toward aggression, temperamentalism, and emotionality. Swedes like to think of hate as infantile, a sign of emotional immaturity, lack of perspective, and an inability to empathize with another's situation—all properly belonging to childhood. Again, the perception may be that "the evil world is far away from Sweden," which is rather like an adult's view of a naughty child. Swedes' most negative judgment of immigrants, a judgment that emerged from a field survey (Öhlund 1982), is that they *bråkar*, that is, they quarrel, are troublesome, unruly.

Swedes are not the only people to have this perspective or to pass such judgments. The attitude that contrasts modernity with the primitive is held by many of the French toward North Africans, Germans toward Turkish immigrants, northern Italians toward southern Italians, African city dwellers toward people in "the bush." Examples are manifold. As often seen, what is typically Swedish is not uniquely Swedish. The content of these notions may have a basis in reality, mainly in terms of differences in degree of industrialization and material living standards, but the stories related about the "others" are marked by coarse stereotyping, great exaggerations, and often bizarre fantasies. Before the enormous postwar immigration to Sweden, similar stories were related about Gypsies, Lapps, and country folk in Sweden. In his studies of modern myths and legends, the Swedish folklorist Bengt af Klintberg has noted people's deep desire to comprehend the discrediting stories as true. Therefore, many people ward off any sort of information that challenges their belief in the veracity of these stories, probably because it is psychologically relevant to have access to material that allows one to look down upon certain groups of people.

Melancholy

Seriousness need not be due to melancholy, but melancholy invariably produces seriousness. Kathleen Nott (1960) noticed a "lack of *joie de vivre*" in Sweden, even though everyone was working like mad to create a good life. The theme of the Scandinavian section at the South Atlantic Modern Language Association's meeting in Atlanta in 1993 was "cosmopolitanism in Scandinavia." It was reported that the University Presses of both Nebraska and Wisconsin had closed down their Scandinavian series, and soon no one would be publishing Scandinavian literature in translation. "Why don't people read Swedish literature, for example, in translation? All the participants at the meeting agreed that the Swedes have only themselves to blame. Someone said that 'Gloom and Doom' from the far North is not popular in the forever young U.S., where people are optimistic" (Tom Conner, *Svenska Dagbladet*, 5 December 1993).

From a representative selection of Swedes in Hans Zetterberg's survey (1985) who described their national character, 5 percent depicted themselves as "melancholy." (They could give three responses; more answers would have given a higher percentage.) One of my old schoolmates who had emigrated to the United States thirty years ago spontaneously mentioned melancholy when I talked with him about memories from Sweden. Melancholy was what dominated his recollections. Lilly Lorénzen ([1964] 1978) cites a French woman who found things in Sweden in perfect order but found the people to be "unhappy, unsatisfied." Similar remarks have been made by many commentators outside Sweden.

Herbert Hendin addresses the question of *inner difficulties*, which he links to discussions conducted in literary magazines while he was in Sweden. The discussions concerned whether life in Sweden was boring.

> Foreigners complaining about Stockholm in this manner may largely refer to the fact that the city is not a playground, which is probably a compliment rather than an insult. However, when such a complaint is made by Swedes, it has to be taken more seriously. The usual ascription of *trå-kighet* (boredom) to external conditions seems incorrect. Boredom is more likely a sign of internal affective difficulties and the consequent diminished capacity for enjoying life. (Hendin 1964, 70)

The reflection warrants closer scrutiny of the main subject of Hendin's book *Suicide and Scandinavia* (1964), an examination also necessitated by the widespread stereotype of the high frequency of suicide in Sweden, which is often (critically) interpreted as a consequence of "Swedes' angst." However, what is often not mentioned is that Sweden occupies the ninth place in the accessible (and partly unreliable) European statistics (1990), eighth place for women, tenth place for men. (It is worthy of note that countries like Switzerland and Belgium are higher on the list and that France comes close to Sweden.) Hendin's explanation (1964, 72–73) is as follows:

> The [Swedish] child's early separation from the mother stimulates anger and at the same time deflates self-esteem. The control over anger and other strong affects requires that anger be handled with a great deal of detachment. Few combinations provide such fertile soil for suicide as affective deadening combined with, and based on, the need to control aggression. In the male, competitive performance is an acceptable salve for his self-esteem and may serve as an outlet for his aggression if he can so channel it. Because of rigid expectations for his own performance, however, the man becomes vulnerable to self-hatred and suicide if he fails in this area.
>
> In the female, greater affectivity serves as a protective device. Although likewise damaged by early separation from the mother, her self-esteem can be restored by a stable rela-

tionship with a man if properly handled. However, her low self-esteem is not particularly helpful in arousing and sustaining the man's interest in her. Male attitudes toward women tend to aggravate the situation still further. Similar difficulties in dealing with aggression may be the woman's undoing if her relationship with the man develops poorly.

In both male and female cases, whenever the injury from the maternal relationship is more severe or the reaction to it more profound, an active paranoid attachment to the mother may become more important than any tie to work or to the opposite sex. In such circumstances suicide often represents a destructive act aimed at both the patient and his mother.

The etiology of suicide is complicated and difficult—as is the statistical reporting of suicide (see Waldenström et al. 1972). Presumably, wise advice to anyone dealing with this area would be to raise a cautionary banner saying, "Here are some of my views on this subject" (Shneidman 1984).

Statistical comparisons are indirectly affected by the secularization that has presumably helped to make the bases for statistics covering the causes of death especially thorough in Sweden—which is not the case everywhere (Link 1969). Regarding causes of suicide in Sweden, a study has shown that problems at work and in one's finances entered into the picture in at least half of the cases involved (Rudenstam 1970).

In a 1964 follow-up study of suicide attempts, Ruth Ettlinger found among those committing suicide an overproportion of "social minus factors" compared with these factors among a control group. In certain cases, these factors were described as "insufficient welfare" (Ettlinger is cited in Farberow 1972, 42). Over recent decades, abuse of alcohol and drugs has increasingly been included in causes of suicide, but the abuse itself is often caused by failures in working life. Both suicide and addiction are responses to a psychological condition, but neither drug abuse nor failure in working life inevitably leads to suicide. A contributing factor in suicide can be the experience of shame, which is mentioned by Elfstadius and Pressner (1984, 75) with reference to Levin (1967). Levin describes the masochistic defense developed by those who suffer feelings of shame.

One element in the existential condition I call melancholy may be problems that many Swedes experience in social relations—even at a safe distance from situations provoking suicide. According to Elfstadius and Pressner (1984, 36), "The contentious picture emerging from high expectations on the one hand and low self-confidence on the other (typical of shy people) is also analogous to Kretschmer's psychiatric description of the sensitive personality, which he describes as permeated by tension between the sthenic and asthenic poles."

Asthenic personalities are dutiful and ambitious, and their asthenism is often counterbalanced by and hidden behind efficiency, according to Clarence Blomquist ([1969] 1975). Blomquist goes on to sketch a character type, the compulsive neurotic, or anankastic, which brings to mind many Swedes—not unlike as Susan Sontag's description of them. This personality comprises elements such as punctuality, thoroughness and caution, stiffness, and lack of spontaneity. "These people have a pronounced ambivalence, and thus their defence mechanisms are stiff and rigid and their whole personality suffers from lack of spontaneity, adaptation and flexibility. . . . They are not only rigid in their thoughts and views but also physically" (Blomquist [1969] 1975, 74).

To these personality characteristics Blomquist adds moods or states of mind that are also common among Swedes, albeit by no means among *all* Swedes. These include feelings of "insufficiency and inferiority," of "sensitivity and concern about prestige," a condition that is frequently counterbalanced by "thoroughness, dutifulness, and diligence"—traits that often help such people "to do well, sometimes very well." However, according to Blomquist ([1969] 1975, 74–75), success seldom gives these people much satisfaction: "The anankastic neurotic has a stiff, cold, controlled, and blocked emotional life. . . . He can be miserly and ungenerous. . . . But miserliness can be transformed into generosity, and interest in the impure can be sublimated into a struggle for purity, veracity, refinement, nobility."

To describe the "significant Swede" in this way assuredly distorts the picture; its exaggeration can easily be taken as a malicious caricature. However, my hypothesis is that this character type is more common in Sweden than in many other countries, where instead other extreme personality traits reflect other social relations, other cultures and histories. Every population presumably contains people among whom pure traits like those described above exist only vaguely. This means, for example, that if a "rigid, cold, controlled, and blocked emotional life" distinguishes some Swedes, then the same applies to a considerably larger portion of the population though only "to a certain extent" or "relatively."

It is important to understand that people characterized by a blocked emotional life, for instance, do not generally "suffer" from it consciously (Casriel 1972). They rationalize their personality traits—that is, give themselves rational reasons for their attitudes and behavior. They can even idealize their own egos: submissiveness is seen as goodness or love; being closed equals being wise and independent (Horney 1951). The features typical of their culture confirm them; they are often surrounded by people who exhibit or follow the same pattern, and thus this pattern is experienced as entirely normal. Characteristics such as diligence and thoroughness can, as has been mentioned, contribute to success in working life. So people with these traits, when asked about quality of life, generally answer that life is good and interesting—which is what most Swedes say (Allardt 1975; Bernow 1985).

With regard to these psychic handicaps, however, neither humankind as a whole nor the small part composed of Swedes consists of a majority of "healthy" individuals on the one hand and a minority of "unhealthy, disturbed, deviant" individuals on the other. All people are formed—or perhaps deformed—by their living conditions, their upbringing, and the course of their lives. The borderline between healthy and unhealthy is difficult to establish even if there are manifold attempts to do so. Certain traits or conditions usually defined as disorders in psychiatric and psychotherapeutic contexts occur very frequently. According to the psychiatrist Daniel Casriel (1972, 13), "Most people demonstrate a combination of neurotic problems and personality disturbances."

Given this, Swedish mentality is perhaps not so bad off as it may seem when immigrants describe Swedes as "spiritually empty" and incapable of love: "Swedes pretend to love because they lack the ability to show real feelings" (Bergman and Swedin 1982, 204). Other people are prone to other personality disorders. Casriel, who has interpreted what is healthy and unhealthy in the spirit of Abram Kardiner's analysis of culture (see Kardiner 1939), points out that there are thousands of ways to be "human," but he emphasizes that civilization (or cultural patterns) is not always adapted so that it corresponds to people's emotional or even biological needs. So culture can create a larger or smaller proportion of disturbed personalities, even though these personalities do not feel they are disturbed. "Most closed people do not know they are not open," but they are often "aware that something is lacking in their lives" (Casriel 1972, 85).

Casriel distinguishes between the neurotic and the character-disordered personality type, although in practice they more or less blur together. Casriel states that the character-disordered personality is typical for modern, urbanized, mobile society. For several years, 80 percent of his patients exhibited such personalities; the rest were mainly neurotic.

In Freud's lifetime, it was the opposite. Strict values kept behavior under control, and the neurotic was the predominant personality type. One important factor in the transition from a neurotic to a character-disordered society, according to Casriel, was the dissolution of the old (extended) family and the advent of the modern family that, considering itself self-sufficient, isolated itself from the rest of the world. Among the features of modernity (both in Sweden and the United States) is that individuals shield themselves or flee from situations that can upset them—for example, dealing with a troublesome neighbor, or with one's partner, or with one's parents.

All this does not immediately increase our knowledge of typical Swedish character traits. The aim is primarily to offer an alternative *perspective* on those personality traits and cultural patterns that have already been described in this book. My impression is that rather few attempts have been made to use "Swedish culture" as a variable in psychiatric research (but see Hagnell et al. 1982). Yet another aspect of what Swedish culture has to do with Swedes can be found in Richard Lynn's studies of different degrees of anxiety. That Swedes can be placed in the category of "low" anxiety means that deviations across the Swedish psychic spectrum typically express themselves in psychotic depression and schizophrenia—when the patient is more or less apathetic, despondent, and devoid of feeling, energy, and hope. High anxiety, on the other hand, is typified by manic conditions and neurotic depressions; patients are, if anything, oversensitive.

The 1961 health-care statistics that Lynn used, covering eighteen countries, show that Sweden is high on the list for admissions to mental hospitals (4.8 per 1,000 inhabitants), along with three other low-anxiety countries: the United States (4.3), Great Britain (4.5), and Ireland (7.3). The explanation for this is that the number of psychotically depressed and schizophrenic patients in mental hospitals is much greater than the number of neurotics or manic patients. Assuming that there is no sharp line of demarcation between healthy and nonhealthy behavior but instead that a large portion of any population can be found in between, in a middle stratum, we may also assume a tendency among many Swedes to feel gloomy, weak, and hopeless occasionally (characteristics of psychotic depression and schizophrenia) rather than terribly upset and aggressive (characteristics of manic conditions) (see Lynn 1971, 7).

The Influence of Climate on Mood

No theory about Swedes' putative melancholy has been as widely disseminated as that in the book *De l'ésprit des lois* (The spirit of laws) written by Charles de Secondat, baron de Montesquieu in 1748, in which the author presents ideas about the importance of natural conditions for the formation of the national psyche and, hence, also the state. Swedes frequently refer to this so-called climate theory—albeit often in jest—in the dark winter season.

There are two ways to use climate to explain the national psyche. One can be called ecological: climate is seen as a part of the conditions shaping people's lives, and in its turn, one's life affects one's personality. I return to this in the next chapter.

The second way is physiological. This has to do with climate's "direct" effect on body and soul through temperature, light, humidity, wind, and so forth. Even if many Swedes know about the climate theory, its significance for Swedish culture has not been much discussed, despite the fact that the international biometeorological literature is extensive.

For example, in his book *Vädersjukdomar och luftjoner* (Weather-related illnesses and airborne ions) (1981) Doctor Bertil Flöistrup primarily deals with the situation of people sensitive to weather, giving particular attention to the effects of atmospheric electricity, or ion balance. He writes about the Atlantic low-pressure front, which begins to move toward Scandinavia at the latitude of the

British Isles, and discusses how the positively charged small air ions, the so-called cat(catheter)-ions, reach us twelve to forty-eight hours before the front and torment the sensitive with all manner of physical and psychic problems—what he calls "climatosis." Symptoms include vascular spasms, colic, asthma, and headaches.

It is reckoned that one-third of the population is weather sensitive. According to Artturi Similä and Björn Forslund (1978), who have also written on this subject, strong young people in their twenties and thirties are less sensitive. Even psychic problems such as "unexplained anxiety and tension" can be climate related, although many sufferers blame stress at work or even "domestic quarrels." Flöistrup (1981, 95) notes that life can feel meaningless and that stress symptoms can appear like "a cloud of anxiety, worry, or apathy."

It is worth mentioning that weather is not the only thing affecting airborne ions. Urban air pollution, industrial waste, and household machines, as well as the indoor climate created by cement buildings, ventilation systems, and synthetic materials, all play a part.

Low air pressure is not confined to the chillier climes, but Sweden is definitely one of the countries frequently subjected to it. For many, the consequences of this include "migraines of a diffuse, protracted kind and a slight nausea. Psychic resistance is broken down, life seems hopeless, and one labors under feelings of meaninglessness and inferiority" (Flöistrup 1981, 95).

Similä and Forslund's presentation is both more concise and broader than Flöistrup's. Similä and Forslund emphasize the differences between town and country, that, for instance, because of air pollution, it rains more in urban than in rural areas. This means that the number of hours of sunshine is reduced by 10 to 20 percent: "With regard to health, particularly serious is the lack of ultraviolet radiation, which in the summer decreases by 30 to 40 percent, in the winter by 60 to 100 percent" (Similä and Forslund 1978, 11). Even with the onset of a warm front, when the temperature rises rapidly, people react negatively: they need more sleep; they are more irritated, depressed; their reactions are slower; they are more powerfully affected by alcohol; and so on. The type of weather people tolerate best is calm, basically high-pressure, without cloud, rain, or storms.

Another aspect of Swedish conditions is the winter darkness. Its negative consequences for some people have provided the point of departure for a research project on light that is being conducted at St. Göran's Hospital in Stockholm, led by Professor Lennart Wetterberg. Treatment methods based on the effects changes in light have on the pineal gland are being tested there. Using blood tests, amounts of the hormones melatonin and cortisol, a stress hormone, are measured. "When the balance between these two is disturbed, we can suffer abnormal fatigue, depression, sleeping problems, and anxiety. . . . Autumn and spring depressions can be related to the fact that certain individuals have problems adjusting to rapid changes between light and darkness—in the spring, from dark to light, in the autumn, from light to dark" (Ljusbehandling mot depression [Light treatment of depression] 1987, 16; cf. Wetterberg 1994). Since the end of the 1980s, coordinated investigations have been going on all over the world to ascertain how light affects melatonin and well-being, and how this explains seasonal variations in depression, stomach ulcers, alcoholism, and migraines.

Physiology aside, the Nordic winter darkness offers an explanation of moods on another level. Consider its symbolic and suggestive powers, its real as well as imaginative connections with death and corruption. Trees lose their leaves, flowers die, darkness descends upon everything, "as if in the grave." The brief Swedish summer is a reminder of life; a bad summer profoundly disappoints many Swedes—or, as Bertil Flöistrup (1981, 38) has observed, "Quite simply, we have difficulties accepting our climate."

Puritan Morality

It is quite common in Sweden to begin certain comments with the word "no." For example, at a dinner party, when the hour is approaching midnight, someone may say, "No, dear friends, now we really have to thank you." The same "no" is used in expressions like "No, now I've really got to get going," or "No, now listen, now I think we should take a break," or "No, now I'm going to settle the matter."

How are we to explain these initial negations? To my mind, there is a connection between these negations and the concept of guilt with its inner voice—the conscience that may impose something other than that which is offered by the circumstances. One's conscience points a finger and denies the prevailing conditions ("No, now we must get a move on," "No, now we must make a decision") or reminds us of necessities—the way we prod or instruct our children ("No, now I have to sleep"). This "no" indicates a dialogue, two wills—for and against. Negation also operates in melancholy, in the guilt-laden attitude toward life in which conscience makes itself felt: do not be proud; enjoy things in moderation.

The brand of Lutheranism that is stamped upon the Swedish church has exerted profound influence upon Swedes' basic view of life. Like the climate, Lutheran puritanism is often referred to in order to explain Swedes' alleged lack of *joie de vivre*. For a long time it was deemed sinful—and is still not considered altogether respectable—to let oneself go, allow oneself to be overwhelmed by joy or sensuous pleasures, much less intentionally strive for such states. In contrast with Catholicism, Protestantism is deeply involved with questions of sin and guilt. In Sweden, the nineteenth-century evangelist movements reinforced the view of earthly existence as a heavy burden (trials and tribulations) one longs to be rid of. Since we are full of guilt because of our human faults and inability to live as God has instructed us, suffering is more legitimate than joy. The "primrose path" leads to perdition.

An individual with these attitudes probably views trials and tribulations as natural, possibly even reassuring and less risky. Against such a worldview so permeated by troubles, happy moments stand out as something even a sinful person has a "right" to. An attitude like this should encourage feelings of *thankfulness* on those occasions when the individual happens to feel completely happy. For a typical healthy Swede, everything's being as it should be feels rather like a favor or a gift. Puritan morality in the very marrow of one's bones demands humility: pride is summarily punished. In the Swedish seventeenth- and eighteenth-century *Farmer's Almanac* readers were admonished to heed its precepts and examples carefully: "[H]appily and thankfully . . . follow all predictions and practical wisdom handed down through the Holy Spirit. . . . So that when we have been blessed with a fruitful and salubrious year . . . we do not then become proud, self-satisfied, and assured, as if we already had everything in hand and as if things could not be otherwise" (*Den gamla svenska bondepraktikan* 1979, 20).

Max Weber's theory of Calvinist Protestantism can help us understand the Swedish variant of Lutheranism. According to Weber, "worldly asceticism" is a combination of asceticism and worldly activities buttressed by the work ethic and expressed in industriousness and the desire to succeed. This combination contrasts with the dualistic Catholic doctrine of an ascetic ideal directed toward another, transcendental world, the object of only a minority of the population, allowing the majority of ordinary people to accept the pleasures of this world (see Peabody 1985).

It is not difficult to find in popular literature reflections of a guilt-ridden view of life, in which suffering—not happiness—is seen as natural. For instance, note the gloom expressed in the well-known Swedish Christmas song from the early nineteenth century, *Hej tomtegubbar* (roughly, "Hi, little elves"):

> The little time we have to live
> is full of toil and trouble

In the beginning of the 1980s the popular Swedish musician Robert Broberg wrote and sang a song about "warming my frozen soul" and "being inspired to live on." The reaction of one southern immigrant to this song was that one can indeed be inspired to poetry and singing and much else—but to live? Every healthy person should by definition be inspired to live; it is an integral part of life to want to live. Broberg's lyrics would be difficult to comprehend translated into many other languages.

The person who ponders life's trials and tribulations and anticipates disappointments will inevitably become serious, at worst be "weighed down" by it all. After visiting Sweden the Bulgarian writer Jordan Raditjkov described how people "drag themselves around" when the weather is "unobliging." We can consider the metaphorical kinship between the expression "drag themselves around" and melancholy, which can be so aptly associated with that slowness in both walking and talking that has previously been denoted as typically Swedish.

In poetic language, happiness is usually quick, frisky like a spring breeze, whereas sorrow weighs down the body, similar to the stillness of death. People who often ponder the trials of life and expect the worst invariably become grave. Gloominess is nourished by introspection, while cheerfulness is (if sometimes childishly) open to impressions. Melancholy arises in anxieties about making mistakes, failing, getting lost—fertile soil for Swedish bards. Melancholy more-over acquires further legitimacy by being elevated, awarded higher value than "superficial" happiness. The well-known Swedish litera-ture critic Ruth Halldén once wrote that a "poem written by an ass is usually considered a much more valuable product than a feature column written by a genius" (cited by Mårten Blomkvist, *Dagens Nyheter*, 3 January 1985). And David Jenkins remarked that Swedish social planners "are not so eager that [people] have fun" (1968, 267).

A young American woman related the experience of going to the movies in Sweden:

> When I go to see a movie, I throw myself into it; I sigh and groan and laugh aloud, and then my Swedish friends tell me it's only a film. But I *want* that powerful experience, I don't want to think it's only a film. . . . I don't want to give up my culture; I want to be American. I interrupt people when I get enthusiastic, but I see that's not appreciated. In groups only one person talks at a time, and for a while I thought people were stupid when they couldn't talk to two people at the same time about different things. . . . I have been influenced by people in Sweden being so serious, so that it's almost impossible when I go home to my family in California, where they only tell jokes the whole time at the dinner table. They've never done anything else. I hadn't learned to be serious until I came to Sweden.

Different social groups experience different degrees of melan-choly. Seriousness and moroseness have been established as a style within the Swedish bourgeoisie and among intellectuals, even though individual variations can be great. Reserved, controlled behavior and emotional discipline is mainly—but far from exclusively—evi-denced in the upper echelons of society, as is the earnestness many think should accompany responsible posts in society. Therefore, the style of communication in Stockholm, which is a civil service city, is generally more formal and detached than the style in Gothenburg, much more of an industrial and working-class town. Power legit-imizes itself through solemnity and gravity (very likely a univer-sal tendency).

There is between genders, too, a difference in workings of melancholy. Men tend to legitimate their power positions vis-à-vis women through being more solemn, which requires career women to adapt and acquire a certain amount of "male" assertiveness. However, women take life more seriously than men do, according to the psychologist Henry Montgomery at Stockholm University.

Generational differences are also worth examining. Many Swedish youths think adult seriousness especially loathsome, whereas to a great many adults seriousness is a positive quality because it indicates a mature person's insights into "life's problems and realities." The psychologist Lars-Olof Persson has found no less of a correlation between mood and age—the older, the happier (Persson 1988).This may seem to contradict the previous sentence about older people's being more serious. However, happiness should be associated with being "at ease" or having the capacity to "cope with" life's circumstances, which comes with age and experiences. Being happy does not primarily mean to be gay or joyful.

The Work Ethic and Work as the Creator of Identity

Despite the generation gap mentioned above, Swedish youth basically do not differ from adults in their relation to their work. They are not noted for their frivolity. In the international youth survey of 1983 (Prime Minister's Office 1984), the youth of eleven countries were asked whether they would work anyway if they had enough money without working. Only 12 percent of the Swedes replied that they would choose *not* to work, whereas, for example, 40 percent of the young people in Switzerland and France and 38 percent of the youth of West Germany made the same reply. The European Values System Study, aimed at the whole of the adult population of different countries, contained the question, "Do you really look forward to work when the weekend is over, or do you regret that the weekend is over?" The Nordic countries appeared here as particularly work-oriented, with an average of 44 percent looking forward to going back to work (37 percent of the Swedes, even more among the other Scandinavians). The average among other Europeans was 26 percent, with the lowest in West Germany (18 percent) and Belgium (17 percent).

There are good grounds for claiming that to many Swedes work and industriousness constitute the foundations of their social identities. This is of course not the only reason more Swedes than any other group among the eleven countries in the European Values System Study feel great pride in their work (52 percent): their working conditions are important here too. Norway and Sweden had the greatest proportion of people who never felt exploited or used.

The emphasis on work and the desire to be productive and *duktig* (capable, with a morally praising connotation) do not necessarily lead to melancholy; on the contrary, to many Swedes work gives pleasure and meaning to life. But performance is psychologically the opposite of sensuous pleasure, and therefore stressing it can in certain instances hinder pleasure. It can be difficult after a day's work all of a sudden to "act out" one's feelings—at least for many Swedes.

I have heard Swedes say that when on vacation it usually takes them a few weeks before they are able to "wind down" and take advantage of their free time, and many think it is good to be back at work after vacation.

From the vantage point of certain other cultures, the impression given by Swedish modes of living can be dramatic. A Kurdish refugee once described Swedes to me as follows: "An industrious people. They work, they're like robots. Work like machines, lock themselves in in the evening with their TV sets." After the war, however, the pivotal importance of "work" dwindled, to be increasingly replaced by "leisure" (Zetterberg 1977).

"Mood and Expectations"

So far in this chapter I have served up a veritable smorgasbord of research reports, parts of interviews, survey data, and diverse theories—all in varying degrees speculative. No clear-cut answer to the question whether Swedes should be depicted as typical melancholics has been forthcoming.

That foreigners often consider Swedes gloomy should not necessarily be taken as a general truth. The frequency of suicide in

Sweden—ninth in Europe (1989), according to international statistics—reflects the psychic condition of a very small portion of
the population. What it may indicate about the population as a
whole is unclear.

However, my personal view is that extreme deviations such as
suicide, alcoholism, certain psychic disorders, overemphasis on work,
and the like, are linked to general personality traits among the population. I would also claim that folklorist material, such as song texts
and jokes as well as fiction and films, can be helpful in studies of
more generally occurring psychic conditions. Even though such material is often produced by nonaverage people, it is still basically
anchored in the collective.

The palpable connections between climate and mood in different
countries support the assumption that climate in one way or another causes differences in mood among peoples living in different
parts of the world.

I think there are sufficient empirical grounds for the assertion
that a streak of melancholy and gloom runs through Swedish culture and through sufficient numbers of Swedes for it to be listed as a
frequent characteristic, expressed in music, poetry, and painting,
and in social gatherings without alcohol. Melancholy need not
be characteristic of a majority of the population to be typical of
Swedes; it is only necessary that it be more common in the Swedish
mentality than in that of other comparable nationalities.

But I am also prepared to accept the objection that what can be
interpreted as expressions of gloom may be better denoted as expressions of seriousness. On the basis of his research on moods, the
psychologist Lars-Olof Persson has written in a letter to me that
"Swedes are serious and aware of risks, which I consider to be the
opposite of frivolous. . . . In comparison with other nationalities, I
think that we Swedes prevent ourselves from being too frivolous,
which could be interpreted as [a streak of] melancholy" (Persson to
Daun, 4 May 1988). The self-assessments Persson presents in his
Ph.D. dissertation provide an empirical basis for the conclusion that
most Swedes are relatively happy, which primarily means "that
their basic needs are satisfied." International research on the quality of life supports Persson's conclusion.

The question remains, however, whether the responses to the
questionnaires on happiness measure people's attitudes toward the

concept of happiness as it is conceptualized in our culture. Swedes are motivated to answer positively because they live in the sort of material conditions that correlate with central values in Swedish culture. Yet it may be objected—with reference to Persson's studies—that *expectations* reinforce mood (state of mind, humor), so that it becomes self-fulfilling: if one expects to be happy, one tends to be happy. If one believes one's living conditions—work, secure employment, good wages, long vacations, good housing, having a car, and so forth—constitute reasons to feel happy, one will be inclined to be happy. Material welfare is not essential for psychic well-being, but it helps in a materially oriented culture.

Proverbs
and Mentality

Can proverbs help us to capture the Swedish "soul"? One widely held notion is that folkloristic material generally—sayings, legends, ballads, riddles, proverbs, jokes—provides insights into a nation's mentality, basic values, and view of life. It is thought that folklore can reveal a fundamental tone in the voice of the populace—not the generalizations of the researcher but those of the masses, their thoughts and feelings. One need not go along with the sentimentality that may be attached to folklore as source material; personally, I have a fairly detached attitude to "the people" and the "soul of the people."

One complicating factor is that folkloristic material is so often universal or borrowed. Much of it expresses a general humanitarianism and hence relates things about the human soul, but less or nothing at all about a specific people or what is culturally demarcated. A proverb like "Pride goes before a fall," which for the purposes of argument may be called specifically Swedish, comes from the Bible (Prov. 16:18). It may have a special meaning for Swedes; it may be psychologically relevant for a particularly great portion of the population—but that we cannot measure.

In the introductory chapter of his book *Svenskarna i sina ordspråk* (Swedes in their proverbs) from 1926, Fredrik Ström confirms that proverbs and sayings tend to have a universal content. Themes are conveyed by similar messages all over the world. Although Ström points out this limitation in the source value of proverbs, he still finds in Swedish proverbs "an echo of the popular spirit": "Proverbs are important in order to interpret correctly a people's character, views, development, habits, and customs and to understand the positions and attitudes of classes in order to obtain the right tone for historical periods and epochs" (Ström 1926, 7).

There are obvious complications here. In order to interpret development one needs to fix a given proverb in time. It would of course be fortunate if one could find out when a proverb first cropped up, when it was most popular, and when it began to fall into disuse. This is not possible. Nor can one from a proverb always detect norms of behavior. Some proverbs have antitheses, for example, "Alone is strong" and "Union is strength"[D].[1] Ström (1926, 12) mentions "conflicting proverbs that wage hopeless battles against each other. Neither can win, for both are right, both reflect the constant flux and paradoxes of life." One measure of the relative strength of one proverb compared with its opposite might be the number of its variations. The variants of "Alone is strong" include "If you want a thing done well, do it yourself"[D], "You are your own best friend"[D], "A good man depends on himself," "God helps those who help themselves"[D], "Every man for himself, and the devil take the hindmost"[D], and a rather common one, "Help yourself and don't give a damn about others—that's the best path to take." Proverbs generalize. However, like many national stereotypes, proverbs contain—despite exaggerations—a hard core of truth: for instance, "The more knave, the better luck"[D].

The meaning attributed to a proverb depends on the context—who tells it to whom and for what purpose—and consequently, no proverb always means the same to everyone. If a proverb is used in an intelligence test, which has happened, the result can be misleading if the proverb means different things to different categories of test subjects—for instance, individuals from different social classes or ethnic backgrounds. In North America the "correct" interpretations of certain proverbs have in fact been found to be those of the white American middle class. Black youth "misinterpret" these proverbs insofar as they do not interpret them "the prescribed way"—that is, the way prescribed by the culturally dominant, white middle class (Mieder 1978).

Divergent interpretations of one and the same proverb may arise depending not only on individual lifestyles and values but also, as Barbara Kirshenblatt-Gimblett (1973) has pointed out, on the meaning derived from a specific context of performance. Moreover, the

1. As the reader will note, some proverbs have their counterparts in the English language, in the text marked [D].

"correct" interpretation out of several possible can be indicated by intonation, for example—in other words, by a specific "interaction strategy," which, of course, cannot be conveyed by published collections of proverbs.

What Is Swedish in Swedish Proverbs?

In the following, when I comment on Ström's statements on the specifically Swedish in Swedish proverbs, I am forced to trust his knowledge of proverbs in other countries. For example, he writes that in comparison with other European proverbs, the Swedish (and Nordic) are distinguished by a "certain inner heaviness, mitigated by humor." This characteristic sets them apart especially from the Slavic and Latin and, to a lesser extent, from the German and Dutch. I do not try to verify Ström's erudition, but I scrutinize his conclusions in the light of Swedish cultural studies that use methods and sources other than his. Comparing Ström's conclusions with my own is also a way of checking the source value of his material.

That proverbs convey knowledge of a culture that verbally cannot otherwise be easily mediated or, in any case, explicitly formulated is made clear in the following: "The Swedish proverbs express everything that concerns mankind, but above all, they mediate the joy and misery of life, sorrow, and happiness, rising to greatness and falling into abjection, honor and shame. Not least, they concern the great questions of life. . . . Proverbs try and judge, comfort and condole, punish and forgive, mock and praise, jest and chasten" (Ström [1926] 1929, 21). Whether or not this is an adequate description, it touches upon something that is generally considered part of the Swedish psyche, namely, seriousness—a hypothesis that seems to me better bolstered by qualitative material than quantitative.

Humility

According to Ström, in contrast with many other peoples, the Nordic, and especially the Swedish, popular imagination avidly circles around fundamental existential issues. "The Swedish psyche exposes itself . . . in its way of dealing with these things: humbly without excessive timidity, uprightly without boasting" and, he adds, with humor and a glint in the eye (Ström 1926, 22). It seems clear that Ström is indicating a characteristic trait, a generally embraced Swedish value (despite many individual deviations)—namely, humility, modesty, lack of vainglory. Even Swedes who are braggarts are probably often conscious that their boasts are not appreciated by others. This culturally entrenched value is also interesting in that humility is *not* included in Swedish self-stereotypes. Very likely, most Swedes think that humility is equally important everywhere in the world, which is not the case. Like many other values, vainglory is condoned in some cultures, accepted to a degree in some, and not tolerated at all in others.

Humility is a central value in, for instance, Japan, and exemplified by all the ritualized expressions depreciating oneself and one's family. In Japan arrogant behavior is considered deeply aso-cial (Lebra 1976). Chile has its own *Jantelag*, (described earlier, in my discussion of shyness) called *cachetear* (literally, "puffing up the cheeks"), deriding pridefulness. Norwegian culture is also well known for resembling Swedish (and Chilean) culture in this respect. The contrast between Norwegian and American students' desire to attain "status and prestige" is dramatic (Jonassen 1972).

The emphasis on humility is illustrated by the Scandinavian habit of frequent thanking. Thanking can be described as ritual subordination. When a Swede is asked whether he or she would like more to drink, the positive answer is "Yes, thank you," whereas in many other languages it would be "Yes, please": in German, "Ja bitte"; in French, "Je vous en prie"; in Spanish, "Por favor"; in Greek "Oriste"; in Russian, "Pozjalujsta" or often simply "yes." In Italy the answer in this situation might be "Yes, thanks," but thanking is generally less frequent in Italy than in Sweden. The Italian practice is also characteristic of Hungary. Between friends in Hungary the answer might very well be just "yes."

Significantly, the Japanese language deviates from this pattern. The answer in "normal situations" is said to be "Yes, but just a little, thank you," which even more than the Swedish "Yes, thank you," minimizes the individual (see Daun 1986). The exaggerated thanking in Sweden may be depicted as "servility," as "slave behavior," as a kind of subordination. However, there are Swedish proverbs countering this, such as "If thanks cost money, there'd be less of it," or "Take your thanks and stroke your cat and see how fat he gets."

The habit of thanking (the host) for his last invitation and thanking the host for the food is specifically Swedish. In shops in Sweden, customers regularly say "thank you" when concluding a purchase or when they leave the premises. In many other countries, it is the salesperson who thanks the customer—*not* the other way around and not a mutual exchange.

Such explicit thanking is diametrically opposite to arrogance or self-seeking. In Sweden immigrants from countries where great generosity is simply assumed are sometimes surprised at this redundant thanking, which is actually an acknowledgment that it would be bold to take generosity as self-evident.

Swedes interpret such boldness as a sign of conceit. Ström writes that "[t]he opposite of wisdom is ignorance. Ignorance is composed of conceitedness, garrulousness, all sorts of foolishness." Proverbs such as "Wise men have their mouths in their hearts, fools their hearts in their mouths" [D]; "Fools do what madmen ask"; "Broken pride reeks"; and "Tall trees easily blow down" are germane here. According to Ström (1926, 44), "The question is whether for Swedes conceit is not the most odious quality in the world. Much can be put up with, but not that." This heavily negative attitude is clear in the Swedish term for conceit *narraktighet*—literally, *foolishness*: to behave like a fool, to be an object of ridicule.

One sign that this negative evaluation is important to Swedes is the plethora of proverbs on the subject: for instance, "Pride is the queen of vices"; "Pride with pride will not abide"[D]; "Pride destroys itself"; "Pride and grace dwelt never in one place"[D]; "Pride is a flower that grows in the devil's garden"[D]; "The devil wipes his tail with the poor man's pride"[D]; "Humble poverty is better than being rich and proud"; "Pride and little power are products of the devil"; "The devil shines his shoes with the poor man's pride"; "When pride is in the cottage, the fall is at the door."

Making fools of others may be an expression of conceit or arrogance—rather than the opposite. In a comparative study of Italian and Swedish mentality using the Cesarec-Marke Personality Scheme, 76 percent of a sample of Italian students answered yes to the question whether it amused them "sometimes to make fun of other people," whereas only 35 percent of the Swedes answered positively. The same question was answered in the affirmative by as large a proportion as 74 percent of a sample of students from seven American universities. The Swedish responses to the question, "Does it amuse you to ridicule your opponents?" indicate how reluctant Swedes are to hector or give themselves airs: only 13 percent of the Swedish students, but 26 percent of the Italians, answered yes.

In the European Values System Study, respondents from thirteen countries were asked to choose from among seventeen character traits five they considered most important to inculcate in children. "Tolerance and respect for other people" were selected by a larger proportion of Swedes (72 percent) than any other nationalities (compared with, for example, Italians—43 percent). The figures for the other Nordic countries were also significantly lower (Denmark, 58 percent; Finland, 53 percent; Norway, 31 percent). A related character trait, "unselfishness," was mentioned by 10 percent of the Swedes but only 2 percent of the Italians.

A methodological comment needs to be made at this point: low figures are a consequence of the particular significance awarded to other alternatives. When the number of answers that can be given is limited (in this case limited to five out of seventeen), each selection involves a rejection, and thus also a rejection of answers that the interviewees would have been motivated to select had they been able to.

Democracy and Justice

There is an old notion that all national self-stereotypes are self-glorifying. As a generalization, however, it does not hold: nations have both negative and positive self-images. Proverbs tend, moreover, not to make pronouncements on a particular nation or its inhabitants. On the contrary, they are composed as universally or generally applicable wise sayings. It is when making comparisons between various nationalities' proverbs that scholars can discern different tendencies in their messages.

According to Ström, another special value in Swedish proverbs is "an extraordinary demand for justice," which "may even be invoked in the defense of a great sinner." Each person should be treated fairly, whether or not he or she has previously demonstrated bad sides. Ström (1926, 27) writes that "[t]o obtain justice in every detail, the Swedish peasant may conduct ruining legal processes." In their proverbs, Swedish people are "much more tolerant, liberal, and democratic than the Pope," and "[Swedish] popular ideals are justice, truth, and freedom above all others. Veracity is admonished, lies condemned" (Ström 1926, 24, 41).

The values of truth and justice may be illustrated in the following: "Right is right, even if it costs you your head"; "One hundred thousands years of injustice is not made right in a minute"; "If you bend justice it breaks." The encroachments of power on justice are referred to in "Power lasts till the morrow" and "Power stops at the gates of hell."

Of freedom it is said, "Freedom is the people's soul." Freedom is accentuated even more clearly in "To receive charity is to sell your liberty"[D]. As Ström remarks, "Swedes prefer hardtack in freedom to plenty in bondage"; or as expressed in the proverb, "Lean liberty is better than fat slavery"[D].

What sort of data do I have on which to base international comparisons? Not much, but in the European Values survey, a very large proportion (84 percent) of the Swedes interviewed—in comparison with other Scandinavians—indicated "complete" agreement with the commandment "Thou shalt not bear false witness against thy neighbor"—that is, the commandment to revere truth. The lowest percentage of agreement was among the Finns (61 percent).

An interesting test of justice as a supreme value is revealed in the CMPS question, "Can you, when it concerns people you like, toss aside your principles of impartiality?" From two large samples of the population, somewhat more Finns than Swedes answered yes to the question, which not only says something about their view of justice but also—or rather—something about Finns' greater dependence upon friends (Daun, Mattlar, and Alanen 1989).

When we require people to choose between two good things, we should not expect any sort of dramatic inclination toward one or the other, but the differences can nevertheless be linked to one or another distinguishing variable. In the European Values survey two assertions were presented: one placed personal freedom above equality; the other placed equality first.

Fifty-six percent of the Swedes chose the first alternative, and 35 percent the second. Only 43 percent of the Italians chose freedom first; 45 percent equality. Because striving for equality is so well established among Swedes, and because in Sweden economic equality has progressed further than anywhere else, the preference for freedom should probably be interpreted as a powerful expression of the value ascribed to liberty in Swedish culture. This is in accord with Ström's description. The greater emphasis on equality among the Italians may be seen in light of the Communist sympathies that have long existed there (more than in any other Western country). According to the European Values Study of the early 1980s, the feeling of "often being exploited at work" was three times as common among Italians as among Swedes (Daun 1992). However, somewhat different interpretations are also possible—for example, that equality has progressed so far in Sweden that some Swedes now think that the principle of freedom is being disregarded. In the survey these people would choose the freedom alternative. In a follow-up survey conducted by SIFO (Svenska Institutet för Opinionsundersökningar) in 1990 (about nine years after the European Values Study of the early 1980s) an even larger proportion of Swedes (63 percent) chose the freedom alternative, and significantly smaller proportion (27 percent), the equality alternative—logical, considering the changes in political opinion that have occurred. It may also be speculated that, in contrast with Italy, the absence of a feudal system in Sweden and the dominance of free, landowning farmers have made freedom a historically more established principle in Sweden than it is in Italy.

There are other grounds as well for expecting that freedom would be especially underlined in Sweden. Self-sufficiency and independence, that is, freedom from social dependence, are documented and explicitly expressed values in Swedish culture and well illustrated in Swedish child-rearing principles. Ström (1926, 41) notes that "[t]he old Swedish yeomen were proud, and they treasured their total independence."

We can obtain another perspective on the concept of freedom by looking at "unity," group affiliation, group feeling. Ström claims that the theme of unity crops up less often in proverbs than that of liberty, except in those proverbs relating to the modern working class—for instance, "United we stand, divided we fall"[D]. In proverbs, the relative absence of a specific value should be taken as a negative indication.

Furthermore, historically, equality has been nourished by the relatively egalitarian agrarian society in Sweden and in the general stress on similarity or sameness (reflected in the Swedish word *jämlik/likhet*) (see Gullestad 1989). The emphasis on this value has probably been upheld by the relatively slight cultural differences prevailing in Sweden (see Daun 1991). The general group orientation, the collectivism in Sweden, is not reflected in proverbs. This is because a proverb is used in situations where the value or norm it expresses is challenged, threatened, or questioned—or in any case needs underlining. Probably there must be opportunities for competing messages, expressed both in the simultaneous occurrence of proverbs with directly opposite messages ("Alone is strong" versus "Union is strength") and in the so-called Wellerisms, where one makes a comic mockery of proverbs.

The question which is most important to Swedes—freedom or equality—may not be clearly ascertainable, despite the survey data given above. The concepts are too large. Freedom from what, we may ask. Independent in what respect, equal in what context? What the survey responses indicate is simply the occurrence of very general attitudes toward these two concepts. But are we only interested in what people say? Are we not also interested in what they express in actions? Actually, cultural patterns are more exactly revealed in people's attitudes as these are expressed in actions. However, carrying out, for example, participant observation studies of individual efforts to achieve freedom and equality would most likely involve, to say the least, immense problems.

Truth Rather Than Beauty

Ideal beauty is not a prominent theme in Swedish proverbs: according to Ström, beauty is mocked—"Prettiness dies first"[D]. Truth as an ideal is more in line with the Swedish character: "Truth keeps its color" and "Better suffer for truth than be rewarded for lies."

If we think of ideal beauty as an expression of general sensuality, does this dichotomy between truth and beauty not touch upon something central in Nordic culture? In which case, truth may be said to be rooted in the concrete, material, earthbound. Frivolity has an inferior position, but according to Ström, some southern peoples sing its praises. Swedes do not dismiss joy, but feel it should be controlled—euphoria can be dangerous: "When joy's in the house, sorrow's on the threshold" or "The end of all joy is sorrow." Liquor is condemned in many proverbs: "With the last drink comes the first clout."

Equally, games and jokes belong to the world of amusement—and of temptation. Truth may be boring, but it gives an adult a firm foundation: "Do not jest in earnest"; "Many jests end badly"; "Knock in jest, open the door in earnest"; "At the end of the game the devil will play."

The sense of gloom emanating from such expressions would earlier have been attributable to grim living conditions. "The evening knows what the morning cannot imagine"; "Time takes away the ticking from the clock, the song from the bird, the yoke from the ox, the rose from the girl." The content of these is the same as that of the enormously popular Christmas song "Hej tomtegubbar"—that is, "The little time we have to live is full of toil and trouble." Such an "earthbound" tendency exists even in proverbs casting a critical eye on love and marriage: "The one who marries for love has lusty nights and heavy days"; "Love me little and love me long." In the collection in the Nordic Museum I have found the following proverb from the province of Småland: "One should never be happy about anything, for then it will be bad"; another along the same lines is "The food of pleasure is served on a platter of regret."

The Swedishness Within

Each individual life, in its form and content, is unique. Many private details and meandering pathways from our earliest moments of life to the present distinguish us from our neighbors. Yet we carry about us collectively shared experiences. We are unique individuals, but culturally we are related to one another. Even immigrants acquire, in this case, "an inner Swedishness"—whether they want to or not— as soon as they learn to use the Swedish language and to participate in Swedish contexts.

Immigrants who have lived a few years in their new country are often struck by the fact that they start thinking in their new language—even dream in it! Since a language conveys attitudes and values and equips people with tools for interpreting their environment, it helps to transmit new ideas and grounds for judgment. Both language and the immediate surroundings implant new ways of looking at things and new interests. Encounters between two cultures generate a third: for example, a Greek Swede not only is a mixture of Greek and Swedish culture but is also stamped by the special experience of being outside, apart. However, first-generation immigrants are still primarily the bearers of their original (native) cultures.

This is even more so for those who are born into and remain in the culture of their forebears. However much Swedes deepen their personal interests and inclinations, however much they may attempt to detach themselves from the general populace and cultivate eccentricities, they carry "Swedishness" inside them. They are products of basic qualities of Swedish culture, and with their lives, they present individual versions of that collective pattern.

Such ties to Swedish culture do not necessarily mean that Swedes are unaware of possessing national characteristics. Consider several self-stereotypes from a survey among fifteen- and sixteen-year-old students in the ninth grade (see table 3). The Swedish students in the sample gave responses to the question of what they considered prominent characteristics among Swedes in general.

Table 3   Swedish Students' Evaluations of Swedes

Characteristic	Percent
Stressed	69
Interested in sports	61
Well dressed	60
Modern	57
Stiff	45
Technical	43
Peaceful	43
Happy	42
Sexy	40
Friendly	40

Source: Takac n.d.

Since the respondents were young people, their responses reflect in part the way youth view the adult world, which they have not yet entered, and in part their special interests. When they (69 percent) describe Swedes as "stressed," it probably reveals their view of their parents' generation as well as their own parents' efforts to accomplish as much as possible. They may have made comparisons with certain immigrant groups' way of life, which seems more relaxed and sociable.

"Interested in sports" (61 percent) may very well reflect young people's self-image—indicating the importance of sports in their own lives. It is conceivable that Swedish outdoor life is especially popular and activity oriented, especially in comparison with the stereotype of the southern European, who sits at café tables playing cards. The Swedish term that was used in the survey, *sportig*, is difficult to translate. It does mean "interested in (conducting) sports," but the term also refers to a certain personality type: active, sound, pleasant.

Among people in other European countries, Swedes are generally not known for being "well dressed" (60 percent). Rather, they are known to dress informally and "sloppy" (Phillips-Martinsson

1981). The survey participants' view of Swedes as well dressed may be based on the image of the Swedish high standard of living; it may also contain a comparison with certain immigrants' deviating, less fashion-conscious styles. The stereotypes "modern" and "technical" are in accord with the widespread view of Sweden as a technically and socially advanced country.

"Stiff" (45 percent) is the sole negative stereotype on the list. It is part of the constellation "shy-reserved-taciturn," familiar to Swedes who have experience of other people and foreign countries.

Most Swedes would agree that they are "peaceful" (43 percent). Generally, the policy of neutrality is considered a powerful expression of efforts to maintain peace—more than, for instance, being a member of a defense pact such as NATO. It is worth remarking that this attribute is mentioned by youth, who seem to experience the issue of peace as particularly acute (cf. Mead 1970). However, "peaceful" is not mentioned in a survey taken among adults (16–74 years old), a fact I return to.

In the 1986 IPPNW study of young people's attitudes toward nuclear arms, the question of peace was placed first. The nationally representative sample of Swedish youth from elementary school through high school was asked to answer the question, "If you were able to have three wishes, what would they be?" They were given complete freedom to write whatever they wanted. Seventy-five percent answered peace, disarmament, no weapons, no nuclear arms, and the like.

The attributes "happy" (42 percent) and "friendly" (40 percent) may be connected with Swedes' view of themselves as peace-loving people. These characteristics also appeared in Charles Westin's major interview survey in which "happy" and "nice" were the most frequently mentioned adjectives (Westin 1984).

"Sexy" (40 percent) can certainly be partly explained by the relatively liberal Swedish view of sex, but it also reflects young people's special interest in sexuality during puberty. In the previously mentioned SIFO survey, directed toward adults, sexy was also mentioned as a Swedish attribute, but by only 0.5 percent of the respondents.

SIFO (the Swedish Institute of Public Opinion Research) conducted an interview survey with a representative sample of Swedes (Zetterberg 1985). According to the survey, the characteristics listed in table 4 may be said to describe Swedes.

Table 4 Swedes' Description of Themselves (16–74 years old) (N = 1096)

Characteristic	Percent
Envious	49
Stiff	33
Industrious	24
Nature loving	19
Quiet	14
Honest	14
Dishonest	11
Xenophobic	11
Proud	9
Fair/equality oriented	8
Nationalistic	7
Politically interested	7
Technical	7
Inventive	6
Worldly	6
Stubborn	6
Melancholic	5
Unaware/unconscious	5
Just	5
Solidaristic	5
Humble	4
Interested in culture	4
Happy	3
Child loving	3
Authoritarian	2
Aggressive	1
Feminine	1
Masculine	<0.5
Sexy	<0.5
Artistic	<0.5

When interpreting these figures, we should bear in mind that the respondents were asked to name "three attributes that describe Swedes." Hence it may be that the respondents actually thought that many of the other characteristics mentioned were also typical for Swedes. For example, "technical" was selected by 7 percent, but we do not know how many others would also have listed it if they had been able to mention more than three attributes.

None of the students in Takac's survey mentioned "envious," which was mentioned by 49 percent of the adults in the SIFO survey. One possible explanation for this is differences in income, which can induce envy. In the SIFO study, 53 percent declared that envy arose when "one person is richer than another," and 20 percent said that when "people pay no tax because they have so many deductions," others envy them. It is in light of one's own income and social ambitions that such questions acquire significance, which of course does not mean that school children cannot feel envy. Twelve percent of the Swedes asked believed that envy was due to "one person being more powerful than another."

The paradoxical figures for "honest" (14 percent) and "dishonest" (11 percent) should be noted. The former is in accord with the traditional stereotype of Swedes; the latter relates to the more recent notion that Swedes have become cheats. Finally, it is worth pointing out that "xenophobic" (11 percent) seems not to have cropped up among the students, and this is confirmed by other studies (Westin 1984). Since the first edition of this book in 1989, however, xenophobia has been on the rise among young people as well as among the population as a whole.

A third survey comes from Swedish businesspeople with experience abroad. In her courses for Swedish export firms, Jean Phillips-Martinsson usually asks the participants to note down what they themselves consider typical for Swedes. At one of these courses (1985), the following characteristics were mentioned, without any particular rank order: well organized, reliable, rational, effective, punctual, well educated, correct, socially conscious, quality conscious, honest, polite, industrious, asocial, overbearing and smug, materialistic, narrowminded, envious, inhibited, have difficulties making friends, nonnationalistic, boring. As one might expect, many of the qualities mentioned by these businesspeople are traits considered beneficial to Swedish foreign trade: well organized, reliable, honest, rational, effective, quality-conscious; well educated—possibly also polite and correct. For a Swedish businessperson, to behave "correctly" is to behave honestly, to be reliable (stand by one's word, not demand private benefits or perks) and factual (keeping to facts, not talking "rubbish"). Behind the negative judgments—for instance, smugness, inhibited, boring—lie values stemming at least in part from the Swedish businesspeople's personal experiences of other nationalities, and in part from that national self-criticism common among well-traveled Swedes.

By "socially conscious," most Swedes mean Swedish welfare society, its social caring, its social and equal rights policies, a picture with which many immigrants would concur. "Materialistic" is a Swedish stereotype shared by Swedes and immigrants. In the 1985 SIFO study, "worldly" was referred to in more or less the same vein. The basic tone is negative, but there is a positive element in Swedes' pride in their high standards.

The contradiction between "nationalistic" in the SIFO study and "nonnationalistic" in the businesspeople's response is paradoxical: both terms encapsulate tendencies in present-day Sweden. The relative disregard for Swedish history (for example, in schools) compared with the nationalistic rhetoric in many other countries (for instance, in the United States; or consider the national delirium prevailing in Norway on its National Constitution Day) is considered avowedly "nonnationalistic." The same can be said for the seemingly weak protests against the submarine violations of Swedish waters (which "violations" probably, as well as ironically, were not made by submarines but by minke whales, according to a 1995 military analysis). Another sign of the lack of nationalism is the fact that many Swedes do not know their national anthem by heart. At the same time, marked "nationalistic" currents have been observed recently. Dramatic displays of anti-immigrant sentiments have been interpreted as indications of a nascent nationalism of the kind arising in other European countries, for example, in France and Germany. Since the writing of this book in 1987–88, nationalistic values have contributed to ethnic conflicts, even to open warfare, for example, in the former Yugoslavia and Soviet Union.

Most of the stereotypes mentioned in the three studies correspond in one way or another to real, or behavioral, tendencies comprehended as Swedish by Swedes when compared with their counterparts in other countries. At the same time, there is a tendency to deny the existence of a "national character," partly because the term sounds antiquated, partly because of its negative associations with racist ideologies. National character—is there such a thing? I have been asked this question many times. Swedish features such as rationality, efficiency, and punctuality are interpreted by many simply as aspects of modern industrial societies and consequently characteristic of many countries. So can these attributes in due course characterize all countries that approach Sweden's level of development? Many seem to think so.

Moreover, there is the notion that the Swedish way of "not being loud," declining conflicts, and compromising is generally good and desirable behavior. Other countries' deviations from these ideals and norms are considered just that—deviations—or possibly an inability to attain the same civilized level of behavior. This has to do with morally charged prejudices about what is "correct" and "mature" behavior. Ethnocentrism is a universal phenomenon, but it becomes particularly strong when it is bolstered, as it is in Sweden, by high living standards and by the absence of bloody conflicts.

Despite an inclination to deny the existence of a collectively shared culture (Austin 1968), it is, as I have shown, entirely possible to induce Swedes to list a number of Swedish character traits. But in their understanding of themselves Swedes seem generally to lack a historical perspective. Many Swedes are socially stiff and practically minded—why? There are few popular theories: one is climate. We Swedes do not sit in sidewalk cafés but huddle inside our houses. It is said that we are still an agrarian folk, practical but socially inept. Even within social science research, there is a relative dearth of ideas about how Swedish mentality came about. Theories concerning the effects of child-rearing on personality formation, which were so important in the early history of psychological anthropology, appear to be lacking in Sweden.

Be that as it may, I would postulate a "Swedishness" in the Swedish population: essentially a collectively shared way of behaving and comprehending the world—a fairly consistent or unified context of ideas, values, and feelings, in spite of all variations and deviations. This context has arisen from a common history and similar living conditions. Taking these factors into consideration, many of the Swedish peculiarities that have been described in this book—and many others besides—should be susceptible to a better understanding than that at present.

What can explain the regulations covering lit headlights in the Swedish traffic laws? Is the emphasis on security, both individual and institutional, that separates Sweden from its neighbors Norway and Denmark, a consequence of an inner insecurity and thus a compensation? Or is the emphasis on security only the most extreme consequence of policies steered by rationality, that is, the conviction that society must be shaped by practical, goal-oriented principles? What effect does the absence of any direct experience of two world wars have on the Swedish way of looking at things?

David Jenkins (1968) devotes an entire chapter to the recurring subject in foreign discussions of Sweden, namely, the "initiative issue." In his summary he suggests that individual initiative is not as developed in Sweden as it is in some other countries, but this is probably of less importance than one may think. Jenkins's point is that this does not make Swedes less happy; rather, it is a matter of taste. Lack of individual decisiveness may irritate some non-Swedes, but there is no sense in demanding that Swedes arrange their society to content foreigners (see Jenkins 1964, 131).

Many of the foreign observers who have written critically of Sweden and of the Swedes seem not to have properly understood that every nationality lives and experiences things on its own terms and within its own frames of reference. This, however, does not mean that certain foreign observers do not put their fingers on the truth when they contend that Swedes are more melancholy than some other people. At the same time, paradoxically enough, most Swedes declare they are happy, pleased with their lives. To a Swede, as to everyone, how people in other parts of the world look at life—that is, with what degree of pleasure they view their everyday existence—is largely unknown. People do not and cannot apply others' existential experiences and frames of reference to their own lives. People build their lives largely on their own expectations and knowledge of how others in their immediate surroundings live. Pretensions adapt to both individual and societal prerequisites.

In a study by Roger Bernow (1986), which measured subjective experiences of the quality of life, the following interview question was posed (to a nationally representative sample): "Are you generally satisfied or dissatisfied with life just now?" Only 7 percent admitted to be more or less dissatisfied. Fifty-five to 62 percent were "[f]or the most part satisfied," and 14 to 21 percent were "[e]ntirely satisfied" (the two figures represent responses to the same question asked on two different interview occasions). Another question was, "Are you generally happy or unhappy?" Of the 1,171 interviewed, 18 percent answered "very happy"; 58 percent, "fairly happy"; 18 percent, "neither happy nor unhappy." Only 2 percent answered "rather unhappy"; and 1 percent, "very unhappy."

One more way of measuring individuals' overall judgment of the quality of their lives was used when those interviewed were asked to indicate where they would place themselves on a scale regarding various experiences. The results, shown in table 5, indicate a pattern of response similar to those above. Bernow's results confirmed Allardt's Nordic study (1975), in which Swedes revealed a high degree of satisfaction with their lives.

Table 5 Subjective Experiences—Semantic Differential (in percent)

Always alone	1	3	4	14	9	29	39	Never alone
Empty	2	1	4	14	19	33	37	Full
Trusting	26	24	15	26	4	3	2	Distrustful
Boring	1	2	4	17	20	32	23	Interesting
Enjoyable	19	30	20	23	5	2	2	Miserable
Meaningless	2	2	3	15	16	33	30	Meaningful
Little possibility of realization	5	4	5	28	18	23	16	Many possibilities of realization
Many friends	31	24	16	20	5	3	1	No friends
Successful	29	31	17	18	3	1	1	Unsuccessful

Source: Bernow 1986, 18.

Even if the total impression of my description of certain typical personality traits—melancholy and social insecurity, for example—seems negative, it does not confute the experienced positive quality of life revealed by the responses to questions in these surveys. As has been mentioned, we are most likely dealing with two different things.

There is, however, a theoretical complication with regard to people's self-declared happiness, a complication similar to that of the Marxist thesis of the false consciousness of the working class. Some people are so "alienated" that they cannot experience alienation. Joakim Israel has noted that "[o]thers experience normal feelings of alienation, but they do not consider this psychological condition as anything extraordinary. Either they have not pondered [these feelings], or they believe they are 'normal.' At some point they may see that something is wrong, but do not think they can do anything about it" (Israel 1968, 57).

The psychoanalyst Daniel Casriel (1972) holds that "human emotions today are pretty much as they were half a million years ago, whereas the nature of culture has geometrically multiplied the complexities of our civilization. As civilization becomes ever more dehumanized, the individual becomes more isolated, alienated from a world that appears to require him to anaesthetize himself from his most deeply felt emotional needs." Casriel (1972, 111) goes on to say that

> [t]oday this thought has been stated so frequently that it is a cliché: The demands of civilization are at odds with man's vital emotional needs.
>
> Forced to repress the expression of these needs, the alienated person either retreats behind a socially acceptable facade or behaves in a distorted, often destructive way that temporarily relieves some of the pressure of his buried needs. Neither "solution" really works; neither is a direct expression of that person's emotional core. An important part of the individual is denied expression. He is alienated from himself and from the world in which he exists.

There is a theoretical-needs perspective that postulates that humans have certain fundamental psychic—"psychogenic"—needs. Culture, or civilization, disposes of various possibilities for satisfying these needs. Culture also contains a number of conditions or circumstances that help to form a predominant personality structure in a society. Personality does possess a biological basis, but it is also shaped by the surrounding environment, which is both individual and collective.

The shaping of the personality begins in the first moment of life, initially in interaction with the mother, then with others in an ever widening social circle, from childhood through adulthood. The individual always responds by adjusting to surrounding conditions in one way or another, and this imprints itself on the personality. Although culture strongly influences the personality, there are great variations because all individuals are not equally equipped biologically and because each life progresses in its own particular way from its inception.

Casriel views the people he describes as "character disordered," as in part victims of their culture. "They are emotionally immature, self-centered, low in empathy for all except those who share their own emotional orientation" (Casriel 1972, 166). The key to the symptoms of character disorder lies in behavior. According to Casriel, many symptoms are strikingly destructive, but others seem positive: outward perfection, for instance, exemplified by hardworking professional people, often successful in their careers, or women who have impeccable homes, where everything shines and everything is in its place and where they put on perfect dinner parties.

Casriel's concept of character disorder encompasses features of the modal Swedish personality: heavy stress on *duktighet* (being capable, efficient), punctuality, outward order, and "emotional immaturity"—that is, egocentricity and detachment. This may seem an unfriendly caricature, to say the least, but I think the perspective worth considering.

It is remarkable that many character-disordered personalities actually manage to perceive that something is wrong. If they go into therapy, they can be motivated to relate their symptoms and their past, but they rationalize and defend themselves and resist the therapist. They can be in individual therapy for years without making any progress. They seem basically to consider their behavior normal, which it is in that it is shared by a significant portion of the population and is part of a cultural pattern. Like Abram Kardiner and Karen Horney, Casriel underlines the cultural influences on the human organism.

In addition to "flight" and "fight," Casriel discerns a third way to react to danger, a way characteristic of neurotics and of the character-disordered and included in Kardiner's psychodynamic theory: "freeze"—freezing or paralyzing. "This is the repression of emotion—which I call 'detachment'—and the thought and behavioral intent of isolating oneself from the source of danger." As examples, Casriel mentions patients who as children learned to suppress anger or who as boys learned that they should not cry but should instead show "manliness," not cry for help but sort things out themselves. Casriel describes American masculine ideals, but they sound familiar, recognizable also as essentially Swedish. The result of detachment can amount to a neurotic condition, full of the pain of anxiety, but the reaction can go a step further, into a condition of feeling neither pain nor anger. The character-disordered person has completely suppressed all emotions.

When faced with emotional stresses, the character-disordered personality, like the tortoise, seeks protection under his or her shell. This defense may take the form of an attitude that effectively shields one from all people other than one's own small group—family, one's few close friends. (Is a Swedish cultural pattern discernible here?) Other reactions may involve single-mindedly devoting oneself to a professional career or building up a high material standard of living—but also, now and then, going on a binge. Even nymphomania is a shield that is used to reinforce the suppression of fear and rage.

A character-disordered person can be withdrawn and behave mildly, passively, reservedly, politely—again, features we recognize as Swedish. They can also be aggressively angry as a defense against attempts to change their behavior. Behavior is experienced, after all, as self-evident, which it is because it is a product of certain circumstances, partly stemming from culture. So character-disordered persons generally answer in the affirmative when questioned whether they are satisfied with their lives—that is, when given the sorts of questions Bernow and Allardt posed. They lack the neurotics' "insight into" or presentiment of a problem or an illness, claiming that they are healthy and normal.

However, Casriel maintains that it is self-destructive constantly to withdraw from one's feelings. Impassivity is a pathological defense, but a "vulnerable" one. This impression of Swedishness belongs to the field that has been especially remarked by non-Swedes. I have met immigrants who have expressed deep sympathy with Swedes because the immigrants see this pattern so clearly in Sweden, where so much energy is devoted to protecting oneself.

I have generously, even uncritically, quoted from Casriel's description of character disorder. Possibly one should differentiate between *character neurosis*, originating in unconscious conflicts rooted in early emotional lacunae, and such *characters*, as, for example, the obedient character, *inter alia* with a compulsion for order, which Casriel describes and which may be better explained in terms of the psychology of learning. However, I have not referred to this theoretical perspective to demonstrate that Swedes are character disordered—that would be an altogether too simple conclusion. Casriel talks about Americans, and even if his definition of character disorder can be applied to Swedes, it can as well be applied to people in other Western countries. This is what one should expect from other sides of the psychiatric picture. It would be interesting to know how common character disorders are in various Western countries. It is in the distribution, the frequency, that conditions indigenous or specific to a given country are expressed.

I have presented Casriel's ideas for another purpose: *to show how problematic it is to employ subjective well-being indicators.* What is interesting about Casriel in this respect is his description of patients' lack of self-awareness; *they basically consider their behavior as normal simply because it is part of a cultural pattern*—whether or not the behavior stems from a character neurosis or is learned.

Irrespective of future conclusions concerning culture's effects on people living in Sweden, it is important to understand that culture— at most, the total environment: people, society, the state, technology, nature—actually pervades our thoughts, feelings, and actions. Culture can make us cruel, cynical, anti-intellectual, egocentric— effects the social anthropologist Jules Henry has likened to those of a Greek tragedy, but without the gods (Henry 1973).

It may seem that people today have become more cruel and more self-centered than they were before, even though making such historical comparisons is hopeless. But cruelty need not go hand in hand with self-centeredness. War provokes cruelty and insensitivity, but it can also create solidarity and unity within the ranks. In present-day Sweden the tendency is rather the opposite: respect for human life is great, but "love [for] thy neighbor" is on the wane, if by that we mean a concern for immigrants and foreigners, for one's neighbors, consideration of others, and so on (see Nisbet 1953). Disregarding for a moment how these things are empirically measured, we can affirm that the ruling tendencies in a culture may be negative and destructive (consider the "paranoid" Dobu people described by Bock [1980], or Jules Henry's critical book on the United States [1964], or the historical explanations [e.g., Masur 1975], based on German mentality, for the Germans' support of national socialism).

If now indeed many Swedes are shy and socially insecure, if they strive for autonomy, feel extremely uneasy confronting personal conflicts, have difficulties expressing and receiving strong emotions, feel all the more secure with matter-of-factness and rationality—it comes from somewhere. If they truly conceive of themselves as individualistic but are not all that happy without the support of a collective, it is not just by chance. If many Swedes are comparatively quiet, slow, serious, possibly even gloomy—in any case hardly lighthearted even though theirs is a self-image of being nice, cheerful, and happy—then all these tendencies are consequences of Sweden as a social organization and historical product, of those institutions and natural preconditions that apply in our part of the world. The cultural pattern, whatever it may be (varied and partly inconsistent), has not been developed from any sort of collective intention. On the contrary, it is the consequence of historical processes over which no government rules.

In my opinion, the most appropriate attitude to all this is respect, not condemnation, possibly not even criticism. Insight and self-knowledge are most important. Efforts to reform or change are not meaningless, but neither are they very effective. We are not omnipotent and cannot like gods reshape the world according to our own designs.

Is There a Swedish Cultural Code?

Is it at all possible to distinguish a Swedish cultural code, or perhaps a set of several codes (or principles) that cover all the domains of culture and that characterize Swedish society? As Kaplan and Manners (1972) pointed out, it is as difficult to detect uniform traits as it is to discern a modal personality (although attempts have been made in the early history of anthropology). One might expect that psychological anthropologists would employ psychological instruments and sampling techniques to expose these mental complexes. However, such is hardly the case.

In his study of child-care centers (1983) Billy Ehn has distinguished insecurity as a characteristic of this Swedish subworld. I have complementary data from entirely different areas that point in the same direction but with different nuances, depending on the context. I have felt it important to secure a quantitative basis for this and other hypotheses. Even if support could be found, I decline here to answer whether there are grounds for postulating an "insecurity syndrome" as a *Swedish cultural code*. There is the smell of the conjurer around such propositions, as there is around Ruth Benedict's concept of configuration. But as a research subject it certainly is tempting.

Perhaps "deconstructing" the concept of culture as a coherent cognitive system is warranted. I see an important point in this post-modern view, but empirical studies show that actual patterns and regularities do exist, though certainly not corresponding to the traditional concept of culture as a consistent and clear-cut entity. Present-day, modern, multicultural Sweden is tending to become considerably more differentiated and culturally heterogeneous.

The anthropologist Anthony Wallace (1961) has discerned some advantages of such a cognitive multiplicity. He claims that it serves two important purposes: (*a*) it allows a system to evolve that is more complex than most are able to comprehend, and (*b*) it liberates the participants in the system from the heavy burden of knowing one another's motivations. But above all, no "fundamental personality" or cognitive framework, shared by all, is needed for classes, groups, colleagues, parties, families, or clans to have anything to do with one another. What is needed is only that their actions be predictable and equivalent.

Wallace's reflection, however, does not exclude the possibility that certain common preconditions in history, social strata, demography, social composition, language, nature, and so forth, have actually provided the grounds for certain patterns that represent a kinship in personality, view of the world, and cognitive orientation.

The History of Swedishness

Why have Swedes become as they are? It is difficult enough *to describe* certain features of Swedish mentality, but at least there are accessible data to turn to for support; *to explain* these features is infinitely more difficult. Even so, the question *why* continually crops up.

To explain a culture is a well-nigh futile enterprise for research. As young students in social anthropology, it was pounded into us that we should take culture as "given": our business as anthropologists concerned what happened *within* the framework of culture. A culture is formed by countless elements or circumstances interacting in intricate patterns that available historical sources seldom permit us to follow.

Nevertheless, explanations for particular features of national mentalities do exist. To a degree these are speculative, some empirically better anchored than others. However, the only method of explanation is to ascertain whether historical conditions have existed from which the patterns we wish to explain can be deduced; that is, the only method of explanation is to propose a theoretical model. As long as the sources offer no alternative causal connections, we have to accept "the present standpoint of scholarship." All research results are preliminary—what we have "so far."

To explain Swedes' practical talents David Jenkins (1968, 20) suggests the "many centuries of battle against the hostile elements in a vast, cold, damp and sparsely settled country." He contends that harsh conditions have produced a specific psychological adaptation. Historically, Swedes have continually had to find practical solutions. Jenkins finds it perfectly understandable that "some of the most notable Swedish advances have been in the field of hydroelectric power" and that "the Swedish genius should express itself primarily in the mechanical arts." Moreover, "this interest in the mechanical has had a gigantic impact on life in general: the goal in organizing society has tended to be the same as that in constructing a machine—i.e. to get it into proper working order" (Jenkins 1968, 21).

We should not dismiss this hypothesis too hastily. It is hard for people today to perceive or immediately comprehend the consequences that living so far north had not so very long ago. Even into the present century, Sweden was one of the poorest countries in Europe, among other things because of its particularly harsh climate with long winters and short growing seasons. Today, Swedes mostly complain about occasional problems getting their cars started and high heating bills, while shopping in comfort in well-stocked supermarkets.

In preindustrial Sweden, time was almost completely occupied with battling natural forces, and relations between people were primarily working relations in which both children and old people participated. The Swedish household was first and foremost a unit of production.

I have deliberately presented an unnuanced picture of conditions in this agrarian society in order to illuminate its character. "Leisure time" existed, even though the term did not. People went to church, went to the markets, and got together at annual festivals like Midsummer and Christmas, and at events like weddings and funerals.

Nevertheless, life was dominated by work. There was probably little opportunity for developing a rich emotional life (see Maslow's theory of needs hierarchy, in which basic needs are satisfied first), and the prerequisites for openly exposing one's feelings hardly existed either. This is not to say that people could not be filled with rage or despair or feelings of joy and love. But it is likely that the relatively subordinate position of feelings and emotional expressions in present-day Sweden originate in past existential conditions. We know from modern sociology of work that people doing heavy, strenuous physical labor are generally incapable of much except rest during their free time.

To sum up the psychological consequences of the above observations: people who do not have time, energy, or motivation to be interested in other people's nonmaterial sides tend to communicate with each other about practical matters and establish relations more through actions than through words. And words tend to be the vocabulary of requests, questions, factual information. Children are instructed, warned, reprimanded. Adults discuss work—the distribution of labor and its results—and the caprices of nature. This is a simplified picture, but previously in Sweden, it was only by very hard labor, "the sweat of one's brow," that one survived the winter. There was no mercy for the idle.

People worked in the fields, in the forests; they fished. They worked in barns and outbuildings, in the cabin or farmhouse repairing things, doing carpentry and woodwork, sewing—days and evenings alike. In such circumstances they basically met only their own household members and their nearest neighbors.

The advent of popular movements—evangelical churches, the temperance society, the labor movement—generated another sort of communal life. However, these contexts were also very goal oriented and pragmatic: people worked together, albeit some latitude was given to socializing, involving the same people one worked with—mainly people from the village or the immediate district. One was part of a collective experience and shared with others a traditional perspective on life and the world at large.

Such was the Swedish countryside, where the vast majority of the population lived until well into the twentieth century. Those who moved into the growing urban areas (in large numbers as late as after World War II) were relatively taciturn and practically oriented people. They had lived in farmhouses, cottages, and farmworker's dwellings and were used to meeting primarily with people of their own kind. Their world was formed by working life and practical contingencies: *getting things done.* The emphasis on the practical aspects of work was distilled into a particular attitude toward life and people, which was directly reflected in child-rearing:

> In extreme cases, the infant should be chastised and purified from original sin. The child's will must be broken as soon as it shows itself. In this system, work was the most important factor in child-rearing. This accords with the spirit of the times. Mercantile texts often assert the advantages of early

forced labor for children. Discipline and work were different sides of the same coin. Harshness toward children was
often explained and defended by citing the Bible. (Szabo
1971, 20)

Playfulness, tenderness, and anger over "not getting what one
wants," which today are recognized as basic elements of children's
psychology, were given much less attention and were much less accepted in peasant society. Rather, newcomers to the community had
to bite their tongues and learn the skills they had to learn as quickly
as possible. This perhaps leads us to some of the historical background to Swedish restraint, to the fear of making a fool of oneself,
to emotional control, to the stress on industriousness and visible
achievement, and to a particular conformist adaptation.

Let us look at present-day archetypical Swedish mentality—even
though it naturally contains elements that in varying degrees appear in other cultures. A relatively introverted and socially insecure
Swede can be expected to strive for independence and self-sufficiency, that is, endeavor to retain his or her peace of mind through
being socially closed while also being "opportunistically" inclined
toward the collective view and afraid of taking an individual stand.

Akin to this is the Swedish avoidance of conflict, the verbal defen-
selessness of the taciturn and factually minded against expressions
of rage, but also the stiff clumsiness when trying to be affectionate.
This in turn leads, it seems to me, to taciturnity or reticence (the
foremost characteristic of shy people), slowness (the irresolution of
the socially insecure), and seriousness and melancholy (the state of
mind of the dutiful and grave). That many Swedes deviate from this
pattern renders it no less a Swedish modal personality pattern.

Among the secondary factors are the institutions that carry the
Swedish mentality on and through which the socializing process,
commencing in the treatment of children during their infancy and
early childhood, is realized. The (psychologically) early "separation" from the mother, training in self-sufficiency and independence, fits theoretically into this outline.

The adult modal personality is confirmed on a daily basis by a
socially norm-fulfilling style. This means that individuals whose basic personality deviates from the modal—the most common—are
prone to imitate the prevailing style because of the punishment-and-

reward system exercised by social control. Those people who are more aggressive than most soon discover the benefits of restraint, "grit their teeth and bite their tongue." Garrulous people are given reasons for thinking twice. All this applies not only to Swedes but also to immigrants who, intentionally or not, approach the common or Swedish way of being.

The Swedish pattern appears like a theme with variations, and this should be kept in mind when considering all generalizations about Swedish mentality. "To portion out milk in the local coop does not provide the same experiences of class as does standing behind the perfume counter in a department store," note Frykman and Löfgren in *Moderna tider* (Modern times) (1985, 96).

Certain traits appear more uniform than others—for instance, the practical, factual orientation—but also here differences may be observed.

Other socializing institutions include public agencies, the organizations and authorities that issue from the collective. To an especially high degree they seem to synthesize and shape basic patterns of culture. In Swedish bureaucracy, Swedish "impersonality" becomes even more impersonal, and the fidelity to rules and the neutral, standardized treatment of each individual are shaped by a supreme principle—no longer tendencies with many exceptions. In health care, technical treatment becomes the prime aim; in child-care centers or kindergarten, avoiding conflict becomes a pedagogical dogma. The public institutions thus acquire a culturally socializing function that etches itself into immigrants' conception of their new country.

The insights of research into shyness as a personal problem can be applied to Swedish social structure and history. When confronted with new types of people whose norms and expectations are not well known, one becomes anxious about their reactions. This can happen when, for example, one moves from the countryside into the city. Those who change social class and consequently encounter people in situations and with expectations they are not familiar with feel social anxiety. Shyness also follows in the wake of dramatic changes in society itself, in which the individual is forced to handle encounters with people in new contexts and with new demands on personal performance.

Sweden exemplifies all three phenomena. Urbanization arrived late but dramatically. The leveling of income, changes in the labor market, and educational reforms have combined to produce a particularly pronounced social mobility. In a study covering 1975–85 it was found that every third person in higher management or administration came from a working-class household (Vogel 1987, 109).

Also in other respects Sweden has been transformed over the last fifty years to a degree that has few parallels in the world. According to Hofstede's previously cited study of forty countries, Swedes demonstrate the least resistance to change. During the postwar period, Sweden has acquired an international reputation as an experimental workshop for social reforms. The similarities to the self-declared but not culturally accepted communication anxiety that has been documented among Americans can be explained by the enormous—and similar—changes that the United States has undergone during the same period.

Taciturnity and Swedish History

Despite the similarities in the occurrence of communication apprehension among Swedes and Americans, there is less "willingness to communicate" in Sweden than in the United States, probably because Americans are far more extroverted than Swedes (Daun, Burroughs, and McCroskey 1988). Americans' generally greater willingness to talk gives us an interesting perspective on the peculiarities of Swedish society. In American social history from colonization onward, personality characteristics like progressiveness and strength have been fostered. The person to whom these features do not come naturally is motivated to appropriate them, or in any case to conceal such a handicap. Sweden's political and cultural history has been very different. Both secular and religious authorities have implanted personal humility or modesty and erased pride and self-assertion from people's social manner.

In the particularly heterogeneous America, with its reputedly "lawless" Wild West, personal address or greeting functioned as a way of ensuring a stranger's friendly intentions (in the same way that in Sweden it feels safer to offer greetings when encountering an unknown man on a dark and isolated forest path). In homogeneous

Sweden, such a need to address or greet strangers has never acquired anything like a comparable institutionalized form.

Against this background, it is understandable that the population of the United States has developed a social pattern encouraging or favoring social intercourse, and a social history that promotes extrovert personalities as well as norms disapproving of shy behavior. This is the case even though other sides of American social development—social and geographic mobility, for instance—have resulted in *feelings* of shyness that in scope resemble the Swedish.

The Formalized Swedish Society

Compared with many other countries, in modern Sweden people need to use informal contact networks much less to find work and housing, to obtain papers and forms from public authorities, and so forth. Swedish society is heavily technically formalized and is meant to treat everyone the same: individuals line up in a queue, register their interest or requests on a form, order papers or forms from public agencies by telephone. These arrangements involve a minimum of social contact and do not in principle presume any active engagement on those occasions requiring face-to-face contact. Certain personal characteristics can indeed be an advantage in Swedish bureaucratic contexts, but generally the informal side is less important. Unlike in France, for example, and in Mediterranean countries in general, in Sweden a shy, reticent, and socially inactive person is not unfairly treated in contacts with the authorities. Having powerful friends or the ability to argue, offering bribes, being charming or aggressive, and so on, are much less help in Sweden than in many other places in the world. Secondary relations may be reduced to a minimum.

Overall, the Swedish societal system does not encourage the shaping of a socially active and energetic manner of relating to people outside one's family, circle of friends, and workmates. This hypothesis does not exclude the possibility that a previous social order in Sweden, before the advent of our modern technical bureaucracy, did indeed place informal demands on contacts. On this point I can only speculate.

The Boundary Between Private and Public

One theory that occasionally crops up in Swedish ethnology is that the great land parceling reforms of the eighteenth and nineteenth centuries had a major negative effect on cooperation and contacts between villagers (see Ek 1960). Previously scattered allotments and fields were combined into connected units, and even farm houses and other buildings were eventually moved out from densely built villages. In this way were created the dispersed settlements that are today so common in the Swedish countryside.

These reforms resulted in people's not meeting their neighbors as often as they had before. Also, the collaboration that had been required by the mixing of fields disappeared. Previously, villages functioned much more as labor collectives; after the land reforms the pattern of social intercourse was more oriented to each person's family or household. Villagers certainly continued to have social contact and to cooperate but less so than before. Possibly contemporary Swedes' relatively reticent and passive style of communication can be attributed to these historical changes in the economic organization and settlement pattern of rural society.

Very likely, agrarian Sweden generally offered fewer meeting places than most other countries and therefore less social "training" than, for example, countries that created institutions such as the *Bierstube*, *taverna*, *café*, *pub* (that these countries were also much more densely populated should also be taken into account). The few Swedish rural taverns or inns were primarily for travelers. The social environments in temperance meeting halls, missions, and labor movement's *Folkets Hus* (the community, or "people's," hall) came closest to the social atmosphere in cafés in southern Europe. Generally, however, Swedes seem to have spent most of their time in their cottages and within their own farm community. The harsh climate contributed to this, as it did to the necessity of particularly long working days.

Homogeneous Culture

A homogeneous population fairly seldom encounters strangers or foreigners with different lifestyles and values, hardly in church and seldom at the market. Historically in Sweden there were Finns, Jews, Lapps, Gypsies, German merchants, Belgian Walloon smiths, and other minorities, but encounters with these groups in the countryside were relatively rare—except for those with Finns and Lapps in certain regions.

This has thwarted the development of social improvisation in Sweden compared with that in many other countries that for centuries have contained mixtures of ethnic groups and languages. However, homogeneity has probably reduced the risk of conflicts, especially those provoked by differences in values and general group animosity.

In a homogeneous culture like the Swedish the individual assumes that other people are as they seem, that they mean what they say. Outward behavior is presumed to mean the same to others as it does to oneself and one's intimates. Nonverbal communicative signals are probably less important than they are in heterogeneous cultures. Only minimal verbal codes are required to turn people's thoughts in the desired direction.

In a homogeneous culture like the Swedish it is easier to categorize people—the person who says "rowt" for "route" *is* like that: "He is like that because he has such views; she is like that because she dresses like that." Individually conveyed views, ideas, information, and so on, are interpreted as symbols of a uniform and easily classifiable identity. Consequently, we have the caution in speech and generous pauses that distinguish Swedes from other Europeans outside Scandinavia: Swedes are particularly concerned to consider the next step or utterance in their verbal communication. One cannot simply talk and talk without considering how it will be interpreted by others. Words are not like "air," as the saying goes in France; spoken words are heavy symbols.

A great deal can be linked to homogeneity—to the fact that sameness or uniformity is not only general but indeed sought after. From this follows a modesty, humility, the desire not to stick out, caution with everything that can cause people to "stop and stare," the same symbolic reduction of one's own person and one's family that outside of Scandinavia is so typical of Japan (another homogeneous society). The negative side of modesty is codified in the *Jantelagen*—containing not only a tacit proscription of boasting but also the admonition that "you have nothing to be proud of."

The stress on sameness complicates face-to-face disputes, since confrontations divide people, ideas, and meanings. Open conflicts are the greatest enemy of uniformity: the person who seeks uniformity or sameness wants to conceal differences. This also explains why Swedes prefer to socialize with "their own," preferably in small groups that seldom change in composition. In the circle of one's own family and intimate friends, one need not dissemble, adapt, look for common interests and areas of agreement. Unattained sameness—the difficulties expressing one's own uniqueness—explains, on the other hand, the inclination to retire into solitude, the wish to be "left in peace."

Does the Need for Self-Sufficiency Stem from Agrarian Settlement Patterns?

Before the land reforms, farms in Sweden depended upon each other for all sorts of cooperative labor—maintenance of fences, harvesting crops, haying, helping each other with house building and with various other economic contingencies. Some of these ties remained after the reforms and new types of dependency relations arose in tandem with the spread of the crofters' holdings and state system at the end of the eighteenth century. However, households' interdependence generally lessened, and in the present century the development in agriculture has been toward total economic autonomy.

Even so, the "etiology" of the need for independence remains particularly difficult to grasp and is complicated by the fact that very early in Swedish history the special arrangements concerning the inheritance of property (*undantagsinstitutionen*) and the corresponding contract between adult children and their parents expressed the special value awarded to independence and self-sufficiency. An alternative explanation might be derived from the homogeneity of the Swedish population, which supports the stress on sameness, and therefore on independence (because by becoming dependent one becomes unequal). Independence for each individual fosters symmetrical relations.

Social Stress, Past and Present

The meager and precarious conditions for making a living in rural Sweden doubtless caused stress, worry, and anxiety. The relative absence of such conditions in more modern times seems largely to have removed this factor, even though other sources of stress have arisen. The absence of war, revolution, foreign occupation, and political turbulence should have set its stamp on Swedish mentality. Since the Second World War Sweden has been particularly stable and, until the 1990s, economically successful. The development of the Swedish welfare state has given further cause for Sweden to be a "low-anxiety country."

This lower degree of social stress in comparison with that in many other parts of the world may amount to a psychological prerequisite for the relatively low incidence of Swedish interpersonal disputes. The fairly stable mood levels, the relative paucity of worry and anxiety in Sweden, presumably has a positive effect on human relations, which are anyway very much directed toward practical goals. Problems tend not to be taken as emotionally—"sparks fly" perhaps less often in Sweden than in other places.

In a society in which face-to-face conflicts occur relatively seldom, a rich repertoire of aggressions is less likely to be established. A Swede who is exposed to an impertinence usually lacks the habit of swift retort. The lack of ability to quarrel renders a quarrel an even more unpleasant experience—something to avoid.

The pragmatism prominent in so many contexts should work to motivate many Swedes *consciously* to avoid complicating conflicts, for instance, through compromise. Restraining aggressive feelings becomes, together with these and other characteristics, a lifestyle, which is rewarded through achieving the practical goals it promotes so well. The contrast with children's and many foreigners' alleged incapacities in these respects serves to reaffirm this cultural pattern.

Gloominess and the Work Ethic

Levity is fostered neither by the Protestant work ethic nor by an achievement-based identity derived from the necessities of the old agrarian society—industriousness, assiduous hard work. Sensual pleasures could be indulged in (in moderation, of course) as a distraction or as a well-deserved reward, but they should be "earned." According to Peabody (1985), the Protestant ethic tends to expound "impersonal virtues" such as honesty or diligence at the expense of "interpersonal virtues" such as warmth or forbearance.

With a life perspective oriented toward performance, it is probably difficult for many individuals temporarily to adjust themselves to take advantage of opportunities for sensual pleasures; their serious goal orientation remains intransigent. There may also be some guilt feelings, especially if their "indulgence" or indolence lasts too long.

However, alcohol helps many Swedes to relax. Alcohol permits a different identity, even without being very intoxicated. Liberating its user from the norms prescribing emotional control and from the pressures of everyday problems, alcohol acquires a pivotal value. Nevertheless, the next day many Swedes may suffer from a bad conscience. Despite being temporary, the altered identity brought about through alcohol is after all a breach of norms, and the attitude toward alcohol has long been ambiguous.

Changes in Swedishness

What has been discussed in this book is "modern" Swedish culture and personality, more or less from the 1960s through the 1980s. In the present chapter, I have pointed out several historical circumstances that may have contributed to the patterns I described earlier in the book.

Whereas the concept of national character may give the impression of something historically permanent and genetically entrenched, mentality is mutable. In fact, mentality changes in tandem with society. For example, it is likely that present-day youth, born around 1950–55, have better contact with their feelings and are not as uniformly oriented toward logic and factualness as their parents and older relatives. Still, certain environmental factors are particularly stable: climate is one (although climatic changes do occur), as is geographical location and the position of—in this case—

Swedish as a minority language. Sweden has been and still is sparsely populated. Lutheranism still permeates Swedish thinking to a considerable degree. Sweden's fate to have avoided war and military threat for so long is also one of the more enduring historical circumstances to be taken into account.

To this should be added what are usually called "tenacious structures," more commonly termed in French *la longe durée*. Mentality is indeed altered through outside influences, but because it is transferred from one generation to another through upbringing and because it manifests itself in the very construction of society, its organizations and institutions—themselves socializing—a fairly durable historical continuity is guaranteed.

Swedes themselves are no less altered over time. Immigrants who came to Sweden after the Second World War have related in interviews how much more "stiff" Swedes were then. Things seemed more formal, hierarchical, serious. Impulses from the mass media, "Americanization" of, *inter alia*, youth culture, increased mobility (more travel abroad), substantial foreign immigration, the Social Democratic policy of equality (the so-called *du* reform of the 1960s, which erased the need for different forms of address for friends and other people)—all have helped to moderate the Swedish mentality.

If the behavioral tendencies that have long been observed prevail, future Swedes will be even more informal, more superficially extroverted, more adroit at communicating. These changes can already be perceived among contemporary Swedish youth, who seem rather different from what their parents were at the same age.

As a consequence of a less homogeneous society we can also expect a greater degree of indifference to strangers and thus an even more demarcated boundary around private life. Harsher surroundings augment the significance of the primary group for the individual.

In a more heterogeneous Sweden, with fewer internal loyalties and less identification with other people, honesty will also be curtailed. Swedes will be more cynical and less trusting of other people's basic goodness—hitherto a marked Swedish trait. Respect for politics and authorities has been noticeably declining. The stress on work and on the value of work has decreased in favor of family and leisure—a process that has been going on since the end of the war, accompanied by a gradual improvement in living standards, expanded leisure, and greater latitude given to hedonistic ideals.

The belief in rationality will presumably be increasingly challenged, spreading confusion as a result. More and more people have difficulties believing in the "grand modernization project"—that is, building up a modern, humane welfare state, with its quality of life and intrinsic rationality. There is little faith in the goal of completing this project, and indeed, developments generally do not point in such a direction.

Altered attitudes toward society and a diminished belief in the future increase "social stress." More and more Swedes will feel anger, irritation, and frustration and will give vent to these feelings. More and more will disregard verbal etiquette: they will talk loudly, interrupt each other, and so on. There will be a different style of communication, which is already evident among the younger generations.

Sweden and the other Scandinavian countries are becoming more and more culturally split and socially differentiated by being incorporated into a broader European and international context. Currently we see a greater fragmentation, with rather competitive ideologies and lifestyles. The economic gaps between social strata (which in Sweden have long been the most level in the world) have deepened. This will in the end bring about the weakening of the famous Swedish envy in that gaps between people will be considered part of the natural order: it is between equals that envy flourishes.

Appendix:
Two Fundamental Historical Preconditions

Earlier in this book I addressed the question whether there are any codes or principles that could be said to cover the entire domain of Swedish culture and thereby to characterize Swedish society. For example, can one refer to an "insecurity syndrome" as a Swedish cultural code? In the first Swedish edition of this book I left this question unanswered. However, during the editing of the present English edition I have been prompted to return to Anthony Wallace (1961). Wallace admitted the possibility that certain common prerequisites of history, political structure, demography, social composition, language, natural habitat, and so forth, provide the foundations for certain patterns that represent a kinship in personality, worldview, and cognitive orientation. To this Erich Fromm added a dialectic connection between institutions and personality traits.

To exemplify, consider social insecurity, or communication apprehension. This can of course be described as a personality trait with behavioral consequences in very divergent contexts, which hark back to a significant element in "a dominating Swedish cultural pattern." But Wallace refers to a more fundamental analytical level, which for my purposes I would use to distinguish, on the one hand, Sweden's geographical position and, on the other, its demography. Many values and patterns of behavior can be traced to these preconditions, in fact, nearly everything that has been discussed in this book. This means that these values and patterns of behavior can be logically generated in a model, the core of which consists of two conditions—one concerning nature and another concerning people.

Let me briefly explain my reasoning. Space does not allow any exhaustive treatment, but the perspective should be sufficiently simple for more or less immediate comprehension.

1. By geographical circumstances is meant Sweden's northern location: basically only Scandinavians live so far north. Characteristic of this location is an extremely short growing season, about three months long, during which time in the old agrarian society people had to "gather in their stores," to hoard in order to survive the rest of the year. Late springs and summers without much sun and with lots of rain could be catastrophic. The harsh living conditions have already been mentioned, as have some of their consequences, for instance, the stress on work and an active lifestyle—"doing" rather than "talking."

The opposite conditions in climatically more mild regions tend to foster the opposite lifestyle where one's work and occupation constitute less of the basis for one's social identity and where social intercourse and verbal communication play a correspondingly larger role.

This dichotomy has its counterpart in the personality: in the first instance, a "materialistic" orientation; in the second, a "spiritual." The materialistic involves a stress on the practical—"engineering" practical solutions—technical gifts, an aptitude for figures and exactitude, factualness (as opposed to speculativeness), interest in laboratory experiments and in how things actually function, having one's feet on the ground, an emphasis on the concrete (as opposed to the abstract); a need for order, doing one thing at a time, celebrating rational solutions (as opposed to emotional ones); a need for planning, organizational abilities, talking slowly, being reflective, pragmatic; oriented toward action; interested in the body (rather than the soul), gymnastics, jogging, health matters—some more than others being related to time-bound ideological trends.

The other side of this dichotomy, the spiritual personality, stresses ideas; is religious, artistic, speculative (as opposed to factual), strongly emotional; is steered by feelings; likes spontaneity, improvisation, social intercourse; possesses strong feelings of the here and now; is verbal; talks quickly—all of which may be said to be atypical of a majority of native Swedes.

2. Demographically, Sweden is characterized by ethnic homogeneity. Sweden is a "nation state," with one commonly shared language, religion, and, with few exceptions, history. This homogeneity is particularly striking in comparison with many other countries that for

centuries have been multicultural—with two or more languages and religions, and lacking a commonly shared political history. The Swedish population has indeed grown through immigration, but the immigrants have been gradually assimilated and their influence has pervaded Swedish culture as a whole and not led to cultural diversification or divisions. The internal differences that exist in Sweden with regard to gender, generations, social class, regional affiliation, and various subcultural divisions may limit this homogeneity, but they still permit us to place Sweden high on the scale of cultural homogeneity. Homogeneity favors a collectivist personality orientation; a heterogeneous population inclines toward an individualistic personality orientation.

Sweden's relative homogeneity not only constitutes a general pattern but simultaneously represents what is desirable—that is, an emphasis on the collective. Sameness between people is considered part of the natural order to the degree that it is seen as legitimate and worth striving for: the more alike, the better. From this issues a political commitment to equality between social classes and between the sexes, an emphasis on justice and equal treatment (and thus a particularly strong aversion to bribery, unfair benefits, corruption based on ties of friendship—which is not to say these things do not exist in Sweden), a fondness for symmetrical relations (and avoiding debts of gratitude), social independence, modesty, envy, group orientation, conformity of values and behavior, bullying, shyness, stressing politeness and manners through clear ritualistic subordination, speaking quietly, sanctions against interrupting, positive attitudes toward reticence or taciturnity, introversion, a positive view of intermittent solitude, elements of melancholy, conflict avoidance, and a strong aversion to violence.

The opposite of this—relative heterogeneity—provides the basis for an individualistic mentality, signified by a more positive attitude toward differences and individual deviations, toward originality, eccentricity, going one's own way, arguing for one's standpoints, being the object of other's positive attention, being self-assured and extroverted, being demanding and boastful, the tendency to interrupt, speaking loudly, communicative competence, verbal alacrity, being confrontative, the relative acceptance of hierarchical and asymmetrical relations, dislike of compromise, social instrumentality, and a lower degree of identification with strangers.

I could mention more, but my intention is not to make an exhaustive list but to combine seemingly divergent values and behavior into a pattern representing a similarity in personality, worldview, and cognitive orientation. This kinship stems from the commonly shared preconditions on the superordinated geographic and demographic levels mentioned above. However, it should be noted that there certainly are hypotheses concerning connections that are not so easily incorporated into this model of materialism and collectivism.

It is one thing to formulate a single theory that would seem to explain a large number of phenomena—a generally acclaimed scientific ideal. In principle, more important in the present context is that these phenomena can be described as universal human variants, that only on an empirically superficial level can they be described as results of historical serendipity—as unique or almost unique products of chance combinations of certain historical preconditions: for example, the value awarded in Sweden to showing humility or modesty and the different ways in which this occurs. At the same time, such behavior represents a universal relation between people that is emphasized more or less, depending on the particular society. I would suggest that the variation in this emphasis depends on where the society's culture lies on a scale between collectivism and individualism.

From this conclusion we may deduce that cultural variation as a whole is more limited than we think, in any case in contrast with people's experience of an enormous variety. Admittedly, this statement is hardly revolutionary, but it has implications for everyday thought and for politically related opinion formation: for instance, people's attitudes toward other countries, attitudes toward immigrants and refugees, in other words, views of other "cultures." If it may be claimed that people think and act within certain given frameworks (introvert/extrovert, more or less impulse controlling, materialistic/spiritualistic) that are specific to the species Homo sapiens, and that the surrounding conditions in nature and among people determine where societies and groups land on these scales, then the possibilities exist for transforming an existential feeling of chaos into an insight into order. Put another way: in their creation of culture, people react to certain existing conditions. Considering this, when confronting any culture, we lack tenable grounds for giving way to either surprise, rage, or pride.

References

Adler, Peter. 1977. Bostadsnormer i sex länder. Ph.D. diss., Arkitektursektionen, KTH, Byggnadsfunktionslära, Stockholm.

Adorno, Theodor, et al. 1950. *The authoritarian personality*. New York: Harper.

Allardt, Erik. 1975. *Att ha, att älska, att vara*. Stockholm: Argos.

———. 1986. Kring ombytligheter i mänskliga samhällen. In *"Mentaliteter,"* edited by Per Sällström. Abo: Abo Akademi.

Allport, G. W., and H. S. Odbert. 1936. *Trait names: A psycho-lexical study*. Psychological Monographs, no. 47. (Whole no. 211).

Allwood, Jens. 1981. Finns det svenska kommunikationsmönster? In *Vad är svensk kultur?* (Essays from a symposium in Göteborg, May), 6–50. Papers in Anthropological Linguistics, 9. Göteborg: University of Göteborg.

Alopaeus, Marianne. 1983. *Drabbad av Sverige*. Stockholm: Brombergs.

Alsmark, Gunnar. 1984. Landet lagom: Några aspekter på svensk kultur. In *Är lagom bäst? Om kulturmöten i Sverige*, 133–53. Norrköping: Statens Invandrarverk.

Andersen, Bert Rold. 1984. Rationality and irrationality of the Nordic welfare state. *Daedalus: Journal of the American Academy of Arts and Sciences* 13, (winter): 109–39.

Anton, Thomas. 1975. *Governing greater Stockholm: A study of policy development and system change*. Berkeley and Los Angeles: University of California Press.

Austin, Paul Britten. 1968. *On being Swedish*. London: Secker & Warburg.

Baksi, Mahmut. 1976. *Hörru'du*. Stockholm: Författarens bokmaskin (Immigrant-Institutet).

Barzini, Luigi. 1964. *The Italians*. New York: Atheneum.

Berendt, Mogens. 1983. *Fallet Sverige: Förmyndarsamhället får en dansk skalle*. Stockholm: Bonnier Fakta.

Bergman, Erland, and Bo Swedin. 1982. *Vittnesmål: Invandrares syn på diskrimineringen i Sverige*. Stockholm: Publica.

Bernow, Roger. 1985. Livskvaliteten i Sverige: Frågor till svenska folket 1982. Typescript.

——. 1986. *Subjektiva välfärdsindikatorer*. Stockholm: Delegationen för Social Forskning.

Bjurström, C. G. 1984. "Det svenska" från fransk horisont. In *Att vara svensk* (Lectures at the Royal Academy of Letters, History, and Antiquities symposium, 12–13 April 1994, conference 13), 157–67. Stockholm: Royal Academy of Letters, History, and Antiquities.

Blomquist, Clarence. [1969] 1975. *Psykiatri*. Stockholm: Esselte Studium.

Bock, Philip K. 1980. *Continuities in psychological anthropology*. San Francisco: W. H. Freeman & Co.

Brandell, Georg. 1944. *Svensk folkkaraktär: Bidrag till svenska folkets psykologi*. Stockholm: Elffellves Bokförlag.

Brannen, Julia, ed. 1992. *Mixing methods: Qualitative and quantitative research*. Aldershot: Avebury.

Braudel, Fernand. 1986. *L'identité de la France*. Paris: Arthaud-Flammarion.

Briggs, Jean. 1970. *Never in anger*. Cambridge, Mass.: Harvard University Press.

Bygren, Lars-Olov. 1974. Met and unmet needs for medical and social services. *Scandinavian Journal of Social Medicine* (Supplementum 8). Stockholm: Almqvist & Wiksell Periodical Company.

Casriel, Daniel. 1972. *A scream away from happiness*. New York: Grosset & Dunlap.

Cederblad, Marianne. 1984. Barnets första krets. In *Barn i tid och rum*, by Karin Aronsson et al., 24–42. Stockholm: Liber.

Cesarec, Zvonimir, and Sven Marke. 1964. *Mätning av psykogena behov med frågeformulärsteknik* (CMPS manual). Stockholm: Psykologi Förlaget.

Childs, Marquis W. 1936. *Sweden, the middle way*. New York: Penguin.

Cook, Mark. 1984. *Levels of personality*. New York: Praeger.

Cullberg, Johan. 1984. Om mannen och jämställdheten. In *Om man hade känslor* (Report from a symposium, 13 September 1984, on male aggression and other feelings), 8–14. Stockholm: Arbetsmarknadsdepartementet.

Dahl, Gudrun. 1984. Idéer om barndom och barnets natur. In *Barn i tid och rum*, by Karin Aronsson et al., 9–23. Stockholm: Liber.

Daly, John A., and James C. McCroskey, eds. 1984. *Avoiding communication: Shyness, reticence, and communication apprehension*. Beverly Hills, Calif.: Sage.

Daly, John A., and Laura Stafford. 1984. Correlates and consequences of social-communicative anxiety. In *Avoiding communication: Shyness, reticence, and communication apprehension*, edited by John A. Daly and James C. McCroskey, 125–43. Beverly Hills, Calif.: Sage.

Daun, Åke. 1980. *Boende och livsform*. Stockholm: Tiden/Folksam.

———. 1984. Swedishness as an obstacle in cross-cultural interaction. *Ethnologia Europaea* 14, no. 2:95–109.

———. 1985. *Bra och dåligt i Sverige*. (Invandrare i Stockholms län. Stockholms läns landsting. Regionplanekontoret, Rapport 1985:6.)

———. 1986. The Japanese of the North—The Swedes of Asia? *Ethnologia Scandinavica*: 5–15.

———. 1989. Are Swedes as cold as they seem to be? Dimensions of Swedish mentality. In *Tradition and modern society* (A symposium at the Royal Academy of Letters, History, and Antiquities), edited by Sven Gustavsson. Stockholm: Royal Academy of Letters, History, and Antiquities.

———. 1991. Individualism and collectivity among Swedes. *Ethnos* 56:3–4, 165–72.

———. 1992. *Den europeiska identiteten: Bidrag till samtal om Sveriges framtid*. Stockholm: Rabén & Sjögren.

Daun, Ake, Nancy F. Burroughs, and James McCroskey. 1988. Correlates of quietness: Swedish and American perspectives. Paper presented at the annual meeting of Communication Studies, New Orleans.

Daun, Ake, and Nils-Erik Landell. 1982. *Hälsa och livsmiljö. En socialmedicinsk studie av unga kvinnor 20–40 år i en svensk kommun*. Stockholm: Tidens Förlag.

Daun, Ake, Carl-Erik Mattlar, and Erkki Alanen. 1989. Personality traits characteristic for Finns and Swedes. *Ethnologia Scandinavica* 19: 30–50.

de Gramont, Sanche. 1969. *The French: Portrait of a people*. New York: G. P. Putman's Sons.

Den gamla svenska bondepraktikan. 1979. Modern ed. Stockholm: Fabel.

Dhillon, H. S. 1976. Ni är alldeles för lagom! *Ordets makt* 3:44–48.

Doi, Tadeo. 1971. *The anatomy of dependence*. Tokyo: Kodansha International.

DuBois, Cora. [1944] 1960. *The people of Alor: A social-psychological study of an East Indian island*. Cambridge, Mass.: Harvard University Press.

Dundes, Alan. 1984. *Life is like a chicken coop ladder: A portrait of German culture through folklore*. New York: Columbia University Press.

———. 1986. Comments. *Focaal: Tydschrift voor Anthropologie*, April, 33–37.

Edfeldt, Ake W. 1979. *Violence towards children*. Stockholm: Akademiförlaget.

———. 1985. *Aga—fostran till våld*. Stockholm: Proprius.

Ehn, Billy. 1981. *Arbetets flytande gränser* (The shifting limits of work). Stockholm: Prisma.

———. 1983. *Ska vi leka tiger? Daghemsliv ur kulturell synvinkel*. Stockholm: Liber.

Ehn, Billy, and Karl-Olov Arnstberg. 1980. *Det osynliga arvet: Sexton invandrare om sin bakgrund.* Stockholm: Författarförlaget.

Ek, Sven B. 1960. Economic booms, innovations, and the popular culture. *Economy and History* 3:3–37.

Elfstadius, Magnus, and Anne Pressner. 1984. Om blyghet. Graduate paper in psychology, Department of Applied Psychology, Lund University.

Ensamhet och gemenskap: Levnadsförhållanden (Being alone and being together: Living conditions). 1976. Swedish Official Statistics, report no. 18. Stockholm: SCB

Enzensberger, Hans Magnus. 1982. *Svensk höst* (A series of articles in *Dagens Nyheter*). Stockholm: Dagens Nyheter.

Eysenck, Hans J., and M. W. Eysenck. 1985. *Personality and individual differences: A natural science approach.* New York: Plenum Press.

Eysenck, Hans J., and S.B.G. Eysenck. 1983. Recent advances in the cross-cultural study of personality. In *Advances in Personality Assessment*, edited by James N. Bucher and Charles D. Spielberger, 2:41–69. London: Lawrence Erlbaum Associates.

Faberow, N. L. 1972. Cultural history of suicide. In *Suicide and attempted suicide* (Symposium 28–30, Skandia International Symposia, 1971), edited by Waldenström et al., 30–44. Stockholm: Nordiska Bokhandelns Förlag.

Fenichel, O. [1945] 1971. *The psychoanalytic theory of neurosis.* London: Routledge & Kegan Paul.

Fife, Agnes. 1986. *Skal du langveis fare: En guide for norske foretningsfolk i utlandet.* Oslo: Cappelen.

Flöistrup, Bertil. 1981. *Vädersjukdomar och luftjoner* (Weather-related illnesses and airborne ions). Danderyd: Fragaria.

Forslin, Jan, and Reine Hansson. 1978. *Psykosocial arbetsmiljö: Förslag till forskningsprogram för byggbranschen.* (Byggforskningen Rapport R 109.)

Forss, Kim, David Hawk, and Gunnar Hedlund. 1984. Cultural differences—Swedishness in legislation, multinational corporations, and aid administration. Stockholm School of Economics, Institute of International Business. Typescript.

Freund, Folke. 1980. Soziale Konventionen und die phatische Funktion der Sprache: Bemerkungen zu einigen Kommunikationsbarrieren von Schweden in Deutschland. *Studies in Modern Philology* (Stockholm) 6:55–67.

Fromm, Erich. 1941. *Escape from freedom.* New York: Farrar & Rinehart.

Frykman, Jonas. 1993. Nationella ord och handlingar. In *Försvenskningen av Sverige*, by Billy Ehn, Jonas Frykman, and Orvar Löfgren, 119–201. Stockholm: Natur och Kultur.

Frykman, Jonas, and Orvar Löfgren. 1987. *Culture builders: A historical anthropology of middle-class life.* New Brunswick, N.J.: Rutgers University Press.

——, eds. 1985. *Modärna tider* (Modern times). Malmö: Liber.

Gannon, Martin J. 1994. *Understanding global cultures: Metaphorical journeys through seventeen countries.* Thousand Oaks, Calif.: Sage.

Gorer, Geoffrey. 1955. *Exploring English character.* New York: Criterion.

Gorer, Geoffrey, and John Rickman. [1949] 1962. *The people of Great Russia.* New York: W. W. Norton.

Gouldner, Alvin. 1975. *For sociology.* Harmondsworth, Middlesex: Penguin.

Gullestad, Marianne. 1989. Small facts and large issues: The anthropology of contemporary Scandinavian society. *Annual Review of Anthropology* 18:71–93.

Gustafsson, Lars. 1984. Nationallynnet och världslitteraturen. In *Att vara svensk* (Lectures at the Royal Academy of Letters, History, and Antiquities symposium, 12–13 April 1994, conference 13), 23–32. Stockholm: Royal Academy of Letters, History, and Antiquities.

Gustafsson, Gunnel. 1987. Political socialization studies in Scandinavia. *International Political Science Review* 8, no. 3:225–33.

Hagnell, Olle, Jan Lanke, Birgitta Rorsman, and Leif Öjesjö. 1982. Are we entering an age of melancholy? Depressive illness in a prospective epidemiological study over twenty-five years: The Lundby study, Sweden. *Psychological Medicine* 12:279–89.

Hall, Edward T., and Mildred Reed Hall. 1990. *Understanding cultural differences: Keys to success in West Germany, France, and the United States.* Yarmouth, Maine: Intercultural Press.

Hannerz, Ulf. 1983. Den svenska kulturen. Project on Culture Theory for Complex Societies, report no. 9, Department of Social Anthropology, Stockholm University. Typescript.

Harding, Stephen, and David Phillips, eds. 1986. *Contrasting values in western Europa.* Studies in Contemporary Values in Modern Society. London: Macmillan, in association with the European Value Systems Study Group.

Heclo, Hugh, and Henrik Madsen. 1987. *Policy and politics in Sweden.* Philadelphia: Temple University Press.

Hedlund, Gunnar, and Per Aman. 1983. *Managing relationships with foreign subsidaries: Organization and control in Swedish MNCs.* Stockholm: Sveriges Mekanförbund.

Hedman, Lowe. 1985. Invandrare i tystnadsspiralen: En explorativ studie av invandrarbilden i massmedia. In *Invandrare i tystnadsspiralen: Journalisten som verklighetens dramaturg* (A report from the discrimination study), 21–195. Stockholm: Arbetsmarknadsdepartementet.

Hendin, Herbert. 1964. *Suicide and Scandinavia: A psycho-analytic study of culture and character.* New York: Grune & Stratton.

Henry, Jules. 1964. *Culture against man.* New York: Random House.

———. 1973. *Pathways to madness.* New York: Vintage.

Hofstede, Geert. 1984. *Culture's consequences: International differences in work-related values.* Cross-cultural research and methodology series, vol 5. Beverly Hills: Sage.

Holm, Ulla. 1978. *Våga tala.* Study material, State Personnel Education Committee. Typescript.

Horney, Karen. 1951. *Neurosis and human growth: The struggle toward self-realization.* London: Routledge & Kegan Paul.

Huntford, Roland. 1971. *The new totalitarians.* London: Allen Lane, Penguin.

Ineichen, Bernard. 1975. Neurotic wives in a modern residential suburb: A sociological profile. *Social Science and Medicine* 9:481–87.

Inkeles, Alex, and Daniel Levinson. 1954. National character: The study of modal personality and socio-cultural systems. In vol. 2 of *The handbook of social psychology*, edited by Gardner Lindzey. Reading, Mass.: Addison-Wesley.

———. 1969. National character: The study of modal personality and socio-cultural systems. In vol. 4 of *The handbook of social psychology*, 2d ed., edited by Gardner Lindzey and Elliot Aronson. Reading, Mass.: Addison-Wesley.

IPPNW. 1986. "Ungdomar och kärnvapen." International Physicians for the Prevention of Nuclear War, Swedish section of IPPNW, SIFO material. Typescript.

Israel, Joachim. 1968. *Alienation: Från Marx till modern sociologi: En makrosociologisk studie.* Stockholm: Rabén & Sjögren.

Jenkins, David. 1968. *Sweden and the price of progress.* New York: Coward-McCann.

Jonassen, Christen T. 1972. *Values and beliefs: A study of American and Norwegian college students.* Oslo: Universitetsforlaget.

Jonsson, Kjell. 1987. Radikalism, rationalitet, värdenihilism och vetenskaplighet: Anteckningar om sekelskiftets radikalism och den svenska ideologins födelse. Paper presented at the symposium "Komponenter i en nationell kultur—den 'svenska modellens' kulturella ansikte," Umeå University, 14–16 January.

Kaplan, Bert. 1954. *A study of Rorschach responses in four cultures.* Papers of the Peabody Museum, vol. 42. Cambridge, Mass.: Harvard University.

Kaplan, David. 1972. On shyness. *International Journal of Psychoanalysis* 53:439–53.

Kaplan, David, and Robert Manners. 1972. *Culture theory.* Englewood Cliffs, N.J.: Prentice-Hall.

References   223

Kardiner, Abram. 1939. *The individual and his society.* New York: Columbia University Press.

Kawasaki, Kazuhiko. 1984. Negotiating with the Japanese. Paper delivered at Furudal Kursinternat, Japan External Trade Organization (JETRO), Stockholm Office, March 7.

Kirshenblatt-Gimblett, Barbara. 1973. Toward a theory of proverb meaning. *Proverbium* 22:821–27.

Klausen, Arne Martin, ed. 1984. *Den norske vaeremåten: Antropologisk sökelys på norsk kultur.* Oslo: Cappelen.

Klinteberg, Britt af, Lars Oreland, et al. 1990–91. Exploring the connections between platelet monoamine oxidase activity and behavior: Relationships with performance in neuropsychological tasks. *Neuropsychobiology* 23:188–96.

Klopf, Donald. 1984. Cross-cultural apprehension research: A summary of Pacific basin studies. In *Avoiding communication: Shyness, reticence, and communication apprehension,* edited by John A. Daly and James C. McCroskey, 157–69. Beverly Hills: Sage.

Kvinnor och barn: Intervjuer med kvinnor om familj och arbete (Women and children: Interviews with women on family and work). 1982. Information on Prognosis Issues, report no. 4, Swedish Official Statistics.

Laine-Sveiby, Kati. 1987. *Svenskhet som strategi.* Stockholm: Timbro.

Landell, Nils-Erik. 1985. *Hälsa och livsmiljö: Slutrapport.* Psychiatric Clinic, Danderyd Hospital, 30 December. Typescript.

Lanier, Alison R. [1973] 1981. *Living in the U.S.A.* Chicago: Intercultural Press.

Larsen, Tord. 1984. Bönder i byen—på jakt efter den norske konfigurasjonen. In *Den norske vaeremåten,* edited by Arne Martin Klausen, 15–44. Oslo: Cappelen.

Larsson, Gerhard, Mårten Rönström, et al. 1979. *Fritidsboende och fritidsbebyggelse.* Stockholm: Byggforskningsrådet.

Lebra, Takie Sugiyama. 1976. *Japanese patterns of behavior.* Honolulu: University of Hawaii Press.

Lennéer-Axelson, Barbro. 1981. Fem orsaker till varför männen misshandlar: Interview with Barbro Lennéer-Axelson. By Elisabeth Magnuson et al. *Socionomen* 14.

Levin, S. 1967. Some metapsychological considerations on the differentiation between shame and guilt. *International Journal of Psychoanalysis* 48:267–76.

Levinski, H. 1941. The nature of shyness. *British Journal of Psychology* 32, no. 2:105–13.

L'Hoste, Jean. 1978. A fifteen-country study of some factors influencing the number and the severity of road accidents. Second part, Drivers'

attitudes and opinions. International Drivers' Behavior Research Association (France). Typescript.
Link, Ruth. 1969. Suicide: The deadly game. *Sweden Now* 12:40–46.
Linton, Ralph. 1939. The individual and his society. In *The individual and his society: The psychodynamics of primitive social organization*, edited by Abram Kardiner, with a foreword and two ethnological reports by Ralph Linton. New York: Columbia University Press.
Ljusbehandling mot depression. 1987. *Karolinska Institutets Tidskrift* 4:16–17.
Lorénzen, Lilly. [1964]1978. *Of Swedish ways*. New York: Barnes & Noble.
Lynn, Richard. 1971. *Personality and national character*. Oxford: Pergamon Press.
——. 1981. Cross-cultural differences in neuroticism, extraversion, and psychoticism. In *Dimensions of personality*, edited by Richard Lynn. London: Pergamon Press.
Magnusson, David. 1982. Situational determinants of stress: An interactional perspective. In *Handbook of stress*, edited by L. Goldberger and S. Preznitz, 231–53. New York: Free Press.
Masur, Gerhard. 1975. Der nationale Character als Problem der Deutschen Geschichte. *Historische Zeitschrift* 221:603–22.
McCroskey, James C. 1984. Self-report measurement. In *Avoiding communication: Shyness, reticence, and communication apprehension*, edited by John A. Daly and James C. McCroskey, 81–94. Beverly Hills: Sage.
Mead, Margaret. 1942. *And keep your powder dry: An anthropologist looks at America*. New York: William Morrow.
——. 1970. *Culture and commitment: A study of the generation gap*. Garden City, N.Y.: Doubleday.
Mieder, Wolfgang. 1978. The use of proverbs in psychological testing. *Journal of the Folklore Institute* 15, no.1:45–55.
Miller, W. 1960. *Russians as people*. New York: Dutton.
Morris, Jan. 1984. *Journeys*. New York: Oxford University Press.
Murray, Henry A. 1938. *Explorations in personality*. New York: Oxford University Press.
Nakajima, Koko. 1978. Alderdomsförsörjningen i Hagestad, Löderups socken, enligt intervjuer 1978 samt jämförelser med förhållandena i Japan. Seminar paper in ethnology, Institute for Folklife Research, Stockholm University.
Nilsson, Thora. 1985. Les ménages en Suède. *Population* 2:223–47.
Nilsson-Schönnesson, Lena. 1985. Hennes och hans äktenskap? Report no. 1 from the project Relations Between Couples in Families with Children, Stockholm Delegation for Equality Research. Typescript.
Nisbet, R. A. 1953. *The quest for community*. London: Oxford University Press.

Nott, Kathleen. 1960. *A clean well-lighted place: A private view of Sweden.* London: Heinemann.

Öhlund, Marie-Louise. 1982. Har dom turban? En grupp svenskars attityder mot invandrare. Seminar paper, Institute for Folklife Research, Stockholm University.

Peabody, James. 1985. *National characteristics.* European Monographs in Social Psychology. Cambridge: Cambridge University Press.

Perris, Carlo et al. 1985. Cross-national study of perceived parental rearing behaviour in healthy subjects from Australia, Denmark, Italy, The Netherlands, and Sweden: Pattern and level comparisons. *Acta Psychiatrica Scandinavica* 72:278–82.

Persson, Lars-Olof. 1988. Mood and expectation. Ph.D. diss., Göteborg Psychological Reports.

Peyrefitte, A. 1976. *Le mal francaise.* Paris: Plon.

Phillips-Martinsson, Jean. 1981. Swedes, as others see them. Stockholm: Affärsförlaget.

Popenoe, David. 1977. *The suburban environment: Sweden and the United States.* Chicago: University of Chicago Press.

———. 1985. *Private pleasure, public plight: American metropolitan community life in comparative perspective.* New Brunswick, N.J.: Transaction Books.

———. 1988. *Disturbing the nest: Family change and decline in modern societies.* New York: Aldine de Gruyter.

Prime Minister's Office. 1984. Outline of the results of the Third International Survey of Youth. Foreign Press Center, Japan.

Raditjkov, Jordan. 1980. *Träskorna: En liten nordlig saga.* Stockholm: Rabén & Sjögren.

Richmond, Virginia, James McCroskey, and Steven Payne. 1987. *Nonverbal behavior in interpersonal relations.* Englewood Cliffs, N.J.: Prentice-Hall.

Riesman, David. 1950. *The lonely crowd.* New Haven, Conn.: Yale University Press.

Rudenstam, Kjell. 1970. Some cultural determinants of suicide in Sweden. *Journal of Social Psychology* 90:225–27.

Scherer, Klaus R. 1986. Studying emotion empirically: Issues and a paradigm for research. In *Experiencing emotion: A cross-cultural study,* edited by Klaus R. Scherer, Harald G. Wallbott, and Angela B. Summerfield, 3–27. Cambridge: Cambridge University Press.

Scherer, Klaus R., Harald G. Wallbott, and Angela B. Summerfield. 1986. *Experiencing emotion: A cross-cultural study.* Cambridge: Cambridge University Press.

Schilder, P. 1938. The social neurosis. *Psychoanalytic Review* 25, no. 1:1–19.

Shneidman, Edwin S. 1984. Aphorism of suicide and some implications for psychoteraphy. *American Journal of Psychotherapy* 38, no.3: 319–28.

Schönfeld, Friedbert. 1975–80. *Sweden*. Cologne: Bundesstelle für Aussenhandelsinformation.

Shweder, Richard A. 1991. *Thinking through cultures*. Cambridge, Mass.: Harvard University Press.

Similä, Artturi, and Björn Forslund. 1978. *Människan och vädret*. Stockholm: Skogek.

Sjögren, Annick. 1985. Förhållandet till barnen visar kulturskillnader. *Invandrare and Minoriteter*, nos. 4–5:40–41.

Skiöld, Bo-Arne. 1975. Blyghet-talängslan-tystnad—tre steg till invalidisering. Documentation series no. 11, Teachers' College, Linköping. Typescript.

Skogsberg, Christina. 1985. *Jaget och omvärlden: En referensram för vår psykosociala utveckling*. Stockholm: Natur och Kultur.

Smith, Hendrick. 1976. *The Russians*. New York: Quadrangle/New York Times Book Co.

Socialstyrelsen (National board of health and welfare). 1985. *Pedagogiskt program för fritidshem*. Stockholm: Liber.

Solomon, Robert C. 1984. Getting angry: The Jamesian theory of emotion in anthropology. In *Culture theory: Essays on mind, self, and emotion*, edited by Richard A. Shwerer and Robert A. LeVine, 238–54. Cambridge: Cambridge University Press.

Sontag, Susan. 1969. Letter from Sweden. *Ramparts*, July, 23–38.

Stedje, Astrid. 1982. "Brechen Sie dies rätselhafte Schweigen"—über kulturbedingtes, kommunikatives und strategisches Schweigen. In *Sprache und Pragmatik*, edited by Inger Rosengren, 1–35. Stockholm: Almqvist & Wiksell International.

Stewart, Edward C. 1972. *American cultural patterns: A cross-cultural perspective*. Chicago: Intercultural Press.

Stewart, R. A., G. E. Powell, and S. J. Chetwynd. 1979. *Person perception and stereotyping*. Westmead, Farnborough: Saxon House.

Stigler, James W., Richard A. Shweder, and Gilbert Herdt. 1990. *Cultural psychology: Essays on comparative human development*. Cambridge: Cambridge University Press.

Ström, Fredrik. [1926] 1929. *Svenskarna i sina ordspråk* (Swedes in their proverbs). Stockholm: Bonniers.

Suède, la reform permanente. 1977. Paris: Stock.

Sundbärg, Gustav. 1911. *Det svenska folklynnet: Aforismer*. Stockholm: P. A. Norstedt & Söners Förlag.

Szábo, Mátyás. 1971. Barnarbete i agrarsamhället. In *Fataburen*, 19–37. Stockholm: Nordiska museet.

Takac, Mirko. N.d. Report från Invandrarprojektet. Statistics in the archive of Jean Phillips-Martinsson, Cross-Cultural Relations Centre, Stockholm.

Terhune, Kenneth W. 1970. From national character to national behavior: A reformulation. *Conflict Resolution* 14, no. 2:203–63.

Thörn, Kerstin. 1986. En god bostad för det riktiga livet: Den moderna bostadens ideologiska förutsättningar. In *I framtidens tjänst: Ur folkhemmets idéhistoria*, 196–213. Stockholm: Gidlunds.

Thörnberg, Agneta. 1985. Tjugofem chilenare talar om svenskar. Institute for Folklife Research, Stockholm University. Typescript.

Tingsten, Herbert. 1940. Folkstyret i Norden (Popular rule in the Nordic countries). In *De nordiska folkens karaktär och lynnesdrag*, edited by Karl Petander, 50–83. Stockholm: Kooperativa Förbundets Bokförlag.

Triandis, Harry C., and Richard W. Brislin. 1980. *Handbook of cross-cultural psychology*. Vol. 5. Boston: Allyn & Bacon.

Trost, Jan, and Örjan Hultåker. 1984. *Swedish divorces: Methods and responses*. Uppsala: Uppsala Universitet.

van Heerikhuizen, Bart. 1982. What is typically Dutch? Sociologists in the 1930s and 1940s on the Dutch national character. *Netherlands Journal of Sociology* 18, no. 2:103–25.

Vogel, Joachim. 1987. *Det svenska klassamhället: Klasstruktur, social rörlighet och ojämlikhet.* (Living conditions 1975–86.) Stockholm: SCB.

Waldenström, Jan, Tage Larsson, and Nils Ljungstedt, eds. 1972. *Suicide and attempted suicide.* Skandia International Symposia. Stockholm: Nordiska Bokhandelns Förlag.

Wallace, Anthony. 1952. *The modal personality structure of the Tuscarora Indians as revealed by the Rorschach test.* Bureau of American Ethnology Bulletin, no. 150. Washington, D.C.: Smithsonian Institute.

———. 1961. *Culture and personality.* New York: Random House.

Webster's New Collegiate Dictionary. 1977. Springfield, Mass.: G. & C. Merriam Co.

Weeks, David Joseph, and Kate Ward. 1988. *Eccentrics: The scientific investigation.* Stirling, Central, Scotland: Stirling University Press.

Weibust, Knut. 1988. Alternatives in child birth: Questions about active birth and resources of the birth-giving woman. *Ethnologia Scandinavica*, 67–75.

Weiss, Peter. 1964. *Brännpunkt.* Uddevalla: Bo Cavefors Bokförlag.

Westin, Charles. 1984. *Majoritet om minoritet: En studie i etnisk tolerans i 80-talets Sverige.* Stockholm: Publica.

Wetterberg, Lennart. 1994. Light and biological rhythms. *Journal of Internal Medicine* 235:5–19.

Widström, Eeva. 1983. Finnish immigrants and dental care in Stockholm country. *Swedish Dental Journal*, supplement 19.

Wingårdh, Marius. 1958. *Så går det till i umgänge och sällskapsliv.* Stockholm: Natur och Kultur.

Wylie, L., and A. Bégué. 1970. *Les Français.* New York: Prentice-Hall.

Zetterberg, Hans L. 1977. *Arbete, livsstil och motivation.* Stockholm: Svenska Arbetsgivareföreningen.

——. 1984. The rational humanitarians. *Daedalus: Journal of the American Academy of Arts and Sciences* 113 (winter): 75–92.

——. 1985. Sverige, svenskarna och skatten. Paper presented at the annual meeting of the Business Association, SIFO, Stockholm.

Zetterberg, Hans L. et al. 1983. *Det osynliga kontraktet: En studie i 80-talets arbetsliv.* Stockholm: SIFO.

Zimbardo, Phillip G. 1977. *Shyness—what it is, what to do about it.* Reading, Mass.: Addison-Wesley.

Zimbardo, Phillip G., P. A. Pilkonis, and R. M. Norwood. 1975. The social disease called shyness. *Psychology Today* 5:69–72.

Index